More Praise for the Previous Edition, *Portfolio First Aid*

"*Financial First Aid* for Canadians provides comprehensive and sensible solutions to heal any investor's wounded financial plan."

—*Paul Allison, President and Chief Executive Officer, Raymond James Ltd.*

"We all make investment mistakes. *Portfolio First Aid* is packed with advice on how to avoid them—and with profit. Eminently readable and practical, it is a prime and welcome addition to the thoughtful investor's library."

—*John Crow, Former Governor, Bank of Canada*

"The authors of *Portfolio First Aid* have taken the principles of investing, which are often presented in overly complex terms, and made them simple and actionable. Moreover, they have done so in a highly engaging and entertaining style! This book will be invaluable to investors and their portfolios, not just as first aid, but also as preventive medicine."

—*David F. Denison, President and Chief Executive Officer, Canada Pension Plan Investment Board*

"*Portfolio First Aid* offers just what investors need—a deep understanding of financial markets, the right tools to nurture and grow investment assets, and a good dose of tender loving care in its purest form: wisdom, distilled from the co-authors' long investment experience. All of this is put together in a readable style that is accessible and astute. Investors have rarely been treated so well."

—*Dr. Mark Mullins, Former Executive Director, The Fraser Institute*

FINANCIAL
FIR$T AID
FOR CANADIAN INVESTORS

FINANCIAL
FIR$T AID
FOR CANADIAN INVESTORS

**Stop the Bleeding, Start the Healing
and Get Your Portfolio on the Road to Recovery**

MICHAEL GRAHAM, Ph.D., BRYAN SNELSON
with CINDY DAVID, CFP, CLU

WILEY

John Wiley & Sons Canada, Ltd.

Library and Archives Canada Cataloguing in Publication Data

Snelson, Bryan
    Financial first aid for Canadian investors : stop the bleeding, start the healing and get your portfolio on the road to recovery / Bryan Snelson, Michael Graham, Cindy David.

Includes index.
ISBN 978-0-470-73852-8

1. Investments. 2. Investments—Canada. 3. Portfolio management—Canada.
4. Finance, Personal—Canada.
I. Graham, Michael R. II. David, Cindy, 1973– III. Title.

HG5152.S59 2009   332.60971   C2009-904807-8

Production Credits:
Cover design: Ian Koo
Interior text design: Natalia Burobina
Printer: Friesens

John Wiley & Sons Canada, Ltd.
6045 Freemont Blvd.
Mississauga, Ontario
L5R 4J3

Printed in Canada

1 2 3 4 5 FP 13 12 11 10 09

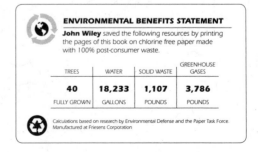

ENVIRONMENTAL BENEFITS STATEMENT

John Wiley saved the following resources by printing the pages of this book on chlorine free paper made with 100% post-consumer waste.

TREES	WATER	SOLID WASTE	GREENHOUSE GASES
40	**18,233**	**1,107**	**3,786**
FULLY GROWN	GALLONS	POUNDS	POUNDS

Calculations based on research by Environmental Defense and the Paper Task Force.
Manufactured at Friesens Corporation

Table of Contents

Preface

"The behaviour of your investment portfolio will be driven largely by your behaviour."
—Dr. Benjamin Graham, author, The Intelligent Investor

The opening decade of what was heralded as a glorious new millennium has brought mind-boggling changes in the world's markets—painful and wealth-destructive ones, too. Whether evolutionary or revolutionary, they are changes once again validating celebrated economist Joseph Schumpeter's theory of Creative Destruction. Concomitantly, they are changes that are bringing an urgent need to rethink long-held approaches and assumptions in the art and science that is investing.

It has often been stated that the financial market is a pendulum that forever swings between unsustainable optimism and unjustified pessimism. Intelligent investors are realists, driven by facts and reasoning. The man often credited as the father of modern securities analysis and value investing, Benjamin Graham, was noted for advising his Columbia University students (including a young Warren Buffett) that the secret to your financial success is inside yourself. By honing your skills and self-discipline you can refuse to let other people's mood swings govern your financial destiny.

Buffett, unquestionably the best-known student ever to have studied under Benjamin Graham, noted in the preface to the fourth edition of Graham's *The Intelligent Investor* that "to invest successfully over a lifetime does not require a stratospheric IQ, unusual business insights, or inside information. What's needed is a sound intellectual framework for making decisions and the ability to keep emotions from corroding that framework." A significant aspect of our mission in writing this book is to give you the understanding of how we've collectively arrived at this point in financial history, and to provide you with some basic framework for making informed financial decisions.

"Those who can not remember the past are condemned to repeat it."
—George Santayana, philosopher, essayist

An understanding of what happened to cause the most severe economic breakdown since World War II, maybe even since the Great Depression, is essential to setting and resetting new investment approaches and starting points. Such an understanding also puts the savage bear market of 2007–2009 into clearer perspective. We hope *Financial First Aid* helps in all of these respects, as well as in reassessing and mounting today's daunting investment challenges.

Besides updating a real-life drama that Hollywood couldn't script better, we wanted readers of our 2005 book, *Portfolio First Aid*, to come away from *Financial First Aid* impressed by its freshness. All investors should also be encouraged by the products and tools available to them in today's investment marketplace—not the structured and derivative products that almost brought down entire financial systems, but genuine products that add value and reduce risk.

Innovative investment products developed by the Canadian life insurance industry couldn't be a better example of the ever-expanding toolbox available to today's investors. We welcome Cindy David for the vast experience she brings to *Financial First Aid* in an area of continuously growing importance.

At no point do we intend to upstage an industry that is more experienced and professional than ever. Nor do we wish *Financial First Aid* to compete with the efforts of dedicated, top-flight professionals who are far better equipped than we are—or will ever be. Instead, our intent is to help you make the most of your hard-earned savings; that means to make them grow the way you want, and need!

To know more about the essentials of investing, to learn from past experience and to capture the excitement of an increasingly globalized world in which investment is more necessary than ever—and in which a "new look" Canada is an increasingly enviable part—these are the goals of the updated three-section "conversation" to follow.

If *Financial First Aid* were to leave you with an improved and excited understanding of what contemporary investing should be all about, this repeat labour of love will have been even more worthwhile.

Michael Graham & Bryan Snelson
Summer 2009

Acknowledgements

Many people are referred to in this work. Some expressly allowed us to use their names and materials. There are also the many others without whose expert knowledge Financial First Aid would hardly have been possible. We are most grateful to them all.

* * *

Bryan wishes to thank his clients for the trust and confidence they have placed in him. He is thankful to his partners on this project; Michael Graham and Cindy David for their keen intellect, good humour and generosity of spirit.

Bryan also wishes to thank the two women who are the backbone of his professional life. Two women whose friendship and wise counsel has meant so much to guide him through a particularly difficult year; Linda Stragliotto and Carrie Hathaway. Above all, Bryan thanks his daughters Laura and Sydney for their love and encouragement. If ever a father needed a demonstration of a child's unconditional love, Laura and Sydney were just that throughout this project.

* * *

Michael particularly wishes to thank Bryan Snelson for his enthusiasm and "we can do it" leadership in getting the manuscript written and submitted within a time frame he would never have believed possible. He is also indebted to Gilda Stein for her electronic input skills and Rena LePage for her ever-willing assistance in preparing his charts and tables. By no means least is his wife, Nancy, for her considerable editing, text-reading and transcribing skills—often in demand late at night or early in the morning—and her invaluable all-round help. The Graham children—Julia, Richard and Hugh—were similarly supportive, with a special tip of the hat to Hugh, who makes his living as a writer, editor and subeditor in London, England, and took a keen interest right from the outset.

* * *

Cindy would like to thank Michael and Bryan for the opportunity to contribute to the book.

Thank you to the many Investment Advisors and their clients who give her the opportunity to make a difference in their financial lives and the tireless contribution of her associate Julia Chung.

Nothing can replace the support and encouragement of a loving husband, thank you Rene.

* * *

A final note of thanks by all three of us is in order to Karen Milner for her constant reassurance and also to the Wiley team for once again steering us ably to the finish line.

PART ONE

DIAGNOSIS

CHAPTER 1

The Past Is Prescient

Let History Be Your Guide

A little knowledge can be a dangerous thing. For investors, a dearth of knowledge could be even more dangerous in times of unprecedented—some might also say revolutionary—change, like now.

History is not a diagnostic tool, per se. But stand back from today's madding crowd, and a working knowledge of what has gone before can only help, not just in the benchmarks needed to compare with and measure against, but also in the compelling challenge we should all be wanting to undertake for the rewards and financial independence it can bring in a McLuhan-like global village whose future is now.

The truth is our savings are needed as never before for deployment in a multitude of different ways. Whether to cover burgeoning government deficits for shovel-ready infrastructure projects, to replenish impaired bank capital, to help clean up the environment, to provide investment for productivity-enhancing plant and equipment, or to fund "lifeblood" research, the demand is almost limitless.

Governments everywhere are awakening to this reality and introducing tax and other incentives designed to encourage fresh savings and investments; this also at a time when chastened populaces, worrying about their futures are feeling compelled to save more for investing anyway. And this time not the toxic type of supposed investments that all but wrecked a greedy and overzealous Wall Street and inflicted massive damage on investors of every stripe—pension funds, registered retirement savings plans, you and us, et al. In fact, don't be surprised if we investors emerge from today's turmoil as "king"—our position is that strong; the need for our savings that great.

It's not that we lack for decision making information now available to us in a dazzling, mind boggling profusion. A search on the Internet, the click of a button or the push of a mouse and you'll have at your fingertips access to investment laden media. In fact, if there is a problem, it is more likely than not one of information overload in our quest for constantly necessary portfolio care—and first aid!

There is also the accompanying challenge of providing for our retirement and attaining personal goals through investments that last longer than we do as our life expectancies lengthen. Keen knowledge of history will enable us to examine what has happened in the past to better prepare for the future. There is also the accompanying comfort of its parallels. Perhaps Mark Twain summed up these sentiments best when he famously declared, "History doesn't repeat, but it rhymes."

PAST AND FUTURE

As we suffer through what may well prove to be the worst economic downturn since the Great Depression of the 1930s, it's useful to know that the Hoover administration set up the Reconstruction Finance Corporation to inject capital into stricken banks, just as the Bush, and now the Obama, administrations have implemented a Troubled Asset Relief Program (TARP) for the same purpose.

Dig deeper and we see that a big difference between then and now is the inflexible resolve back then to keep budgets balanced, even if it meant raising interest rates and taxes at the worst possible time. There was also the fixation that currencies had to be wholly backed by gold, despite the complication of gold reserves varying widely between countries. How things are different today, as pump-priming deficit budgets come back into vogue and money supplies are dictated, not by gold backing, but by central bankers' pens.

It is also useful to be reminded that recessions and bear markets come and go like the seasons, assuredly to be followed by recoveries and bull markets. Sir John Templeton, the towering mutual fund pioneer, lived by 10 steps for investment success, his seventh summarizing that bull markets are born on pessimism, grow on skepticism, mature on optimism and die on euphoria. And following from this, that the time of maximum pessimism is the best time to buy, and the time of maximum optimism is the best time to sell. Past investment history can usefully help gauge these "best times," as we shall illustrate later.

FEAR AND GREED

Human nature being what it is, one can never remove the emotional side of investing. However, history can help us get a better grip on the two most dangerous investor emotions: fear and greed.

Three centuries ago, after losing a fortune in the South Sea Bubble, Sir Isaac Newton lamented that he could calculate the movement of the stars, but not the madness of men. Several decades ago, John Maynard Keynes soberly reminded us that markets can remain irrational longer than you and I can remain solvent. In late 1974, towards the end of a severe two-year bear market that Michael still remembers as frightening him the most, an elder statesman of Wall Street observed that the stock markets of that time seemed to him to be made up of 15% confidence, 85% fear and 0% judgment. We wonder how much different these ratios were in the market swoons of 2008–09.

There are just as many examples of irrationality at the other extreme. Remember the high-tech craze that ushered in the new millennium and took Nortel stock above $100? Also, remember the ill-fated boom in exotic structured products and the improbable returns they were supposed to bring? History can certainly help us get a better grip on fear, greed and judgment during extremes like these.

Vince Lombardi instilled in his Green Bay Packers teams the belief that winning wasn't *everything*, it was the *only* thing. Today's investor well might want to take a leaf from his playbook and think in terms of perspective as the only thing. Better still, combine perspective with history and there'll be even more validation of the warning that those who fail to learn from the lessons of the past are doomed to repeat them.

Black Monday Redux

In a moment of quiet reflection while researching content for this book, Michael was tempted to encapsulate a career spanning 6 recessions and 10 bear markets—and shortly, he hopes, a 7th recovery and an 11th bull market.

There were also his teenager memories of the extreme pessimism that set in after World War II when the economic problems then left many believing the Dow Jones Industrials might never again see 212, its post-war recovery high.

We also thought about the 17 years, from 1966 to 1983, that it took for this most famous of stock market bellwethers to break the 1,000 threshold. Those years included the fear-filled summer of 1982, when even a perennial optimist like Michael was left wondering whether Chicken Little might indeed be right. We didn't know that one of the greatest bull markets of all time was in the process of being spawned.

Black Monday 1987 saw Michael en route to Brandon, Manitoba, to speak at an investment seminar that evening. A call from the Winnipeg airport to check the closing markets brought news that the Dow had closed down 508 points—a staggering 23%, the largest single-day decline in history.

Black Monday 2008 found him passing through Calgary where he experienced a similar numbness as the Dow dropped more than 400 points, or close to 7%, in six minutes as the U.S. House of Representatives voted down the Bush administration's first bailout proposal. Bryan remembers without a trace of fondness the nausea-inducing plunge as he sat staring in disbelief at his computer screen.

How does one give presentations—in Brandon in 1987, in Edmonton in 2008—after stomach-churning declines likes these? By repeating the golden rules of balance and diversification, by putting what was happening into historical perspective, and by being very brave!

In October 1987 it wasn't long before freshly minted Federal Reserve Board Chairman Alan Greenspan (later of "irrational exuberance" fame) reassured investors the Fed would not stand idly by and would provide all the liquidity the markets and the economy would need. Similarly in 2008, Mr. Greenspan's successor Ben Bernanke reiterated that the Fed stood prepared to pull out all the stops to help keep a crisis-hit U.S. economy functioning.

If those fateful six minutes didn't usher in a "new normal," they certainly triggered the unprecedented, coordinated, synchronized, pedal-to-the-metal global stimulus that is described separately in chapter 2. Suffice to say that if the supportive efforts worked in 1987, why not again in 2009 and beyond, given global fiscal, monetary and political unanimity as never before?

Today, Black Monday of October 1987 is but a blip on stock market charts and screens. The jury remains out on Black Monday of September 2008, but if both brought one overriding reminder it was of the bargain-basement opportunities they provided those with properly positioned portfolios and the wherewithal to take advantage. In other words, those investors who could keep their heads—and maintain historical perspective—when all around others were losing theirs.

Icons Speak

Shortly after the September 2008 crash, Warren Buffett wrote that it was a time to be greedy when others were fearful, because "if you wait for the robins, spring will be over." He concluded that both his money and his mouth said "equities." So too did his acerbic Berkshire Hathaway partner Charlie Munger in a separate article written at that time. Mr. Munger concluded the markets could be setting the base for a 10- to 15-year bull run stemming from a repositioned, streamlined corporate America.

It wasn't long before both were being criticized for their poor timing, as the stock markets resumed a headlong retreat that was to continue through October and November, and on into January and February of 2009. They were criticisms that reminded Michael of that same long-to-be-remembered summer of 1982 when Sir John Templeton boldly predicted the Dow, then floundering in the 750–770 range, would reach 3,000 within five years. It eventually reached this target in the spring of 1991, four years later than Sir John had predicted. Nevertheless, what prescience in the depths of investor despair! In a similar vein, history could well prove Buffett and Munger to be right, regardless of shorter-term timing, and what are a few years, give or take, in what should essentially be a long-term undertaking?

John Bogle, founder of the Vanguard mutual funds, reminds that investing isn't just about probabilities, but also about "consequences," for which you have to be prepared. Mr. Bogle believes this to be a very good time to put money into equities—not for short-term trades, but as part of a diversified portfolio to be held for many years. He adds that "if you were to put your money away and not look at it for many years, until you were ready for retirement, when you finally looked at it you'd probably faint with amazement at how much money is in there."

In late 2008, still another respected veteran, Barton Biggs, the former Morgan Stanley international strategy chief, confessed to being wrong on the severity and duration of the panic, and admitted to having no idea when the next bull market would start, but he nonetheless saw us setting up for "the mother of all bear market rallies," after which we would have to see.

Jeremy Siegel, author of the acclaimed *Stocks for the Long Run*, is another who admits to misjudging badly the 2008 decline, but nonetheless believes "today's markets present a rare opportunity for long-term investors to reinvest the proceeds of higher dividend yields at deep-discount prices."

At the one-of-a-kind Berkshire Hathaway annual meetings, Warren Buffett regularly reminds that the future is never clear, investment never easy, and you pay a very high price in the stock market for a cheery consensus. Buffett is fond of stating "uncertainty is actually the friend of the buyer of long-term values."

Is Greed Good?

The 1980s brought the junk bond and its offspring, the leveraged buyout (LBO), along with LBO leviathans like T. Boone Pickens, Carl Icahn and Alan Bond, to drive markets higher in their hunt for the next seductive takeover target. It was an era personified by Oliver Stone's film *Wall Street*, in which Gordon Gekko, played by Michael Douglas, in a classic gunslinger pose declared that "greed is good." How nice if an older, more experienced Gordon Gekko were to repent of this credo in the sequel we hear Hollywood is currently planning.

In the 2000s came two new types of gunslinger—hedge funds and private equity groups—who were to feature front and centre in the next LBO boom and the craze for alternative investment products. It's not that there is anything wrong with sensible hedging against investment risk, or raising needed capital from private sources. It's when these practices are used to leverage returns to extreme—dare we say obscene—levels that financial systems and investment markets become exposed in dangerous ways that can bring down the entire house, as was to happen in escalating fashion in 2008.

The risks became more dangerous still when exacerbated by unregulated, hard-to-measure, specially structured products called derivatives. Some estimates put the national value of what are essentially contractual bets as high as $200 trillion. Never before have financial markets had a "Gordian Knot" like this to unravel, or anything of this magnitude to deleverage. Warren Buffett's 2008 annual letter to Berkshire Hathaway shareholders contains a stark, one-sentence reminder of an oft-repeated warning: "Derivatives are dangerous." There is also—as happened—the risk of a breakdown in that most vital investment ingredient of all: trust. It's a topic we shall return to in the next chapter. Gordon Gekko, we pray you have repented, because greed is not good. As Mr. Buffett keeps repeating, it is also very dangerous.

ENTER THE BEAR

Bull markets are born in the depths of pain and despair, while bear markets tiptoe in at the heights of euphoria, to be succeeded in due course by the returning bull in the timeless market cycle. However, few could have appreciated the gauntlet of troubles that were to lie ahead not once but twice over the opening decade of what was going to be a glittering new millennium and century. The bursting of that grossly inflated tech bubble (the biggest speculative bubble in history); the horrors of September 11, 2001; growing corporate malfeasance and an accompanying breakdown in sacred trust; the Iraq war and its aftermath; a contagious subprime mortgage crisis and banking system breakdown; the humbling of the once mighty U.S. dollar; government bailouts and takeovers of financial institutions judged too big to be allowed to fail; and coordinated, synchronized rescue actions by governments and central bankers—it's all a real-life movie Hollywood couldn't have scripted any better, and continues to play out with no certain happy ending.

BE PREPARED

Rather than a glorious millennium, investors have found themselves pitchforked into their second bear market in less than a decade—a brand new experience for a whole generation of beginner investors, and a painful reminder for the ill-prepared to always be prepared.

Bear markets typically average 12 to 15 months in length and take the stock market down about a third. Two bear markets that stand out are those of 1973–74 (in 21 months, down 48%) and 1980–82 (in 20 months, down 27%). After the great bull market spawned in the depths of despair in 1982 came an equally unexpected bear market to usher in the new millennium, lasting 30 months and bringing a correction of close to 50%. On its heels came the bear market that began in October 2007 and, if it turns out to have ended with the lows of March 2009, will have lasted 18 months for a correction in the broad markets, as measured by the S&P 500 Index, of close to 60%.

Rather than healthy restoration, these successive new millennium bear markets have subjected investors to what could well have been perfect stock market storms, one after the other, in which almost every portfolio lost value big time, and those not properly structured were blown clean over—a great many never to return.

In due course, as they have always done, bear markets end and new bull markets are born. It's a timeless cycle in which the lessons learned and the magnitude of past versus present declines help maintain all-important investor perspective.

WALLS OF WORRY

The lexicon of Wall Street is peppered with phrases meant to remind, inspire and warn, including one that *investors must always be climbing walls of worry*. Over the years of making a living in the business of advising people on how best to invest their hard-earned dollars, we've learned the hard way that if you're not sweating the details—climbing walls of worry—a cavalier attitude and a degree of carelessness can creep into the decision-making process. In retrospect, there can be no doubt this happened again in the leveraged, get-rich-quick-guided, product-driven markets of recent years. Legions of battered investors could painfully testify how the result can be extremely costly—and often also lifestyle altering.

WHAT IF?

Writing in the *Wall Street Journal* more than a hundred years ago, Charles Dow, that great Wall Street theorist and the originator of the Dow Jones Industrial Average, recognized the most basic elements of investor psychology: fear and greed, which we introduced earlier and will return to in chapter 4. Dow wrote that "There is always a disposition in people's minds to think that the existing conditions will be permanent. When [stock] prices are up and the country is prosperous, it is always said that while preceding booms have not lasted, this time there are unique circumstances which will make prosperity permanent."

Eighty years later, Sir John Templeton was to put it even more succinctly when he stated that the most expensive phrase in the language of Wall Street is "this time it's different."

We'll go one step further and say that the two most *profitable* words an investor can utter are "what if." It's often been said that armies are best prepared to fight the last war, yet we know that survival on the battlefield demands extensive preparations and a willingness to adapt to changing conditions once the enemy is engaged.

Economists, academics, portfolio managers and politicians all expend tremendous amounts of time and energy trying to get a fix on where the world is heading. This is as it should be, but who hasn't heard of that guy Murphy and his law? Instead, please remember that for every risk there is an opportunity. In this knowledge, sift through the verbiage and use the resources around you to plan for the future as you let history be your guide. As you do, always be prepared to ask yourself, and your advisor for that matter, "What if…?"

Circumstances do change. In fact, in our world of instant communication and a 24-hour news cycle, change occurs faster than at any other time in human history, leaving no standards to compare with and measure against.

If you've learned anything from this opening chapter, it should be that change is constant and seldom occurs when expected. To embrace this fact of life and to put it in historical perspective is to take a quantum leap forward in your development as an investor. You'll be better able to understand what is happening in the ongoing push and pull of the world's financial markets, the focus in the next chapter. It's all part of the careful planning, vigilance and discipline that makes for successful long-term investing.

CHAPTER 2

Trust, but Verify

"In God we trust; all others pay cash!" So reads the now legendary and often duplicated sign next to a cash register at a long since forgotten American diner. Trust is highly transitory, perhaps more so now than ever before. The best remedy we can prescribe to keep trust from veering into naiveté is knowledge. "If you don't know it, you can't say it." We've never forgotten this credo of Aneurin Bevan, a distinguished Welsh parliamentarian and brilliant orator, who learned the hard way that you lose out if your adversaries across the floor know more than you do.

The same logic applies in investing: if you don't know as much as you should about the overall economy and markets and what you should be investing in, you won't do nearly as well as you deserve to. Your understanding and knowledge needn't be exhaustive. This should be the responsibility of your trusted financial advisor. You should know that the next time you are offered something as off-the-wall as a "high-grade structured enhanced leverage fund," you can say a categorical NO. (We promise you, there will be a next time.) And, more importantly, you should be able to understand what is having an impact on your savings and investments in these times of tectonic change and radically fluctuating markets.

Just as there is a heightening need to look after ourselves financially, there also are emerging new approaches and thoughtful, effective, new investment solutions from the insurance industry that we will outline in a later chapter. You should know about them. With improved understanding, you'll also be able to keep better tabs on your assets and their ability to work within the context of a carefully structured plan.

Trust must feature front and centre in this whole process. It's a vital investment ingredient that has taken a beating lately, yet is more essential than ever in the "new normal" world outlined in chapter 1, and was very likely ushered in on September 29, 2008. Without trust you simply will not be able to get to your predetermined destination safely.

In turn, trust has a polar opposite called greed, the two forever locked in a timeless tug-of-war. Investors the world over have painfully rediscovered what it means when greed gains the upper hand.

BERNIE'S BILLIONS AND MISPLACED TRUST

Bernard Madoff (funnily enough, pronounced "made-off"), a former chair of the NASDAQ electronic stock exchange, was known for his respectable client returns. Year in and year out, good markets and bad, they were steadiness epitomized. Bankers, brokers, dealers, investment managers and clients from all over fed him business, and the referrals kept on coming. Unfortunately, as it turned out, his exemplary records were falsified, and the steady profits and returns he supposedly earned for his clients were merely an illusion.

This Ponzi-like swindle on a scale as never before could be kept going as long as the new cash inflows exceeded outflows. But it became a different matter, and by Mr. Madoff's own admission the game was up, when the stock markets crashed and cash inflows began shrinking. Stealing from new clients to service existing clients could go on no longer, and in late 2008 a fraud of somewhere between US$50 billion and US$65 billion over 20 years was exposed as Wall Street's largest ever.

The list of names feeding Madoff business and entrusting him with their savings reads like a "who's who" and begs many greed-related questions. At the same time, we tip our hats to those who did their due diligence and decided against investing with him. One individual in particular questioned how an auditor so small and obscure could handle a firm so large. Not satisfied after getting to know more, he wisely walked away.

THE AMERICAN DREAM . . .

If Bernie Madoff wasn't bad enough, how about a scheme on an ultra grand scale that all of us were probably indirectly and unknowingly involved in?

You know the story about realizing the "American dream." Enter Wall Street and its creation of a "factory" through which billions of dollars worth of subprime mortgages were processed, thereby helping finance the biggest-ever U.S. housing boom on the easiest and most irresistible of purchase terms.

Take infamous NINJA ("no income, no job, no assets") and "no doc" (no documentation) loans, with nothing down and nothing to pay for the first year or two and low initial interest rates on the easiest of payment terms—with nary a mention of the triggers later on. Bundle or "securitize" these subprime mortgages into fancifully named investment packages, get them a top rating from the credit rating agencies, and sell them to banks, pension funds, hedge funds and private equity groups leveraged to the hilt to take maximum advantage. Even swindlers like Charles Ponzi would have been envious.

There was something in it for everyone—fat commissions for originating brokers and lucrative fees for the rating agencies, participating banks, investment firms, hedge funds and private equity groups. There also was highly profitable counter-party insurance provided by AIG. All of this was on the IBG ("I'll be gone") principle, with everyone on the take, creating a huge new subprime-based gravy train for predators of all types.

It was also a demand that could be handled readily through the short-term money markets. Never mind that every Economics 101 student is taught not to borrow short and invest long—the prospective pay-offs were just too tantalizing.

AND THE GLOBAL NIGHTMARE

Everything went swimmingly until U.S. interest rates began edging upward, triggering reset mechanisms in core mortgages. Homeowners, many of them also speculators in their own homes, began defaulting in droves and, horror of horrors, housing prices started to fall. It didn't take long for businesses, from the smallest to the largest, to no longer be financed—or re-financed—in money and credit markets that had frozen. No longer were those securitized and supposedly collateralized debt and other obligations worth their underlying value, which had always been difficult enough to determine anyway. Just as suddenly, the biggest boom in housing became the biggest bust, leaving in its wake a wave of unfathomable but heavy investment losses and write-downs.

A contagious fallout was to spread internationally, particularly to Britain and Europe where participating banks turned out to be leveraged much higher than at first had been thought. Impossible-to-determine losses in the derivative and insurance markets, i.e., in contracts (or bets) "derived" from these investments, brought further complications for a banking system that had become a complex mass of leveraged, intertwined counter-party lending.

Layering product upon product, extending the chain between user and investor, traders simultaneously going long and short—it was mind-boggling, even for the experts. The late Tony Furgueson of Furgueson Capital Management expressively likened it to the pick-up sticks game we played as children. Considerable dexterity and skill were required to build structures higher and higher, but the smallest miscue and it all came crashing down.

As mentioned in chapter 1, Sir John Templeton always believed the phrase "this time it's different" to be *the* most expensive in the investment language. Except there couldn't ever have been a time when the world's banking system became quite so contaminated by illiquid, unmarketable toxic assets. Or when banks and other financial institutions, hard hit by difficult-to-measure mortgage-related investments and anxious to shore up their damaged underlying capitals, cut back on lending and lifeblood credit the way they did. Or when trust broke down to such an extent that they wouldn't even lend to one another!

A forbidding list of banks and financial institutions judged too big to be allowed to fail and needing to be saved from summary bankruptcy included not just AIG, but iconic names like Citigroup, Merrill Lynch and, internationally, Royal Bank of Scotland, and Lloyds Bank. But thankfully not in Canada where a mostly asset-backed commercial paper (ABCP) problem outside the major bank orbit needed to be resolved, (refer to Chapter 8), but there was never any need for government bailout or takeover, and key capital ratios could be readily maintained.

In all, it was almost as if George W. Bush had found his long-sought weapons of mass destruction, only they were financial rather than nuclear and in his own back yard. Furthermore, when the wherewithal to finance payrolls, receivables and working capital becomes ever harder to maintain there is an ever-widening ripple effect. This time the wave that rolled over the crucial automotive industry and its legions of related and satellite businesses was of the killer variety. Economies the world over were sideswiped too, some like Iceland, Ireland, and in Eastern Europe to the point of national bankruptcy. How an artificial and recklessly-financed housing boom could go wrong—and what lessons to be learned!

THERE *IS* A SILVER LINING

On the positive side, the credit crisis and the economic hardship that followed in its wake are also bringing far-reaching adjustments and corrections for the better. It may be a far cry from Ronald Reagan's inaugural declaration that "government is not the solution to the problem, government *is* the problem." Or, his contention that the most terrifying words in the English language are "I'm from the government and I've come to help you." Nevertheless, seldom—maybe never—was there such an all–out and co-ordinated attempt by governments everywhere to get credit flowing again and to assist stricken economies get out of recession: also to resolve trust in badly-shaken banking and financial systems.

In capital markets there is the growing benefit of heightened investor awareness and scrutiny learned the hard way. For a time, opening your monthly investment statement became something to dread. But you and your financial advisor have learned from this experience: you manage the bear rather than allowing the bear to manage you.

One such lesson unquestionably would be to better select and identify with companies that have the balance sheet and cash flow strength to not only survive recession and hard times, but to come through for you all the more strongly and better positioned within their industries. So much the better if they also pay regular and rising annual dividends. You'd be amazed how the yield on the cost of your investment rises over time.

INFORMED CONSENT

Even if owning individual stocks is not your style, there is much to be said regarding the benefit of buying or adding to holdings in sound securities when they too are swept over a cliff in rollercoaster market corrections.

You'll be in a much better position to make the distinction between an undervalued but sound security and appropriately priced junk when armed with some basic understanding of what it is your hard-earned money has been invested in. Simply put, you become a better investor by knowing more. If you work with a financial advisor, you know that all he or she can do is advise. Advisors cannot make decisions for you. The best financial advisors don't want clients who blindly give their consent to any and all recommendations. The best clients give their advisors *informed* consent.

CHAPTER 3

Self-Inflicted Wounds

The Most Common Strategic Errors Made by Investors

As we discussed in chapter 1, memories of a market reversal fade in direct proportion to the speed and altitude of that market's advance. Not surprisingly, this also has the tendency to lead to heightened levels of bravado among investors who then begin to unwittingly take on greater degrees of risk.

In the course of our work with legions of individual investors, a number of potentially painful themes appear repeatedly. Many of these self-inflicted wounds, if left untended, can fester, growing into substantially more serious and costly problems. That's the bad news. The good news is that most if not all of the wounds we've tended to are, with time, fairly easy to treat. Should you recognize some of your own foibles nestled among those chronicled here, take comfort in the fact that you are not alone. These are injuries that are easy to fall victim to. You certainly weren't the first casualty, and neither will you be the last. Our message is to not give up in the face of adversity; giving up metastasizes something entirely treatable into something terminal.

In this chapter, our focus is on strategic errors, most of which involve our own basic human failings. Some of these portfolio ailments also may have a certain ring of familiarity. Once again, take heart, as we show you how to stage a complete recovery.

THE NUMBER ONE ERROR OF OMISSION: WHERE ARE THE BONDS?

Though this chapter will deal largely with errors of *commission*, it is not uncommon for us to review a wounded portfolio only to discover that the root problems stem from what the owner overlooked or omitted. All too often this can be as simple as a dearth of fixed-income securities and, following from this, a portfolio lacking the all-important requirement of proper balance.

During the late 1990s, in what turned out to be the last phase of the greatest bull market of the 20th century, it became fashionable to shun bonds. What had happened was that as inflation came under control, central bankers became able to bring down lending rates to levels not seen since the times of Eisenhower and Diefenbaker, which meant that bonds provided relatively poor returns in the eyes of investors who had in years past become accustomed to much more lucrative yields. The net result was that many investors felt compelled to recapture some of what they used to receive in the form of yield by entering the stock market—many indirectly via mutual funds, and many for the first time in their lives. Early successes by these investors chased away any butterflies the typical investor may have had when making his or her first investment. The sometimes substantial gains realized by these neophyte investors quickly changed the way they looked at bonds and all other fixed-income investments. Suddenly, bonds were like the contestant who wins Miss Congeniality at a beauty pageant. Equities, meanwhile, had won the Swimsuit Competition.

Flying Without a Net

Even in an era of ultra-low interest rates like now, the tragedy is that running a portfolio without fixed-income securities is a little like the Flying Wallendas—performing without a net. Too often, starry eyed investors were trying to make apples-to-apples comparisons between bonds, which have a fixed rate of return, and equities, which were in rapid ascent. Just as often, the illogical conclusion was that having bonds in their turbo-charged growth portfolios served the same purpose as aerodynamic drag: unnecessarily slowing things down.

To stretch this tortured metaphor a little more, the reality is that having a fixed-income segment in a growth portfolio is not so much *aerodynamic drag* as having a *drag chute* on a top-fuel racer. It's understandable, and desirable, to want to achieve maximum velocity when market conditions permit. There will come a time, though, when the stock markets will falter. At that point, you will recognize the need to be able to gear down to navigate through the difficult market conditions that inevitably will get in your way.

Grandma's Got Her Game Face On

Investors in need of income, such as retirees, also can fall victim to the temptation of forgoing bonds in favour of a growth strategy that they think will meet their needs more easily. This is invariably the case in advanced bull market phases like the late 1990s. Early in a bull market, these self-described conservative, income-dependent investors still retain vivid memories of market downturns. We've seen time and again, however, that these memories quickly fade. As the major market averages scale new heights, the terms used to describe one's risk tolerance start to become increasingly subjective. All of a sudden, Grandma has a portfolio stuffed full of growth stocks, and she's on the phone to her broker demanding to know why Millie at the bridge club is getting more growth on her portfolio than she is.

Bryan vividly remembers his office's Christmas potluck luncheon in 1999 when the brokers gathered around the massive mahogany boardroom table, nibbling on nachos, nursing lukewarm beer and swapping stories of "irrational exuberance." Every broker had at least one story to tell of a verbal tongue-lashing from a stereotypical little old lady for failing to deliver growth that kept pace with a day-trading friend (despite asset allocations and risk tolerances geared to conservatism and income generation). Michael remembers similar examples of clients objecting loudly when he recommended cutting back on suddenly disproportionately large holdings in Nortel Networks as it kept reaching for the sky.

The stories one year later couldn't have been in more stark contrast. By December 2000, a bear market had begun taking hold in earnest, and those same Jekyll and Hyde investors were reverting to their conservative personas with a vengeance. Many investors became paralyzed with fear. They fervently hoped that the decline was nothing more than an aberration. During the market's rise, they had been able to draw income from their portfolios without eating into their capital, thereby gaining the mistaken impression that growth investments were also suitable for income-dependent investors. Then cold reality began to set in: drawing income from a portfolio that is declining in value is akin to compounding in reverse. As a consequence, investors who are the least able to withstand a downturn suffer significantly greater harm than others. This is exactly what happened with a vengeance as the ferocious bear market took hold in 2000–2002 and again in 2007–2009.

Bonds as a Buffer

This brings us back to the true purpose of fixed-income investments. Even for growth-seeking investors, fixed income plays the role of a buffer, smoothing out the inevitable peaks and valleys in portfolio performance and providing the liquidity to fund fresh investment when the market opportunity arises.

For the income-seeking investor, fixed-income investments, with their set maturity dates and regular interest payments, offer a degree of income and capital preservation commensurate with the degree of credit risk that can be run. As a rule, we tend to avoid any debt instrument with less than an "A" rating.

As bonds mature, the continual adding of new maturity rungs to a ladder of maturities can keep this process going indefinitely. Laddering a portfolio of bonds is another way to smooth out the ups and downs of interest-rate changes.

What's a Bond Ladder?

A bond ladder, or laddered bond portfolio, is a series of bonds that each have a maturity date later than the bond prior in the succession. Think of a laddered bond portfolio as the investor's version of a vertical wine tasting. We'll talk more about bond ladders in chapter 8.

Even if you do not yet rely upon your portfolio to provide you with an income, this chapter is still worth a visit. Suffice it to say that a representative fixed-income component should be a mandatory prerequisite in each and every portfolio.

CONCENTRATION:
A CLOSER LOOK AT EGGS AND BASKETS

The collapse of Houston-based energy trader Enron was, to say the least, tragic for all of its stakeholders, both direct and indirect. Arguably, the greatest harm was suffered by scores of Enron employees who, in addition to losing their jobs, watched helplessly as their retirement savings, which had been pumped full of their employer's stock, came crashing down. We're not referring here to those senior executives under indictment for the criminal actions and inactions that led to Enron's demise; we're referring to the rank-and-file workers who continued to invest in good faith at the urging of their employer, in the process concentrating their retirement savings accounts to an ever-greater degree in the shares of one company: in this case, Enron. For many Enron employees the collapse of their company meant a permanent shift in their standard of living to something far less desirable than what they had worked and saved for.

The lesson in the Enron catastrophe and other high-profile collapses that were to follow is that a portfolio can become dominated by one stock or market sector. This is a situation that often occurs in the portfolios of long-serving employees at major corporations. Most publicly listed corporations offer employee share ownership programs and/or structure their compensation programs to include an equity component. Over time, this can be deservedly rewarding. And, as a result, it is not at all unusual for a disproportionately large portion of an employee's net worth to become represented by the shares of their employer firm, a development that can also appear entirely logical. After all, if one of the cardinal rules of investing is to *know what you own*, then does it not make sense to have your largest holding in the shares of the company you likely know better than any other? Within reason, yes, but not excessively, and most definitely not to the point where the portfolio structured to help finance your retirement future is put at unnecessary risk.

Know Where to Draw the Line

All too suddenly the employee-shareholders of fallen giants like Enron came to rue their extremely painful over-ownership of their company's stock. While employees usually fare well in their employee share ownership experience, these employee-shareholders unwittingly became part of spectacular, life-altering disasters. It is a lesson that is applicable not just to those who own shares in the companies they work for, but to anyone who has excessive exposure to any one stock or market segment.

Although we've already stated that a cardinal rule in investing is to know what you own, clearly this easily can be taken to extremes when it comes to employee share ownership. Stop to think for a moment how many times you have watched in amazement as another apparently invincible corporate bellwether is brought to its knees by changing technology, economic hardship or even scandal. Think back to the autumn of 2008 and the decline of so many financial icons that had once seemed invincible. Though tragic for shareholders, the problem is magnified many times over when your largest investment is also your place of employment and primary source of income.

A disciplined approach here is essential. Stop to consider the degree to which your employer's stock occupies your total net worth. You will need to have a discussion with your advisor (even if you are your own advisor) about the magnitude of employee share ownership that is appropriate for you. The investment policy statements outlined later in this book can help to clearly map out what the limits should be, but are useful only if you are determined to stick to your own guidelines.

A Little Off the Top, Please . . .

Harm from portfolio concentration can manifest itself in other ways. If the company in question is part of a cyclical business (natural resources, consumer discretionary products, etc.) and as such the company's shares are subject to a high degree of price volatility, you'll need to be prepared for major fluctuations in the value of your nest egg. To mitigate volatility, you'll need to occasionally trim back the size of your position by regularly stopping to take profits on the way up. This will serve two purposes. The first is that it will force a discipline of not allowing any single position (or sector) to become an overwhelmingly large aspect of your portfolio. The second is that you'll be adhering faithfully to that old investment adage: You'll never go broke taking a profit.

The prudent investor must set limits on how much of his or her portfolio should be dedicated to any one security or sector of the economy, regardless of how promising it may seem. This speaks to the issues of asset allocation strategies and investment policy statements, which we will explore in greater detail in later chapters. Again, it boils down to knowing where to draw the line so that the risks to you and your retirement investments are contained.

PACK RAT SYNDROME

Proper diversification may be a cardinal rule of successful investing, but just as there can be too much of a good thing (concentrated positions) there can also be too many inconsequential holdings. Time and again we see portfolios that have far too many holdings for their own good. They may not necessarily be poor investments, but invariably they are too small to have any meaningful impact on the overall portfolio, regardless of how well they do.

Dr. Sharpe's Prescription

We subscribe to the view of the distinguished Dr. William Sharpe that there shouldn't be more than 15 to 20 different stocks or equity holdings in a portfolio at any given time. Why? Because beyond this number the benefits of diversification trail off steeply. Accordingly, Michael's initial advice on many portfolios he is shown is to begin the restorative process by weeding out superfluous holdings, ideally to no more than Dr. Sharpe's prescription. In the process, you'll also find that what's left becomes much more coherent and manageable.

Cut the Clutter

Suppose a portfolio should be balanced 60:40 in favour of equities. Divide 60% by 15 and this gives 4% of the total portfolio value as the optimum size of each individual equity holding. If 12 rather than 15 equity holdings are judged to be the optimum, then the 4% becomes 5%. Individual holdings of this magnitude are meaningful. If they perform well, their overall impact will be positive; if one or two perform sensationally, the impact could be dramatic—and all portfolios should aspire to a grand-slam home run or two. If, however, a position begins to turn sour, the security in question will be much easier to spot if it is not lost amid the clutter of a portfolio that is excessively dispersed.

Plight of the Mutual Fund Investor

Mutual fund investors have a unique plight. It is not uncommon for this breed of investor to suffer simultaneously from both the Pack Rat Syndrome and portfolio concentration. Until the elimination of the foreign content rule in the 2005 Canadian federal budget, this had been an all-too-frequent occurrence among RRSP accounts. Under the terms of the foreign content rule, an investor could invest no more than 30% of the book value of his or her RRSP (or RRIF) beyond Canada's borders. This rule invariably led many investors to stack, one upon another, a series of Canadian-based mutual funds. Each fund was presumed to approach the market from a slightly different angle, with the ultimate objective of additional diversification.

There is merit to this theory of style diversification, at least in principle. There are times when the growth method of security selection is the superior style. Similarly, there are occasions when value investing is significantly more rewarding. Where the theory can run head-first into practice is in a relatively small market, such as Canada's. The net result for investors can often be an unnecessary redundancy of holdings. Without knowing it, mutual fund investors can have concentrated positions in a handful of stocks and/or market sectors because their mutual fund managers all picked stocks from the comparatively limited menu that is the Toronto Stock Exchange. With the elimination of the foreign content rule, mutual fund managers have begun to choose stocks from the much wider global market in addition to that here at home, and this problem should ultimately sort itself out over time.

There remains, however, the central issue of a given mutual fund's mandate. Though a Canadian fund may invest some of its assets outside Canada, the bulk of its investments will be here. If you have an assortment of Canadian mutual funds in your portfolio, take a look at each fund's largest positions to smoke out redundancies. If you hold four Canadian equity funds, each listing some of the big five Canadian banks among their largest holdings, chances are you've got a concentration issue. This is all the more so if, in addition to the mutual funds, you hold a bank stock or two (not a rare occurrence).

Be a Weight Watcher

Keeping asset weightings in line is a good way of maintaining necessary portfolio discipline and of controlling portfolio risk. It often includes a need to limit portfolios to an optimum number of holdings. This can mean adding to exceptionally promising holdings that are proportionately too small, taking them up to the desirable maximum weighting. Always remember there should be no more than an optimum number of equities in most individual investor portfolios. Each such holding must be meaningful in size. Excess holdings should be weeded out to bring the portfolio to the optimum range of holdings (we prefer 15 to 20). This act alone will bring greater clarity to the portfolio, making it easier to spot and remedy problems much sooner than would ordinarily be the case with a cluttered portfolio.

This is not a prescription to give up on mutual funds. In fact, far from it. We're simply pointing out that many Canadian mutual fund investors are not getting the degree of portfolio diversification that they assume they are receiving. This is not the fault of the fund manager. It comes down to sloppy fund selection, which can be easily remedied by looking deeper within a fund family's stable of offerings and choosing funds with the same degree of care as you would individual stocks.

MAYBE KENNY ROGERS WAS RIGHT—YOU'VE GOT TO KNOW WHEN TO HOLD 'EM . . .

There was a dark period in Bryan's youth when his mother developed an affection (an unhealthy one, in his opinion) for the music of Kenny Rogers, specifically, the album *The Gambler*. Day after day, the living room console stereo would reverberate with Kenny's dulcet tones belting out the title song's chorus—which has stayed with Bryan like an unsightly birthmark.

This Kenny Rogers classic lyric—of knowing when to hold on or fold—illustrates one of the most important yet most often overlooked disciplines for successful investing: the sell discipline. All too often we are inundated with suggestions of what should be added to portfolios. Rare is the day when someone rings a little bell and says, "Okay, time to sell International Goose Grappler Inc." There's an old investment adage that says your first loss is your best loss. In his popular book on the fine art of investing, *How to Make Money in Stocks*, William O'Neil expands on the thinking behind the old first-loss chestnut, and recommends investors learn to take losses quickly and profits slowly. In real life, however, many investors do just the opposite, with unfortunate consequences.

Letting your losses run is often the most costly mistake an investor can make. You simply have to accept the fact that mistakes and unforeseen circumstances will make their way into your portfolio from time to time, despite your best efforts. This is something that is difficult, if not impossible, to control. However, what *is* under your control is your response to recognizing these mistakes.

One method of stripping away the emotion from the decision to sell a security is to put in place what is known as a stop-loss point, a predetermined price that triggers the sale of the given stock. This approach has the added advantage that if the security is on a downward trajectory and management is taking concrete steps to correct the related deficiency, then you'll be able to re-examine the company with cool detachment because you cut your losses earlier and are now faced with the question of whether to reinvest at a more attractive price. By then you might well have moved on to an even better, more lucrative investment opportunity and have a doubly nice choice to make, thanks to the discipline of stop-loss selling that automatically triggers action. Having some predetermined plan of action on when to exit a security, regardless of whether it is a stock, mutual fund, exchange traded fund, etc., is vastly preferential to doing nothing or procrastinating endlessly.

A Humbling Experience

Forget your ego, offload your pride and never forget that investing is a humbling experience even at the best of times. You just can't fight the market. The market is not always rational. None of us can afford to fall in love with a company that is losing us money. Remember the words of William O'Neil, even if you have to swallow hard in the process: "Take your losses quickly, your profits slowly."

FALLING KNIVES

Yet another time-tested investment adage states that one should never try to catch a falling knife. That's good advice in the physical as well as the abstract sense, and is even more valuable today against a backdrop of seemingly unending corporate misdemeanours.

Catching a falling knife in the investment context concerns the act of picking up shares of companies that have dropped precipitously, usually after some catastrophic event. Sometimes, the rewards can be very lucrative. Michael likes to put a bit of a twist on the falling knives theory by preferring to pick up *fallen* knives, not falling ones. Using this rationale, investors know that they are not likely to grab on to a stock at its absolute lowest point. Instead, investors who shop among the fallen knives are more likely to buy shares of a company once recovery has already begun. Sure, they will forgo some potential profit, but this class of investor views the forgone profit as a small price to pay for the security of the higher probability that they own shares of a fallen rather than falling knife.

Admittedly, the temptation to grab hold of shares of erstwhile high flyers that have come upon hard times is understandably powerful. Consider the shares of insurance brokerage giant Marsh & McLennan, which in late 2004 dropped by more than 40% in just over a week following allegations of kickbacks and bid-rigging by then New York state Attorney General Eliot Spitzer—the same with the Canadian example of Teck Cominco in late 2008, though for altogether different reasons. A breathtaking plunge like this is just the kind of activity that ordinarily gets the contrarian investor's attention. (A contrarian is an investor who makes a point of going against the crowd.) In fact, many professional "vulture" funds make a living out of buying and trading in the shares of companies in deep distress. However, given the complexities, the successful catching of falling knives has become more difficult and dangerous than ever.

Don't Try This at Home

Knife catching is tough and often best left to professionals rather than casual investors. Bad news is often followed by even more bad news. Knife catchers with full sets of fingers are those who have moved in on a company after all bad news has been disseminated and when relatively good news is starting to emerge. The trouble is that the window of opportunity is exceedingly small and most knife catchers have been nicked more than once by moving too soon in anticipation of a turnaround.

Buying fallen stocks when nobody else wants them can give the savvy investor who has done his or her homework a head start on the crowd. Nevertheless, being a contrarian investor isn't easy for the vast majority of individual investors. If you do like to dabble and prefer the stock markets to lotteries or the horses, and occasionally fancy yourself to be a catcher of knives, by all means set up a separate trading account, but always do so with a specific limit as to how much you can afford to lose. Never try to catch a falling knife in an RRSP or RRIF account. Though gains in RRSP or RRIF accounts are sheltered from tax, the problem is that if the trade turns into a painful loss, you will not be able to write off the resulting capital loss against capital gains on other transactions. In a genuine long-term investment portfolio, "never catch a falling knife" is an old Wall Street saying that is best heeded.

OTHER PEOPLE'S MONEY

Businesses regularly expand their operations through the use of borrowed capital. So do countless individuals. For example, home ownership would not be even close to today's level were it not for the mortgage financing structures that began to be introduced shortly after World War II.

Borrowing money for investment purposes offers a similar ability to gain financial *leverage*. For example, a $100,000 investment made half on borrowed money that rises in value by 10% to $110,000 will provide a profit of 20% on your original capital once the investment is sold and the loan paid off. This is the magnifying capability of leveraging in action. Unfortunately, the same principle applies in reverse as well. Going in the opposite direction, were the same investment to fall in value by 10%, the loss to the investor is actually a much more substantial 20%. Ouch!

Often, a company that has been funding its growth strategy primarily, or perhaps even exclusively, through the use of borrowed capital is referred to as being highly leveraged. Similarly, the act of borrowing to invest is often referred to as the act of leveraging, which, when used prudently, can work like an anabolic steroid on your net worth, adding muscle mass to your portfolio more quickly than would otherwise be the case.

Like anabolic steroids, however, leveraging can have nasty, undesirable side effects, introducing additional volatility to portfolios. The most common of these side effects occurs when a highly leveraged investor fails to meet a margin call and watches his or her equity disappear without the ability to recoup it. A margin call is a "send more money" call from your broker—one that is triggered by a drop in the value of your portfolio so that the account is in a status known as "under margin." Please refer to the upcoming section entitled Margin Trading for more detail on the subject of investing on margin.

Financial Flesh-Eating Disease

When it goes awry, leveraging is more like the financial equivalent of flesh-eating disease, magnifying and accelerating the damage to your financial well-being. It's for this reason that leveraging needs to be handled with great care. The lesson? Using borrowed money to invest can dramatically magnify gains. Unfortunately, it works in the same manner in the opposite direction, magnifying losses and multiplying the degree of risk in an investment strategy.

You're likely familiar with the concept of leverage if you have ever:

- borrowed money to make a contribution to your RRSP
- bought securities on margin from your broker
- used a line of credit or term loan to raise money for investment purposes

Leverage can be applied to RRSPs, margin buying, short selling and mutual fund purchases; in other words, the uses are very wide.

RRSP Loans

Early each year, the nation's financial institutions usually heavily promote RRSP loans in a bid to capture (for them at least) something akin to a two-for-one special. Short on cash after the holidays, and staring into the gaping maw of a potentially big tax bill? Fantastic! Your bank would love nothing more than to lend you the money to make an RRSP investment with them. This is all well and good, provided you don't over-borrow and you resolve that this kind of investment loan should be paid off quickly, even if your bank is offering it at their prime rate. The reason: interest charged on such loans is not tax deductible and can all too readily become an unwelcome millstone.

Margin Trading

In a similar vein, brokerage houses offer margin accounts, which enable their clients to borrow money from the firm against the equity in their portfolio for the purpose of making additional investments. This "loan" works much like a secured line of credit, in that clients are charged interest on the outstanding balances and are free to repay the loan balances in whole or in part without penalty at any time. As long as clients have sufficient equity in their accounts, they are able to re-borrow and repay over and over again. However, under securities law, a brokerage house can only loan you a set percentage of the total value of your investment, and if the value of the outstanding debt exceeds the maximum permissible loan amount, the broker is then forced to make the dreaded margin call. To expand on the earlier explanation of a margin call, that's the unpleasant conversation when you are asked to send more money in order to get back on side the percentage loaned, otherwise your brokerage will be compelled to sell some or all of the investment, even at a loss, in order to make up the shortfall. It is precisely for this reason that margin buying needs to be handled with utmost care.

In addition, being excessively leveraged through margin can rob you of control to effectively decide when certain of the securities held in your portfolio should be added to, trimmed or sold. This position of vulnerability is simple to avoid by making certain that you have plenty of excess capital available before engaging in buying securities on margin.

Dr. Graham's Prescription

One old-fashioned rule that stays in Michael's mind is to borrow for margin buying no more than the previous year's gain in the overall portfolio. And similarly to deleverage (reduce) your margin borrowing by your previous years's losses. Whatever approach you and your advisor decide upon, always set and keep to the strictest of limits on borrowing for investment purposes. Never forget that while borrowed capital magnifies gains, it also magnifies losses.

Short Selling

The act of borrowing, from your brokerage, shares of a company you do not already own in order to immediately sell these shares is called short selling. This is another means of leverage that requires you to tread warily and is definitely not for the faint-hearted. For short selling to be a profitable venture, the shares of the company must drop in value so that you can buy them back on the market at a lower price, repay your broker and pocket the difference. The obvious risk to selling something you don't own is that the shares of the stock in question may rise rather than fall. The implication of this is that eventually you will have to pay back the shares to the brokerage from whom you borrowed. If the stock has increased in value, it will cost you more—sometimes considerably more—to buy the stock for repayment purposes. In the upside-down world of shorting, you make money only if the stock being shorted falls in value.

Margin requirements for short selling are generally much more stringent than for more conventional borrowing, and this can make short selling even more expensive.

Mutual Fund Leverage

During the extended bull market of the 1980s and 1990s, banks got in on the lending act in a big way by providing term loans for investors wishing to invest in mutual funds. Clients were urged to make monthly payments that consisted almost entirely of interest on the loan, the line of reasoning being that steady appreciation in the value of the invested assets would render repayment of the loan principal unnecessary until such time as it could be repaid out of profits.

Investors, lenders and financial planners all benefited. Investors became enamoured with this type of financial planning strategy because it permitted them to effectively "rent" money, leverage their income and earn a profit on the rented capital. Similarly, the banks' security increased as the value of the portfolio increased. Borrowers paying interest only made these investment loans (sometimes referred to as leverage loans) highly profitable for the lenders. Financial planners also loved the strategy because it enabled them to earn a commission on a large lump-sum investment all at once rather than the comparatively microscopic commissions they would make on investors' monthly contributions to their investment accounts. It was a situation in which all three stakeholders remained happy as long as the market continued its steady ascent.

Just as using borrowed money to invest has the positive attribute of magnifying gains, this form of investment can also magnify losses. The added tragedy is that losing money that is not your own doesn't alleviate the responsibility of having to pay back the principal and accumulated interest. In the case of brokerage firms, margin accounts with depleted asset values result in the "send more money" margin call.

We are not fundamentally opposed to borrowing for investment purposes. Countries do it (the international benchmark limit being 60% of gross domestic product) and companies do it, so why not investors? Certainly there are occasions when gaining this kind of leverage can assist materially in building lasting wealth, but always keep the prescribed limits in mind.

- Borrow no more for investment purposes than you are prepared to lose.
- Always remember that borrowing to invest is a strategy that is not for everyone.
- Respect the potential destructiveness of leverage.
- Avoid being seduced by the allure of tremendously magnified profits.

CONSIDER THE SOURCE

The hot tip. The inside edge. The smart money. In a world of supposedly efficient markets, the universal dream of investors is to find and act on information that is not widely available. Unfortunately, this perennial search can be carried to extremes in the hope that some obscure kernel of truth will provide an edge to score big gains in the market.

This isn't to say that great ideas shouldn't come from unconventional sources. Widely regarded as one of the savviest money managers ever to prowl the corridors of Boston-based mutual fund giant Fidelity Investments, Peter Lynch contended that individual investors can find good investment ideas by merely looking in the shopping cart when doing their weekly grocery shopping. Lynch has always been a proponent of good old-fashioned common sense. The father of modern securities analysis, Benjamin Graham (sadly, no relation to Michael), believed similarly that sound investment should be based first and foremost on correct facts. This approach clearly rules out buying investments on a hunch or on a tip, or because an acclaimed guru is recommending it—as with Michael's purchase of IBM, to be related later, a notable, but nailbiting, exception.

Make sure you do your homework before investing. Michael's research training has taught him to look critically at the records of the authors of research reports. He also always makes a point of reviewing the track record of the management of companies whose shares are being recommended. Genuine turnarounds are worth their weight in gold, but are very much the exception rather than the norm. It's much better to invest in a company with a reliable track record. Because it's your long-term retirement future that is at stake, you must have confidence in the source. For more information on research, please see the chapter entitled "The Unfair Advantage."

TRIAGE: GET ON WITH THE HEALING

The injured being brought to a hospital's emergency department often have ailments requiring lengthy diagnosis and treatment. Just as often, however, on-the-spot action can be taken to stop the bleeding before deciding on remedial treatment and an ultimate cure. The same is true of ailing portfolios in need of proper long-term treatment, while self-inflicted wounds that can be dealt with then and there should be. Equally apparent are portfolios that are in obvious trouble because of a hodge-podge of shortcomings despite their owner's best intentions.

For an investment professional, just as hard as making obligatory margin calls is having to look well-meaning investors in the eye and tell them that their portfolios just haven't got it—that they can't possibly bridge that ultimate retirement gap because of an accumulation of self-inflicted deficiencies. This is a state of affairs that also could have come about as a result of too-frequent changing of investment advisors and/or of a legacy of too many ill-suited, over-priced and illiquid investment schemes that looked better on paper than in execution. Even then, it is always better to face up to reality and begin the rehabilitative process as soon as possible. It's amazing how many investors immediately begin feeling better, despite the pain, the financial losses and the lost investment time needing to be made up.

In addition to a myriad of self-inflicted wounds, there's often an even bigger obstacle called "you" that needs to be dealt with in completing that all-important initial diagnosis. Never forget that the ultimate diagnosis depends on you and your personalized investment goals down that long but exciting and satisfyingly rewarding investment road.

Get treatment quickly for your portfolio's various wounds. As with many of life's endeavours, procrastination is often ultimately more costly than imagined. The sooner you embark upon the healing process, the sooner your portfolio will begin to gain momentum that will compound over the years. Over time, your now vibrant portfolio will make all the difference in the achievement of your ultimate goals.

CHAPTER 4

Tactical Errors

Mind Over Matter

To complete our diagnosis we need to look squarely in the eye of the investor's biggest potential obstacle of all: our own human failings. To err is human, but it's amazing nonetheless how we can get in our own way on the road to successful investing.

Like navigating a ship through uncharted waters, the essence of successful investing lies in the myriad of decisions you need to make on your long-term journey. Most of these decisions will come in the regular portfolio reviews and accompanying adjustments that should be at the heart of every successful investment strategy. Others will need to be made in response to the unexpected, a subject we examined earlier in detail and can promise plenty more of in the future.

Even the procrastinator, who ends up like the proverbial deer frozen in the headlights, still will have made a choice. Unfortunately, that kind of decision-making comes at the price of portfolios with weakened potential. Whether active or passive, large or small, all these necessary *en passant* decisions will add up over time to put their imprint on your portfolio and its ultimate degree of success.

FACTS AND REASONING

Benjamin Graham, regarded by many as the father of modern-day investing, maintained that you will be proven right if your facts and reasoning are correct. Following from this belief must be the making of sound investment-related decisions, and the taking of necessary portfolio action, in a world where change now takes place faster than ever before. You can be handed any number of "hot tips," or read a stack of books like this one to learn all you need to know about investing, but if your decision-making is flawed, whether because of incorrect information or failure to act, your portfolio will be as well.

Far too often, we are lulled into believing that someone has the so-called "silver bullet" that will deliver outstanding portfolio performance from here to eternity. Your authors have seen a lot of investment fads come and go over the decades, and often have wished someone did have all the answers. Life then would be so much simpler, more predictable and more profitable—but also more boring.

EMOTIONS IN MOTION

The fact is that managing a portfolio in good times and bad is more a matter of process than of event. Along the way, you'll be asked to make hard and fast decisions. This is where the human element enters the picture, and must be faced and acted upon, rather than avoided. Even so, it's a risk that is all too often easier to recognize than to overcome.

For most investors, it is almost impossible to strip away emotion from the decision-making process. After all, you're likely investing money that has been worked for very hard and at considerable personal sacrifice. There can also be strong emotional ties to portfolios resulting from an inheritance. However, the inescapable truth is that our emotions must be brought under control if our minds are to remain clear enough to make the sound and timely investment decisions that will be called for.

Every 12-step program begins with the premise that before healing and recovery can take place there first must be the admission of a problem. Investors often have no trouble recognizing that a problem exists; for example, when swallowing hard at the bottom-line number on their portfolio statements. That sinking feeling quickly can take away any lingering subjectivity and inexorably bring them face to face with the need to do something about slumping portfolio performance.

It follows, therefore, that recognition of the emotions that cloud judgment and an understanding of how they can manifest themselves in the decision-making process become critical in achieving portfolio goals—and ultimate investment success.

Most if not all of us are psychologically hard-wired to think we are better off than we actually are. It's an ongoing self-deception that inevitably leads to decision-making errors. The tendency to become overconfident can also mean previous decisions being viewed as sound, even when the evidence is to the contrary.

A century ago, Charles Dow, the founder of modern Dow theory and the man for whom the world's most famous stock market index is named, pointed out that the two most powerful human emotions investors can repeatedly expect to bump up against are fear and greed—polar opposites that can have a tendency to drive just about every investment decision and are all too often the root cause of clouded judgment. There are others, too. Highlighted below are these commonplace investor "sins" in what we see as the most logical sequence.

Greed

The 18th century South Sea Bubble fiasco and tulip bulb mania are both searing examples of how infectious greed can overwhelm even the most sensible investor. However, these and other examples of the herd mania that sweeps through the markets with regular monotony pale beside a speculative bubble that history will surely recall as the biggest—and also the most painful—of all time: the tech stock boom of the late 1990s. (We concede others may point to the U.S. property-related, subprime mortgage bubble of 2007–2009 as every bit as catastrophic.)

We've mentioned Nortel Networks before, the Bell Canada spinoff that landed in the portfolios of thousands of rank-and-file Canadians. The timing of this "bonus" couldn't have seemed more fortuitous as technology stocks rocketed up and up and up, in Nortel's case to a peak of more than $120 per share. What a way to begin a new millennium! New-found riches danced before countless eyes. However, that was before the tech bubble burst and a grossly and, as it turned out, falsely inflated Nortel became an icon for corporate malfeasance that sadly ended with a filing for creditor protection. Few Canadian investors emerged unscathed from the Nortel experience. What a painful lesson for a great many veterans and neophytes alike!

In his book *Investment Blunders of the Rich and Famous*, Washington State University finance professor Dr. John Nofsinger addresses the common psychological condition in which people tend to believe they are better off than they actually are. To maintain this ongoing self-deception we tend to filter information to fit preconceived beliefs. Invariably, this leads to overconfidence and a psychological bias that can be devastating, as witnessed by investors in Nortel and a host of other high-tech stocks when the great tech bubble burst, as it inevitably had to.

In a similar vein, consider the popularity of lotteries, to many the very personification of greed. Statistically, lottery players have a better chance of getting hit by lightning than of winning the jackpot; yet, when these odds are mentioned, players will often give a glib response along the lines of "Somebody's got to win, and it might as well be me!" There is nothing wrong with this attitude, provided one is talking about a couple of dollars played at the corner store on a Saturday morning. However, it's a different matter altogether when applied to retirement savings that have taken a lifetime to amass. That's when the danger signals should really start to fly.

Often, the investment industry, in marketing its services to the public, panders to the same emotional biases used by lotteries in their advertising. Is it just a coincidence that many lottery and investment industry advertisements feature luxurious yachts, exotic villas, picturesque golf courses, etc.? The not-so-subtly implied message is "You *can* have it all, if only you turn your dreams over to us."

To be fair, the best investment firms are staffed with gifted professionals who spend their waking hours thinking about how they can better their competitively measured performances and, in the process, the investment performance of their firm's clients. We are happy to record many, many occasions when we've been witness to the kind of lifestyle enhancement that sound investing can bring about. Regrettably, we've also seen the lifestyle destruction that can occur when the investment dream turns into a nightmare. Almost without exception, that nightmare was spawned by greed, one of the most difficult of all human emotions to control.

Pride and Overconfidence

Similarly, the necessary decision to remove a losing holding from a portfolio is often deferred for no other reason than that making such a change would imply that a previous decision was a poor one. We mentioned previously that in his book *How to Make Money in Stocks*, William O'Neil, founder of the widely read and respected *Investor's Business Daily*, advises readers to take losses quickly and profits slowly. Many of the investment decisions we are most proud of were rooted in that simple philosophy.

Regrettably, the instinctive response by the vast majority of investors is to do just the opposite. Pride can often drive investors to sell winning positions early to lock up a gain. This is logical enough, and is personified in that old saying "No one ever went broke taking a profit." The euphoric sense of victory that accompanies having made a good security selection can blind investors to the fact that a good investment is still doing its job within the portfolio. By all means trim successful holdings that become disproportionately large, but as a general rule, it's best to stay with winners and dispose of losers.

Envy: Keeping Up With the (Dow) Joneses

The propensity to fall victim to the demon of greed, and its close relative envy, is greater than ever during times of surging market prosperity. This is the time when friends and co-workers begin bragging about the grand slam home run they hit from an obscure IPO (initial public offering). Greed then is being sparked by the entirely natural human response of envy. It's not unusual for that little voice in your head to pipe up and say, "If they can do it, I must be able to as well; after all, I'm *much* smarter than they are…"

Running a portfolio free of psychological and emotional biases is comparable in many respects to playing golf. The most successful golfers will tell you that your only true competition is yourself. Trying to beat the other members of your foursome can be entertaining for a round or two, but if you're serious about reducing your handicap, you'll have to block out your competitive instincts to outplay those around you and focus, instead, on bettering your own game with every stroke. For investors, there is a similar need to recognize that envy can lead to contemplating levels of risk they might not otherwise have taken on or fully appreciated.

During the tech stock boom, even the great Warren Buffett began taking heat from his shareholders. With the bellwether NASDAQ Composite Index soaring into the stratosphere, and relative investment novices slipping headfirst into great fortunes in what seemed to be the blink of an eye, an increasing number of Berkshire Hathaway shareholders began urging their hero to "get with the times" and include at least a few technology names in the stable of companies held by Berkshire. Instead, the "Sage of Omaha" held his ground, flatly rejecting the idea of investing in companies he didn't understand. If he and his worldly wise partner, Charlie Munger, could not grasp the workings of a company and how it made profits for its shareholders, how could they presume to evaluate the worth of that company and its attendant investment risks?

Buffett not only had to withstand the ire of his own shareholders, but also the disdain of the North American investment media. Similar criticism was levelled at Buffett during the 2007 annual meeting of shareholders. Berkshire Hathaway sat on tens of billions of dollars worth of cash at a time when stock indexes around the world were touching never before seen heights. (Anyone remember the talk of "de-coupling"?) In response to a barrage of questions over just when and how Buffett would put Berkshire's billions to work, the Sage of Omaha calmly replied, "We have more cash than good ideas," meaning that Buffett and Munger found little in the marketplace that met their definition of good value. Ultimately, Buffett was vindicated by his rigid discipline of investing, both in the aftermath of the tech stock collapse and more recently in the credit market fiasco of late 2008. In fact, there was even talk for a short while that Warren Buffett was then president elect Barack Obama's first choice as Treasury Secretary.

Chart Your Own Course

Sadly, the majority of individual investors don't have someone as steadfast as Warren Buffett to guard against the envy that can often blur the otherwise sound judgment of even the most astute investor. This is why having a personal target rate of return for your portfolio is so critically important. We'll return to the vital question of "what's your number?" in more detail in a subsequent chapter. For now, however, we note its importance in determining what's wrong presently, in connecting this with the mapping of individualized portfolio strategies that will follow a proper diagnosis, and in aiming to achieve longer-term, wealth-accumulation goals.

Fear

Benjamin Graham used to contend that "Investing is most intelligent when it is most business-like." These words, taken from Graham's epic work *The Intelligent Investor*, are *the* nine most important words in all of investing according to Warren Buffett, who developed them further to state that "Successful investing doesn't require extraordinary intelligence, but rather extraordinary discipline." Easier said than done, because at the opposite end of the emotional spectrum from greed sits fear.

Fear is the most powerful of emotional biases. A healthy dose of fear can at times keep us from making foolish and costly mistakes. However, just as often, *irrational* fear can paralyze investors and foil decision-making in their best long-term interests.

How many times have we heard the cop-out "I'd prefer to delay investing because…"? The box that follows dates back to our beginning year of 1982 and drives home what dithering like this could have come to mean.

Dithering Diminishes Dollars

Waiting for the "right" time to invest can be costly. There is always some crisis of confidence that successful investors must see beyond to make rational, informed decisions.

1982	Recession, pessimism rampant	1,047*
1983	Stock market recovery premature	1,258
1984	Record deficits, rising interest rates	1,211
1985	Slowing economic growth	1,546
1986	Stock markets ahead of themselves	1,895
1987	Black Monday, October 19th collapse	1,938
1988	Recession fears	2,168
1989	Stock and junk bond market collapse	2,753
1990	Gulf War	2,633
1991	Recession, bear market	3,168
1992	New U.S. political regime	3,301
1993	Too many uncertainties	3,754
1994	Rising interest rates	3,834
1995	Stock markets ahead of themselves	5,117
1996	Inflation fears	6,448
1997	"Irrational exuberance" warning	7,908
1998	Russian default, Long-Term Capital collapse	9,181
1999	Y2K risks	11,497
2000	Bursting of tech bubble	10,786
2001	9/11, terrorism threat	10,021
2002	Severe bear market	8,341
2003	Shattered trust (Enron, WorldCom, etc.)	10,453
2004	Iraq, contentious U.S. election	10,783
2005	U.S. personal savings rate at record low	10,717
2006	U.S. housing market breaks down	12,463
2007	Global economic slowdown begins	13,264
2008	Global credit crisis, sky high oil price	8,776
2009	Another Great Depression	?

* The figures in this column represent closing levels of the Dow Jones Industrial Average at the end of the years shown.

When it comes to investing, there will always be reasons for backing off and procrastinating if you are so inclined, but to move from the ordinary to the extraordinary, we've got to overcome the emotional biases. Fear usually makes its presence known at precisely the point in time when valuations become their most compelling. The birth of the great 18-year bull market in the summer of 1982 and, most recently, the last gasps of the bear market in the autumn of 2002 are but a pair of examples. Just as greed can tempt investors to embrace already soaring securities, so too can fear engender the procrastination that results in missing out on advantageous buying opportunities.

The chart on page 43 illustrates how drastically investment returns would have fallen away had investors been out of the markets in what turned out to be the top 10, 20, 30 and 40 best trading days in the 1980s and 1990s.

Remember, you would have known what the best-performing trading days were only after they happened. In addition, each of these decades began with recession and a bear market, and each was to experience a major stock market collapse. Yet, they worked out sensationally well, with overall U.S. market returns averaging in the area of 17% in the 1980s and 20% in the 1990s. However, you would have shared in this prosperity only if you had stayed invested through thick and thin, using logic and reasoning, and guided by a well-structured investment plan within which to make strategic decisions along the way. This need would have held equally true in the much more volatile first decade of the 2000s.

CREATIVE DESTRUCTION

Every so often a bewildered and none-too-pleased investor comes to see us with a portfolio that reeks of failure. The bewilderment often stems from the fact that at one point in their hapless portfolio's past it was a thing of beauty dancing along with, or perhaps even ahead of, the markets in terms of relative performance. By the time these investors get to us, though, the love has gone because the portfolio is stagnating or, worse still, has been bleeding cash for long enough to warrant a complete overhaul.

It is at times like these that we are reminded of the famous Harvard University economist Joseph Schumpeter and his writings on capitalism's capacity for "creative destruction." Though Schumpeter was referring to capitalism's unique ability to tear down and re-create itself based on the immutable laws of supply and demand, there

Why It Pays To Be In The Market
% Total Returns on S&P 500 – 1980s & 1990s

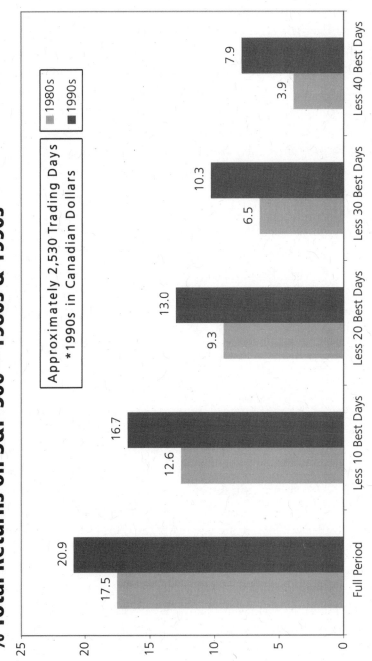

Legend: 1980s, 1990s

Approximately 2,530 Trading Days
*1990s in Canadian Dollars

Category	1980s	1990s
Full Period	17.5	20.9
Less 10 Best Days	12.6	16.7
Less 20 Best Days	9.3	13.0
Less 30 Best Days	6.5	10.3
Less 40 Best Days	3.9	7.9

Source: Berstein Research, CI Global Advisors US

is something very definite to be said for taking this principle into consideration in the management of portfolios.

Steady, long-term investment performance can be achieved only by coping with continuous change. It's the same with companies that accept and adapt to a constantly changing world tending to outperform their peers and enjoying a much longer lifespan than those that cling rigidly to what has worked in the past.

IBM eventually overcame a flawed decision to stick with its mainframe computers when desktop computers were taking over, but not before its stock market price was cut down by two-thirds and a change in top-level management was brought about by a board of directors with the courage to recognize the need for drastic action. There were many times when many doubted whether IBM would ever make the conversion successfully. *Who Says Elephants Can't Dance*, a book by IBM's legendary former chief executive officer Lou Gerstner, tells the remarkable story.

Michael can thankfully attest to how "Big Blue," which he had been prevailed upon to buy by a famous MIT professor at what turned out to be the sunset of the mainframe era, worked out very well for him in the end. Rather than taking the loss, he kept his patience and averaged down. In other words, he purchased more shares at lower prices because he liked what he saw happening. Nevertheless, it took many years for that MIT professor to be proven right, for Michael to get back to his average cost, and for IBM to go on to become one of Michael's most successful long-term investments.

Examples like this illustrate how creative destruction must also be part of the investment lexicon. For too long, the phrase "buy and hold" has been twisted from its original meaning to become code for a style of laissez-faire (i.e., hands-off) asset management that can often have little relevance in a pervasively changing world where strategies and investment tools that make sense today could be outdated in double-quick time. To illustrate what we mean, just think back to how technology-driven investments that were once representative of the tsunami-like force of change, and were believed necessary for growth in the 21st century, quickly became emblematic of devastating losses and fanciful pipedreams when a savage bear market set in to start the new millennium.

At the same time, embracing the concept of creative destruction need not be as radical or as revolutionary as one might think. For one thing, taking it to heart as an investor means much more than tearing down perceived conventional wisdom. Instead, creative destruction should be looked on as acknowledgement that in a global economy where constant change has become the norm, there is also a burning need to remain current on issues that could shape portfolios, as well as on tools to better manage portfolios. Exchange traded funds are a good example. There was a time, not all that long ago, when an investor who objected to the costs and direction of actively managed mutual funds had few alternatives. The emergence of exchange traded funds dramatically altered the investment landscape for those whose preference runs to passive asset management.

It's not enough to have the information at your fingertips. You've got to be prepared to act when the facts tell you that you're in danger of being blown off course. Think of those poor misguided souls who in the early 1980s bought gold as it approached $800 an ounce, convinced that the yellow metal was well on its way to $1,000 and beyond. There wasn't a whole lot creative about gold's spectacular fall from its all-time high, but there sure was a lot of destruction to be found. Schumpeter's vision of creative destruction is just the kind of destruction you want, the kind where you are firmly in the driver's seat.

FORTITUDE

Think back to the first chapter in this book, and the birth of the great 18-year bull market in the rock-bottom summer of 1982. Statistics showed that the tide of individual investor capital began flowing into securities of varying descriptions only once the sustainability of the market's advance had been established beyond a shadow of a doubt, a process that took several years. There was nothing wrong with this, except that the most lucrative investment gains were missed by those who waited for the herd to dictate the direction of their portfolios, rather than by using their own logic and reasoning, and by having the fortitude (one of Sir John Templeton's favourite words) to back their judgment.

THE SEARCH FOR SPOCK

This brings us to the heart of the matter. The downfall of most individual investors involves a decision-making process that is too often coloured by emotion. For most of us, the dollars that reside in our portfolios represent considerable sacrifice and strain over a period of years, if not decades. When we stop to think of the effort that went into these life savings and the lifestyle hopes and dreams that they represent, we would need the emotional detachment of *Star Trek*'s Mr. Spock to remain cool and detached about day-to-day decisions affecting our portfolio's well-being. It's for this very reason that we each need to have our very own Mr. Spock to warn us away from speculative excesses, and to encourage us to see beyond unfounded fears in order to make investment decisions that are rational, not emotional.

Your personal Mr. Spock could be a trusted investment advisor, spouse, business partner or even sibling. Regardless, that person should be someone with a sufficient degree of emotional detachment and expertise to have won your trust. You must then act on their counsel regardless of how hard it might be to swallow, or how painful it might seem at the time.

INVESTOR, KNOW THYSELF!

In the final diagnosis, you know you best. *You* are the owner of the portfolio that is being built and nurtured for *your* own distinct, long-term needs. Take stock of these needs, your ability to commit the time to study the information all around you, and your true comfort level with risk. Ultimately, the success or failure of your portfolio will come down to you. Regardless of whether you are a do-it-yourself investor or choose to work with a professional, you will need to be in tune with your own emotions and needs in order to make the required investment decisions that are most effective. Never forget it's always about *you*.

PART TWO

PRESCRIPTIONS

CHAPTER 5

You Need Professional Help!

In 1962, when Michael joined Wood Gundy as part of that fine firm's original research department, investors who needed professional help certainly didn't have much to choose from. Having been in operation for more than half a century by the time Michael arrived, Wood Gundy was only beginning to shed its image as a bond house to expand its offerings to include (gasp!) stocks. Mutual funds were fringe players, and the entire Canadian mutual fund industry was just a fraction of the giant it has grown to become today. Financial planning was available almost exclusively to the most sophisticated, well-heeled clientele. The friendly neighbourhood bank manager lent money, and could help you to make a little money with one of his bank's certificates of deposit, but was not the one you would turn to for advice on how to plan for your retirement. By comparison, today's range of choice of financial services and the types of professionals offering them is so broad it can be bewildering.

The Way We Were

"When I began my business career in 1962, Canada's financial services were built on four rickety pillars: an archaic banking system hamstrung by lending rate ceilings and other statutory impediments; venerable trust companies providing old-fashioned (even then) fiduciary and transfer services; old school investment dealers awakening to a life and world beyond bonds; and a fortress-like, mostly-mutualized life insurance industry steeped in tradition and actuarial dogma."

Michael Graham

"Money in the Bank"

The MoneyLetter, March 1999/First Report

Yet, in many ways the more things change, the more they stay the same. It's often been said that the two certainties of which we can still be sure are death and taxes. Change should be added as the third element to this time-honoured axiom. Many changes can occur over the course of one's adult life: marriage, divorce, birth of a child, death of a parent or spouse, career opportunities, business ventures. The list is virtually inexhaustible, and we haven't even mentioned the inevitable ebb and flow of markets and economic conditions. Significant changes like these can end up directly or indirectly affecting the financial lives of most people and those who are dependent on them. The importance of investing to provide for our own *independent* financial futures in an environment of seismic change cannot be ignored and makes the need for professional help all the more imperative.

THRIVING ON CHAOS

In 1988, management guru Tom Peters published *Thriving on Chaos*, a book that at the time was considered to be a somewhat radical piece of business writing. In it, Peters prophesied a time when industrialized nations would be forced to defend their high-wage-earner status as Marshall McLuhan's vision of a global village became an increasing reality.

Peters anticipated the need for both blue-collar and white-collar workers to become more entrepreneurial in their approach to work, and for employers to foster an environment that not only encouraged but rewarded the free thinker who was able to quickly adapt to changing circumstances. As you are likely quite aware, that day has arrived.

Not only is change distorting the financial landscape beyond recognition (most often for the better, in our opinion), it is occurring at a speed never seen before. Once again, that diligent, trustworthy partner we stressed the need for at the conclusion of the previous chapter becomes a tremendous asset, and all the more so if he or she has access to timely, thoughtful research and analysis. In a world of constant and rapid change, you need someone to help you to adapt, step around unnecessary risk and seek out new-found opportunities to build (and safeguard) the value of your hard-earned dollars.

EVERYTHING OLD IS NEW AGAIN

To help investors cope with change (and sometimes to unwittingly exacerbate it), the financial industry is constantly dreaming up new financial instruments. The abundance of investment choices alone is a good reason to have a tried-and-true relationship with an advisor who has earned your trust—one who is keenly aware of your needs, wants, desires and fears.

Sometimes new instruments are nothing more than a slick repackaging of existing securities, the purple ketchup of the financial world designed more as a clever trap for fees than as a brilliant means of capturing greater gains for your portfolio. There are, however, just as many instances when a forward-thinking innovator does conjure something original that lives up to the accompanying marketing hype. In both circumstances, having a dependable partner by your side with the experience and expertise to separate the worthy from the unworthy among the plethora of candidates vying for your favour is a significant edge.

FINANCIAL ADVISORS: MORE FLAVOURS THAN BASKIN-ROBBINS

Depending upon where and how they are employed, the types of registrations held, their area of specialty and the infrastructure supporting them, some types of advisors will be more suitable to your own unique situation than others.

Generally speaking, advisors can be broken down into four categories:

1. Financial planners
2. Bankers
3. Investment advisors
4. Investment counsellors

Without a doubt there are highly competent, trustworthy professionals to be found in each category. Having an understanding of each type of advisor will help you to streamline the process of finding the most desirable match.

Financial Planners

Financial planners take a holistic advisory approach that reaches beyond the composition and monitoring of client portfolios to deal with a wider range of financial issues including, but not limited to

- detailed tax planning
- estate planning

- business succession planning
- asset allocation strategies

Financial planners are the one type of advisor to traverse all segments of the financial services industry. Their ranks can include stockbrokers who happen to offer complete financial planning services, and life insurance agents who have joined the fray in order to offer a more comprehensive array of services in an era where the life insurance policy is only one segment of an individual's finances.

The blurring of the lines among what were once distinct, if rudimentary, financial service pillars has not been lost on the nation's bankers, who now possess greatly expanded capabilities compared with as recently as a decade ago. Financial planning has transformed many job descriptions, but perhaps the most dramatically altered one is that of the bank loans officer (a title that was long ago tossed onto the ash heap of history). The banker who set up your car loan would love nothing better than to look deep into your eyes and talk longingly about your retirement plans, all the while gently caressing a chart showing your projected assets in your golden years.

A Word of Caution

Be warned that there are very few restrictions on just who can hang out a shingle and call themselves a financial planner. Some are little more than salespersons. Before you entrust your hard-earned dollars to someone claiming to offer financial planning services, ask a few pointed questions. Later in this chapter we'll offer some questions to ask.

Financial Planning Credentials

A certified financial planner is someone who has been granted the CFP designation by the Financial Planners Standards Council. CFP holders have completed a rigorous course of study, and are required to complete a minimum number of continuing education credits each year in order to maintain their designation.

The Canadian Bankers Association (CBA) has established a parallel program for bank employees engaged in offering financial planning to the public. The CBA designation is known as the PFP, which stands for personal financial planner. Like CFP designation holders, PFP designation holders are required to successfully complete a series of courses and keep up a regimen of continuous education.

Though reassuring, a designation like CFP or PFP is not necessarily a foolproof identifier of a good financial planner. We've been witness to some pretty egregious work performed by people holding designations that would suggest they should know better.

Fee-for-Service Planners

In Canada, most financial planners work on a commission basis, although there is also a small but hardy band of fee-only practitioners. Fee-only financial planners are financial planners who do not recommend specific securities or manage investment portfolios. Traditionally, fee-only planners tended to deal in more complicated financial situations. They have carried a reputation for being able to delve deeper in their analysis than those who offer financial planning as an added service to banking, insurance or securities offerings. The very notion of fee-based financial planning is, however, undergoing a significant transformation, just like every other facet of the financial services industry. Like all of the other changes occurring throughout the industry, fee-based planners are responding to intensifying competition.

For many years, fee-based financial planners charged a fee for only preparing a detailed financial plan. No specific securities were to be sold to the client by this breed of planner. For those concerned about potential conflicts of interest, this was an ideal situation. The client of the fee-based planner would take the financial plan prepared on his or her behalf to a financial institution to execute the investment strategy contained within the plan.

More recently, the ranks of fee-based planners have increased quite dramatically, with a growing number of commission-compensated planners and advisors beginning to offer a fee-for-service component to their offerings. Later in this chapter we'll outline some of the questions that you should ask if you're shopping for a professional advisor, regardless of how they are compensated.

Bankers

In a bid to capture what is known in the industry as greater share of wallet, Canada's bankers have bent over backwards during the past two decades to shed their image as stodgy lenders of capital. In particular, the big banks have moved in a big way into what has come to be known as *wealth management*. Gone are the days of tellers waiting patiently at their wickets for you to come in with a deposit. Everyone in the bank is now an advisor of one magnitude or another. Don't let the bank's size and presumably good name sway how you view the value of their services. You've really got to judge the value of what is being offered on the basis of the person sitting across the desk from you. How? Ask for references. Find out how long they've been doing what they do. How often can you expect to receive progress reports on your portfolio?

There are many diligent, empathetic bankers/advisors. Over the years, both of your authors have developed lasting associations and friendships with bankers who have been of great service and value at one stage or another. Unfortunately, in our experience we have also been witness to many for whom it's just a job and to whom your life's savings represent little more than another file in their "in basket." It's this latter group that must be identified quickly and avoided. Once again, asking the right questions at the start of the relationship will help you to better avoid potential disappointment later.

More often than not, any damage to your portfolio by your advisor will come not through acts of malice or commission, but rather through neglect and ignorance. Remember, it's a fast-paced, constantly changing world in which you really want to have someone who is "on their game" working for you. Unfortunately, and this is unique to the banking environment, banks seem to keep moving their best people around, promoting them to new responsibilities within the bank or to new locations. This type of advisor receives a large portion of their annual stipend in the form of salary, so if the bank tells them that starting tomorrow they are going to work at the branch across town, that's where they'll go. All of a sudden you'll find yourself with a new advisor, but don't assume you've been given the pick of the litter. Ask questions all over again. You're not being rude. Don't you think that same banker is going to ask you a lot of pointed personal questions if you want to borrow a little money? You're simply protecting what you've given a whole lot of blood, sweat and tears to attain. You simply must know who you are entrusting your money to. It's up to you to make sure you have an advisor who is going to do what it takes to help you build your investments and preserve the value of your portfolio.

Now let's say you've done all of your careful questioning and you've found a banker with whom you'd like to do business. Great! Please understand, however, that unless they're private bankers, who we'll come to later, these garden-variety bankers found at every bank branch across the country are trained to be generalists, not specialists.

The banker/advisor of today with whom you'd like to do business is someone who should be able to handle fairly basic, straightforward financial planning issues ranging from saving for retirement to developing a savings strategy for a child's post-secondary education financing. He or she also should be able to assist you with basic tax savings strategies, as well as rudimentary portfolio construction and asset allocation.

We use words such as "basic" and "rudimentary" because of the constraints placed upon the banker/advisor by both the terms of their licensing and the offerings available from their employer institution. Thus, the overwhelming majority of banker/advisors you are likely to run into are licensed to handle little more than mutual funds and term deposits. A small, albeit growing, number are moving to the next step, which is to be fully licensed to handle a wider range of securities, including stocks, bonds, exchange traded funds, income trusts and insurance-related vehicles, such as segregated funds. If you are just starting out, and your needs are not highly complex, dealing with an advisor who works primarily with mutual funds and term deposits is not necessarily a bad thing.

These folks are often required to wear more than one hat over the course of their average working day. Hence, their focus is not always going to be on the portfolios under their care. For this reason it can be a blessing in disguise that the banker/advisor sticks with mutual funds for equity-related investments, whereas a qualified third party (the fund manager) makes the day-to-day decisions over what stocks are to be bought, sold or held.

Private Bankers

Sitting at the high end of the advisory food chain offered by the chartered banks are private bankers. These are advisors specially trained and equipped to service more than just individuals. Private bankers are frequently called upon to work on complex financial situations involving high net worth families and closely held small to medium-sized businesses.

The scope of the services offered by private bankers is quite diverse, placing this category of advisors in a position to become intimately involved in the lives of their clients. At its most basic level, private banking permits the client to have a dedicated banker who can go to greater lengths than would ordinarily be the case to link personal and professional banking, as well as to coordinate investment, tax and estate planning with philanthropic goals.

It is not unusual for the clients of a private banker to have financial needs that transcend international borders. To meet these needs, private bankers also offer offshore services, such as offshore trusts that can sometimes be used as estate planning vehicles and to protect assets from litigation risk, as part of a tax planning strategy.

The services of a private banker are generally limited to a bank's wealthiest clients. Often, the minimum asset threshold is $1,000,000. The banks aim to offer highly sought-after clients like these one-stop shopping for all their financial needs. In some instances, this is ideally suited. It is not unusual, however, for a well-heeled investor to prefer an "unbundling" of services, and to opt to use a private banker for some services, a brokerage house for full service, a discount broker for some other services and an investment counsellor for other facets of his or her financial life.

Investment Advisors

Still known in the industry and by much of the general public as stockbrokers, or just simply brokers, investment advisors ply their trade at the nation's brokerage and investment firms. Traditionally, they did little more in the way of advising than counselling their clients on which stocks, bonds or mutual funds to buy or sell. However, over the last couple of decades, this pillar of the Canadian financial services industry has, like the others, undergone a significant transformation in a bid to offer a more holistic approach to meeting client needs.

The evolving nature of the services offered by investment advisors (and everyone else making a living in financial services) has been in response to intensifying competition and a bid for greater market share.

Customarily, most investment advisors have been compensated on the basis of commissions charged for securities bought and sold, although that too is undergoing a significant change. Growing numbers of clients and their advisors are moving from a commission structure to a flat fee, expressed as a percentage of assets under management, as the preferred method of payment.

Brokers, whether they operate under the title of Investment Advisor, Investment Executive, Financial Advisor or Financial Consultant, are, by the nature of their relationship with their employer firms, afforded considerable latitude in choosing the mix of products and services they may offer their clientele. The better advisors long ago recognized the cold, hard reality that they cannot be all things to all people, and have more often than not tried to specialize in the aspects that play to their strengths, though this is not to say that an investment advisor who is adept at picking stocks is unable to select appropriate mutual funds or recommend an asset allocation strategy.

Variety Is the Spice of Life

Walk into any brokerage office across Canada and you will find as many different ways to manage your money as there are advisors in that office. With a few exceptions, most of the styles offered are quite valid on their own merits. This lack of uniformity is the polar opposite of the advisory experience found at the nation's bank and trust companies. The lack of uniformity is not, however, a structural flaw in the offerings of the brokerage. The greater choice can be quite liberating, depending on your needs and wants. Once again, the selection of an advisor requires great care and diligence. Ask your friends who they have as their advisor. This could be particularly important, since many established advisors do little or no advertising, gaining much of their clientele through referral from satisfied existing clients.

Uncomfortable talking to friends or family about your finances? Take some time to attend a workshop or seminar delivered by a brokerage office. You've probably already found that broker-sponsored and -conducted workshops are pretty easy to find, and are usually fairly close to home if you live in an urban setting.

The Entrepreneurial Edge

Often, investment advisors reach a point in their career paths where the sheer size of their clientele, together with growing competitive pressures, will compel them to take on staff and build teams of specialists to satisfy the needs of a growing and diverse clientele. It's not uncommon to find teams staffed with an administrative assistant, an associate advisor specializing in financial planning and an estate planning specialist. The members of the team are almost always paid for by the lead advisor rather than by the advisor's firm. This highlights a critical point of differentiation between brokers (or whatever else you want to call them) and those bankers/advisors who are employed by banks, trust companies and credit unions. The overwhelming majority of brokers in Canada are required to be listed as employees of their respective firms for tax and regulatory purposes. In reality, though, they are independent contractors, in that this class of advisor makes his or her living solely from the work performed for their clients.

That there is no salary for advisors to fall back on in tough times can serve as both a blessing and a curse for clients. On the positive side of the ledger, the broker or investment advisor, like any small business owner, lives and dies by their clientele, and as such is more likely to be keenly aware of their clients' needs and wants—their livelihood depends upon it. On the negative side is the potential for conflicts of interest, and excessive trading designed to boost commission revenue.

Caveat Emptor

There are many excellent advisors to be found among the nation's large and small brokerages. Just as we stated with regard to bankers, there are some investment advisors who are best avoided. How do you know when you're sitting with a champion for your money versus an accident waiting to happen?

Just as we stated earlier that a bank's size and reputation alone are not necessarily assurances of quality, the same can be said of investment houses. Brokerage firms are required by law to maintain compliance departments, which monitor the work of their advisors, keeping watch for unethical and illegal activity. Generally, though, this is less about quality control than about keeping the advisor's work in line with national and provincial regulations. Most, if not all, compliance departments simply are not designed to extend their oversight any further than that. The ultimate responsibility for ensuring that you are receiving the best of what your advisor has to offer rests on your shoulders. It is, after all, your money.

Investment Counsellors

The standout characteristic of investment counsellors is that they are independent to the point where they have no business affiliations or gainful associations that could prejudice the arm's-length decisions they make on behalf of their clients.

As Michael can testify after 36 years as an investment dealer and more than a dozen years on top of that as the founder and chairman of an investment counselling firm, the focus of an investment counsellor's business is to advise individual clients and, in most instances, to manage client portfolios on a discretionary, fee-paying basis.

Discretionary Vs. Non-discretionary

The overwhelming majority of the investment counsellors in Canada manage client accounts in their care in what is known as a discretionary manner. This means that the counsellor, after having their client sign an agreement, makes buying and selling decisions on individual securities on behalf of the client without seeking approval for each trade. This contrasts with a non-discretionary relationship, which is more typically found with investment advisors and in which the client must approve each trade before it is placed.

Investment counsel firms range from single practitioners to large entities with many partners. For clients of these firms, the appeal, aside from an investment performance track record, is the ability to confer directly with the people making the day-to-day investment decisions. This permits the client to direct the investment counsellor toward or away from certain types of securities. This could be on the basis of closely held personal ethics or for reasons of religion. Though this degree of flexibility is also available with an investment advisor that is picking individual securities with his or her clients, it is not possible if the advisor is using third-party asset managers, such as mutual funds.

Investment counsellors also spend the largest proportion of their time, even as high as 80%, on research for clients' portfolios. This is in marked contrast to others who spend the majority of their time interacting with clients. The investment counsellor model is designed for those who hire managers and monitor them, rather than instruct and direct them. The fact that so many investment counsellors have the Chartered Financial Analyst (CFA) designation only adds to the research depth and the "unfair" research advantage they can bring to their clients.

Investment counsellors can combine unbiased investment advice with the ongoing management of their clients' investment portfolios. For economy of management, investment counselling and management relationships typically work best with higher net worth investors, usually $1,000,000 and up.

THE GOOD, BAD AND UGLY: CHOOSING THE ADVISOR THAT'S RIGHT FOR YOU

Once you meet an advisor with whom you think you might like to work with, there are some basic questions that need to be asked to help ensure you have a good professional and personal fit. Here are the seven questions that we believe should be at the core of an introductory meeting with a potential advisor.

1. How long have you been an advisor?
2. What are your average assets under management per household?
3. How many clients (households) do you serve?
4. What is your investment philosophy?
5. Who is on your support staff?
6. What can I expect from our relationship?
7. What are your credentials?

Now let's look at the seven questions in detail in order to help you to "smoke out" vitally important information at the introductory meeting, and ultimately make an informed decision on choosing the advisor that's right for you.

How Long Have You Been an Advisor?

Pretty self-explanatory here. Pick a number of years' worth of experience that you feel is adequate, and go from there.

What Are Your Average Assets Under Management *Per Household*?

This is important because it will let you know where your family's total assets stack up against the advisor's other clients. Don't believe any altruistic platitude about treating everyone the same. That's one of the all-time great red herrings, ranking right up there with "No, that dress does not make you look fat at all."

Size Matters

Let's not kid ourselves. The simple truth is that larger clients get more time and attention than small accounts. When you work on commission (or fee for service) for a living, it really is a dog-eat-dog world. Ideally, what you want from your prospective advisor is some degree of selectivity. We're not advocating an elitist approach, though. An established advisor with a thriving practice eventually arrives at the point where they need to manage their workload intelligently. That means they've either got to set some criteria for becoming a client, or they've got to take on more help. If the prospective advisor states that they work only with clients who have $200,000 to invest, and you have $225,000, how much attention do you think you will garner? It would be nice to think that an advisor will treat all clients equally, and in some rare instances that is exactly what happens. Often, though, while all clients are treated equally, some are more equal than others. It is preferable to be a big fish in a small pond rather than a small fish in a big pond. Take care to choose an advisor for whom you will not necessarily be their largest client, but you'll not want to be the smallest either.

How Many Clients (Households) Do You Serve?

Let's be practical here. Although Mr. and Mrs. Jones technically count as two separate clients, chances are they are sitting down with the advisor together and therefore they should count as one. What you're looking for is an advisor with a healthy, stable clientele.

In the late 1990s, Merrill Lynch conducted a study in which it found that the optimum number of households an advisor could properly service was 175. Since that time, technology has advanced to a point where we believe the number could be moved up safely to 250. If your prospective advisor responds to your question with a number that is considerably higher than this, ask the advisor if there are any associate advisors on his or her team. Many of the most experienced advisors have one or two (sometimes more) associates on staff to help shoulder the workload. If this is the case, the 250 figure can be raised even higher based on the size of the advisor's staff.

Chances are that an advisor with a small clutch of marginal clients is not going to be around for very long. The exception to the rule is if you are looking at someone still early in their career. More seasoned clients may not want to deal with a relatively inexperienced advisor, regardless of their gold-plated academic credentials (more on that in a moment). However, a young client with fairly straightforward needs often can do quite well with a rookie broker, growing with that advisor over a span of many years as they both grow older and move forward professionally. The risk, of course, is that the rookie becomes one of the many unfortunate "washouts" that don't last long enough to celebrate many anniversaries with the firm. Should this come to pass, your protection lies in the firm that your now-former advisor was employed with. Investment firms have a fiduciary responsibility to you, their client, and as such are obligated to make certain that another qualified individual is in place regardless of whether or not your advisor left the business of his or her own volition.

If your firm assigns your account to another advisor, your responsibility is to take the time to get to know this advisor and to satisfy yourself that this person is right for you. If it's not a good fit, there's nothing wrong with saying so. In fact, it's preferable if you speak up early, calling the branch manager and asking to be reassigned to someone more suitable for you, rather than suffer through a poor relationship. That time spent brooding could wind up being quite costly to you. Once again, it's your money. If you don't speak up in its defence, who will?

What Is Your Investment Philosophy?

With this question, you are trying to ascertain exactly what it is that guides the advisor sitting before you in recommending one type of security over another. Many people are a little too intimidated by their lack of investment acumen to ask this basic question, or back off when the advisor starts to speak in jargon. Don't be—you needn't be Ben Bernanke. If the advisor lapses into some Gregorian chant, spewing acronyms and financial linguistics, stop them dead in their tracks. Ask for clarification. You are not stupid, and more likely than not the advisor is not trying to baffle you with some bullish balderdash. You simply want to ensure that you are both speaking the same language.

Many professionals who work in a technical field have the annoying tendency to slip into their professional mother tongue. Think of your doctor, your auto mechanic or, worst of all, the 17-year-old kid who just fixed your computer. If the advisor and his or her intentions are honourable, when pressed for clarification the advisor should be able to explain his or her investment philosophy in terms that anyone can follow. If the advisor is unable to explain his or her motives in a language you can understand, move on. Good communication is essential to establishing trust, and if he or she is either unable or unwilling to communicate something as fundamental as investment philosophy, you're going to have problems sooner or later.

The advisor you are interviewing may state that he or she uses third-party managers such as mutual fund managers to look after the portfolios in his or her care. Another might state he or she has a value bias, for example favouring the security selection method pioneered by Columbia University finance professor Benjamin Graham and made famous by Warren Buffett. The point of the exercise is not to become an expert on investment styles, but rather to learn whether the prospective advisor is working from a core set of principles that guide recommendations. A serious professional will be.

Who Is On Your Support Staff?

Even the most determined workaholic advisor will inevitably get sick, go on vacation, attend a conference, etc. Who's "minding the shop" while the advisor is away? Who can you call if you need help? How long has that help been with the advisor? What are their qualifications?

Good advisors, like any competent professional, invest back into their practice. That means going beyond the very basic level of administrative support offered by the major firms, and hiring (and paying out of their earnings) additional staff such as associate advisors, estate planning specialists and financial planners. They don't need to have all of these people on staff, but a growing advisory practice is labour intensive, and adequate help ensures that the client experience remains very personal.

What Can I Expect From Our Relationship?

The courting stage is a good time to establish up front what each of you expects from the relationship being considered. Set the parameters of exactly how often you and the advisor are going to sit down and review your money's progress. Will all meetings be face to face? Perhaps some will be done over the phone. How often can you expect statements? Can you take a peek at your accounts via the Web? Is the advisor going to call you with a recommendation and expect an answer on the spot? You should see some evidence of a process that the advisor works through in all client relationships. This process should be flexible enough for some degree of customization, yet not so flexible that the advisor loses focus and spends most of the day scrambling from one emergency to the next.

What Are Your Credentials?

Given a choice between a relatively inexperienced advisor who has gold-plated academic credentials and a seasoned veteran, a veritable graduate of the fabled school of hard knocks, we lean toward the latter. This is not to say that we are dismissive of higher education. If you should happen upon someone with the scrappy instincts of a street fighter *and* the refinement of a rigorous formal education, you may have found just the right combination for you.

"Persistence and determination are," as a famous Calvin Coolidge quote states, "omnipotent." Successful investing is something that is as much an art as it is a science. The instincts and sound judgment that are a necessity for a qualified advisor can be acquired only with the patina of time. The world of investing is not a neat and tidy place. People lie, circumstances change and rules are written and rewritten. Through it all, the desirable advisor continues to evaluate, study and contemplate the most suitable path for his or her clients, sifting all available information through the filter of experience.

Credentials, such as a CA, MBA, CFA or, heaven help us, a PhD, are valuable to say the least. At the same time, as Michael can attest, they are only a complement to experience—not a substitute. Formal education prior to the start of an advisor's career provides an excellent foundation on which to build. As noted previously, we live in a world of constant change in which continuous study is a vital ingredient to success. This includes formal as well as informal study. The formal study is generally found in the continuing education requirements that licensing bodies now place upon advisors. In the course of meeting these obligations, many advisors will acquire professional designations such as the CIM (Canadian Investment Manager), CFP (Certified Financial Planner), CFA (Chartered Financial Analyst) or FCSI (Fellow of the Canadian Securities Institute), all of which are offered by qualified professional organizations. These designations (and others) are a good sign that your advisor is committed to maintaining sharp skills and a well-stocked arsenal of knowledge.

Still, your authors have met some advisors who, despite outstanding academic and professional qualifications, fail to stay abreast daily of changes that can adversely affect the client assets in their care. Keeping up can be as simple as reading the newspaper daily, and can extend as far as membership in professional organizations where an exchange of ideas is possible. Ask your prospective advisor where he or she gets the best investment ideas and how he or she stays on top of developing trends. The answers will reveal a great deal about the level of persistence and determination residing deep in the advisor's belly.

GET HELP

Our bias on this matter is undeniable. Yes, we earn our living from providing advice to investors on what they should be doing with their money. We are, arguably, in a good position to speak to the importance of having proactive, professional and ongoing counsel on the management of your nest egg from someone you know and trust. Change, as we noted in the opening paragraphs of this chapter, is constant, and occurring more rapidly than ever before. We have seen countless examples over the years of investors who have been caught "offside" with their investments when circumstances have changed quickly, or when investment decisions have been made with dated information.

We do live in the information age, and while we may be more informed than ever, the sheer volume of available information can lead easily to clutter and ultimately confusion. This is where a dedicated professional, one whose interests are inextricably linked to your own, can cut through that clutter, keep you abreast of shifting circumstances and put you in a position to make more informed investment decisions.

CHAPTER 6

It's Always About You

Working With an Advisor

The start of the title of this chapter could be mistaken for an accusation hurled during a marital spat. Our context is much less contentious. We like to think of the client/advisor relationship as being a little more comparable to the kind of close-knit, trusting relationship that you might have with your family doctor (minus the request to turn your head to the right and cough). The common denominator in both kinds of relationships is the focal point: you.

In the last chapter, we underscored what we believe to be a very strong case for having some kind of professional advisor by your side to assist you in making intelligent investment decisions on a consistent basis. Here we continue the line of reasoning to describe the working parts and responsibilities inherent in a successful working relationship with any type of advisor.

A PROCESS—NOT AN EVENT

There exists a widely held misconception that declares successful investing to be composed of a series of unconnected, random events. The hot tip, the discovery of the savvy fund manager and the high-concept investment all come to mind. The truth of the matter is that successful investing is really much more of a process than an event or even a series of events.

THE STARTING POINT: FINANCIAL TRIAGE

The first step both of us take when consulting with a "wounded" investor is to embark upon a process to uncover the investor's wants, needs and risk tolerance. Most advisors, to varying degrees, employ these same basics of the financial planning process in work with their clients.

At its core, financial planning is a six-step process, and is evolutionary by nature. Simply put, the process should be flexible to adapt to changes in your financial circumstances. The six-step process we subscribe to can be summarized as follows:

1. Fact finding: The first step in the process is for you and your advisor to have a very frank conversation about your current financial situation. The more information that you can bring to this meeting, the more value you'll receive in return. The advisor will look at your financial life from several different vantage points, and will need to have an up-to-date snapshot of your investments.

Before this advisor can perform an effective analysis of these investments, though, it is important that they place the information in the proper context. It is for this reason that you should let the advisor know the details of your debt obligations, your income and your income source(s). The discussion of the source of your income is important because the advisor will want to determine whether there is much risk of an interruption to your cash flow. If so, special attention will need to be paid to the issue of liquidity and an adequate emergency reserve.

There are a growing number of advisors who have taken to using a detailed questionnaire to gather information. This is over and above the mandatory Know Your Client (KYC) form. Often this is quite useful for both you and the advisor. The questionnaire is usually sent out to the client in advance of the initial, fact-finding meeting, permitting you to take your time to complete the forms in detail. The questionnaire helps to ensure that important information is not overlooked during the initial meeting and can evolve into a wide-ranging dialogue.

Though we are not opposed to the use of such questionnaires, we caution that the questionnaire itself is not to be used as a replacement for a fact-finding meeting itself. There needs to be that all-important human interaction. This is particularly true when it comes to the measurement of your tolerance for risk. Too often, attempts have been made to try and boil down an assessment of an investor's appetite for risk by putting forward a series of questions, each designed to "smoke out" the respondent's true attitudes toward risk. More often than not, this form of risk measurement offers little more than a means of "pigeon-holing" the investor to a specific, predetermined profile, and ends up doing more to save the advisor's firm from litigation than getting at the heart of the matter.

One of Bryan's clients is a retired psychometrist (someone who does psychological testing/evaluation). Her concern regarding the use of questionnaires to assess a client's attitudes toward risk and reward is that while they may represent a fairly accurate portrait of the investor's deep-seated beliefs, the responses can be tainted by recent successes or failures in the market. Bryan's client recommends, and we concur, that if a questionnaire is to be used at all, it should be revisited at regular intervals (semi-annually or annually) to ensure that the responses given during the initial meeting are still a valid reflection of the respondent's viewpoints. Use these questionnaires as the tool they were originally intended to be: an adjunct to a vigorous discussion on the issue at hand—*you*.

2. Objectives: Once your advisor has a firm grasp on where you stand today, the next logical step is to have a discussion about exactly what it is you wish to achieve. This can be a fairly wide-ranging conversation, and should encompass everything from your medium- to long-range financial aspirations to the "terms of engagement" with the advisor.

Any investment/financial plan worth its salt should be guided by a rational set of objectives. Should your objectives prove to be unrealistic, it is the responsibility of the advisor to bring reality into focus. A good advisor will not tell you only what you *want* to hear. The truly professional advisor will tell you what you *need* to hear.

As part of the objective-setting process, you and the advisor should establish some fairly basic ground rules over the degree of risk you are prepared to withstand. The advisor will talk through some hypothetical situations with you. Suppose, for example, that you purchase an investment for $50 per share and a month later it is worth $100 per share. How responsive will you be to an advisor's suggestion that you trim back a portion of this wildly profitable position? Going in the opposite direction, let's assume for a moment that you purchased income trust units at $19 each. A week later the Bank of Canada increases interest rates by 50 basis points and as a consequence, the units drop in price to $14. Assuming that nothing has changed with respect to the income trust itself, how willing would you be to permit your advisor to purchase more units for you at the new, substantially reduced price? For your own sake, it's a good idea to be brutally honest. There's no medal for bravery to be had. Too often, we've seen clients exercise ill-placed bravado only to learn too late that they are not the reincarnation of J.P. Morgan they had fantasized themselves to be. If you're going to make a mistake, it's a far better thing to err on the side of caution than hubris.

3. Analysis: It is at this point that you and the advisor may wish to go your separate ways for a few days while the advisor analyzes the information provided to him or her at the initial meeting. An assessment of your assets, liabilities and cash flow will allow the advisor to put your present financial state into context with your objectives. This will permit your advisor to map out a strategy that is unique to your own needs. This strategy will likely but not necessarily include a tune-up of your portfolio, recommending the elimination of some investments in favour of others, corrections to errors of omission and the scaling back of positions that have become disproportionately large (or too small to be meaningful) in relation to all other securities in the portfolio.

4. Asset allocation: After completing a thorough analysis and its attendant recommendations, the advisor will be able to wrap the investment strategy around a comprehensive asset allocation strategy. We'll delve into the art and science of asset allocation in detail in the next chapter. For now, let's simply describe what asset allocation is, and set it within the context of the six-step process.

Asset allocation comes in two forms: *strategic* and *tactical*. Recognizing the risk and reward characteristics of the three main asset categories—stocks (equities), bonds (fixed income) and cash—strategic asset allocation seeks to strike an appropriate balance among the categories to meet at the intersection of a particular client's need for growth and tolerance for risk. Tactical asset allocation begins to take shape after the strategic asset allocation has been established. With tactical asset allocation, the primary goal is to spread the assets within the equity component among various market sectors or geographic regions in order to maximize investment performance while managing risk.

Strategic asset allocation tends to remain more rigidly fixed in place over an extended period of time, and is usually only dramatically altered if and when the client faces a significant change in their objectives brought on by a life-altering change such as retirement.

The objective in this stage of the process is to sketch out the broad parameters of the strategic asset allocation. Details as to when rebalancing should occur will be covered in the Investment Policy Statement, which we will focus on in chapter 16, Follow the Yellow Brick Road.

5. Security selection: When the process is running smoothly, the effort expended in step four should flow seamlessly into step five. This is where tactical asset allocation enters the picture, and the detailed work of building an Investment Policy Statement begins. The advisor will draw upon his own analysis of your agreed-upon needs and overlay his understanding of asset class characteristics to narrow down the range of appropriate securities. From there, the advisor can lay out his recommendations for your approval.

6. Maintenance: Warren Buffett has been lionized as a monumentally patient investor, so much so in fact that he once famously answered the question "What is your ideal holding period?" with one word—forever. It would be a mistake (and a tragic one at that) to assume that buy-and-hold investors do not need to periodically make adjustments to their investment holdings in response to changing developments that can affect the values of their investments. Even Mr. Buffett has been known to do this. Over time, some securities will grow more quickly than others. Though we are advocates of the theory of letting one's winners "run," on occasion it will be necessary to scale back positions that have become disproportionately large. This takes us back to asset allocation. A well-thought-out asset allocation strategy will recognize the need to make adjustments, and will set out guidelines for when and if rebalancing should occur.

THE FINANCIAL FULL MONTY: YOUR RESPONSIBILITIES AS THE CLIENT

The quality of the advice that you receive from your advisor will be determined in large measure by the quantity and quality of the information you provide to him or her. You really need to open up to this person, letting them know exactly what you hope to achieve. Of equal importance is the need to disclose your deepest, darkest financial fears.

Investors with significant financial holdings occasionally wish to have their assets spread among a handful of institutions and/or advisors. Depending on your situation, this often turns out to be a less-than-ideal situation for both you and the advisor. You simply *must* provide full disclosure. The advisor must be able to see "the big picture," including assets that you may not yet be ready to bring under his or her responsibility. The primary advantage of this financial "full monty" is to permit the advisor to offer recommendations that are set within a proper context and to avoid redundancies and errors of omission.

Letting your prospective advisor in on your deepest fears allows the truly professional advisor to have a good understanding of your tolerance for risk, and your need (if any) for growth. Opening up completely alerts the advisor to any potential life-altering changes that could prompt a significant change in the investment strategy you have asked him or her to formulate for you. If you suspect, for example, that the company you work for may be coming out with an early retirement package in six months, and you are a likely candidate, put that on the table. Even though the anticipated event may never come to pass, you will be far less prone to disappointment if the advisor with whom you have trusted your life savings has a contingency plan in place all the same. Remember: the more you give, the more you receive in terms of reliable advice.

WHAT'S IN IT FOR ME?
RESPONSIBILITIES OF THE ADVISOR

As we discussed in the last chapter, the advisor has a responsibility to provide you with a clear understanding of his or her investment philosophy. He or she should also provide you with a plan for managing your portfolio and ultimately helping you to reach your goals. There should be no deviation from the plan unless the proposed changes are first discussed with and approved by you. Just as your communication with the advisor needs to be frank and complete, so too does the advisor's communication with you. The advisor needs to outline which services he or she will be bringing into the relationship personally, and which services will be contracted out.

The benchmark(s) against which your portfolio's performance will be measured should be set out in advance by the advisor and agreed to by you. Most advisor/client relationships are non-discretionary. This means that the advisor makes adjustments to your investment holdings only after consultation with and approval from you. In order to make it easier for you to make well-informed investment decisions, your advisor will want to periodically provide you with an overview of the current market and general economic climate. Without having the relevant facts before you, how can anyone reasonably expect you to make sound investment decisions? A little client education will make both the advisor's job and yours significantly easier.

COMMUNICATION BREAKDOWN

To have the most productive, lasting relationship with any financial professional, it is imperative that expectations from the relationship (for both you and the advisor) are clearly articulated at the outset. One point that often leads to relationship-ending friction between client and advisor is the matter of personal contact. Of course, it is reasonable to expect that your advisor will proactively get in touch with you if and when circumstances demand your immediate attention. It's during those occasionally lengthy periods when there is no pressing matter to attend to that problems creep in.

You need to ask yourself how often you want or need to meet with the advisor. Is it reasonable for you to expect a quarterly portfolio review? Perhaps, but be prepared for the possibility that the advisor, eager to retain your business, could make promises that he or she may not be able to keep. Ask how often the advisor thinks portfolio reviews should be conducted and negotiate from there, if necessary, to arrive at a frequency of contact that you can both live with. If you're considering working with a busy advisor who has a large clientele, there may be associate advisors with whom you can connect if your need for contact is greater than the amount of time the advisor ordinarily can spare. Having occasional portfolio reviews conducted by a competent associate and supervised by your advisor is preferable to inconsistent contact from a harried, distracted advisor. The emphasis here should be on the consistency and quality of reporting your portfolio's progress beyond the regular statement. This accountability should include proactive advice when necessary.

You and your advisor also should have a blunt conversation regarding your expectations for portfolio performance. An ethical, professional advisor will not permit you to set unrealistic expectations, nor will they prey upon the basic human instincts of fear and greed.

KEEP IT REAL

Avoid setting hard targets, such as "I need a 10% return on my money every year." The markets are in a constant state of flux. You will be far less prone to disappointment if you set a range of returns in relation to previously agreed-upon market averages, or if you set a long-term rate of return. For more information on setting performance targets, please refer to chapter 15, What's Your Number? Benchmarking Performance.

Just the Two of Us

Some of the principles that apply to a happy, long-lasting marriage can also apply to the functioning of a happy, long-lasting and mutually rewarding relationship with your financial advisor.

- Full disclosure: Let the advisor see all of the working parts of your financial life, but don't stop there. Speak openly about your hopes and fears.
- Demand feedback: Regularly scheduled progress reports serve several purposes. They keep the advisor accountable to you, reduce the chances of something important "falling through the cracks" and raise your level of awareness. This last point will, over time, make it easier for you to make well-informed investment decisions, resulting in fewer regrets.
- Set goals: How will you know you're winning if you don't keep score? Work with your advisor to set attainable goals that reflect your overall objectives.

IT'S A TWO-WAY STREET

Solid, enduring marriages are built on a foundation of good communication and trust; so too are long-standing, mutually rewarding relationships with financial advisors. Once the trust has been established and the communication flow agreed upon, respect is the next ingredient called for in this recipe for success. Respect needs to extend from both parties in the relationship. You, as the client, need to remain mindful of the fact that the professional with whom you are working is likely devoting most of their waking hours to their craft. The terms of their licence require the advisor to engage in many hours of ongoing study. Through the firm at which your advisor is employed, there is access to timely analysis of securities and market trends that most individual investors have neither the time nor inclination to source out on their own.

In a similar vein, it is imperative that the professional financial advisor demonstrate the utmost respect for you, their client. Regardless of the corporate name on their business card, it is the client for whom the advisor works. The advisor needs to remain mindful of what often has been many years of hard work and sacrifice that went into amassing the capital that is now being put before the advisor to care for. The best advisors carry an attitude that the client is doing the advisor a tremendous favour by bringing their business to him or her, not the other way around. The professional, conscientious advisor never loses sight of just whose money is at stake and what those dollars represent. The finest advisors always remember that it's always about you.

CHAPTER 7

Balancing Act

Asset Allocation Strategies to Minimize Risk and Maximize Return

Winemakers will often blend specific quantities of various grape varietals to create a wine that has certain unique characteristics—something that is more than the sum of its parts. This is the essence of asset allocation. By putting together certain combinations of stocks, bonds and cash, the three main asset classes, an investor should be able to create a portfolio that is unique to his or her own tolerances and preferences for risk and reward. Like the wine that is the result of a careful blending of grapes, a portfolio successfully blending divergent securities should result in something much more valuable than the sum of its parts.

STAY SHARPE

William Sharpe is a professor emeritus at Stanford University who rose to international prominence with his Nobel Prize–winning work in 1990 on measuring investment risk and expected return. Sharpe's advice to a Toronto audience in 2002 was to be certain to "diversify, diversify, diversify." His accompanying view: "We're looking at a risky future, and the question is what price we are going to pay to hold stocks." The entire objective of asset allocation is to give the investor the greatest opportunity for gain with the smallest degree of risk, something Dr. Sharpe has spent much of his adult life studying.

There has long been a misconception, though, that getting the asset allocation right outweighs the importance of careful security selection. It's a misconception fuelled in part by studies that have shown asset allocation to be a critical determinant in portfolio performance. Though we agree that getting the right asset mix is highly important to a portfolio's long-term success, sloppy security selection still is going to hamper progress. However, get the two working in harmony and you will have a thing of beauty.

We'll cover the selection of both fixed-income and equity investments in the chapters to follow. For now, let's keep the focus on how these asset classes can work together for the common good.

STOP SWINGING FOR THE FENCES

To be an active investor is to be an optimist. Even though we've been investing for ourselves and for clients for many years, we still can't help but get excited at the opportunities each day brings. It's also human nature to want to knock the proverbial ball out of the investment ballpark. Experience has taught us, however, that swinging for the fences every time results in little more than a whole lot of strikeouts. The more sensible strategy, to carry on the baseball metaphor a little longer, is to strive to get runners on base every time and to advance runners through consistency. A successful asset allocation strategy will help you to do just that. Ultimately, it's consistent returns that you should be seeking from your overall portfolio.

ZIGZAG

The three main asset classes behave differently at various points in time. Ideally, you want some portion of your portfolio to zig while the other zags. By studying the historic patterns of various types of investments you will notice that the three main asset classes seldom move in a synchronized manner. Sometimes they even move in opposite directions. This is what is known as an inverse correlation, and is central to the risk-busting attributes of asset allocation theory. The net result of the entire exercise is to give you more consistent portfolio performance by having less dramatic peaks and troughs in value.

Study after study has shown that in periods of 10 years or more, equities provide the best total return on investment. Bonds, by comparison, offer stability and income-generating potential. Cash (and its equivalents) pay little, yet offer safety and are useful for meeting unexpected liquidity needs. Various combinations of these three distinct asset classes will deliver differing quantities of both risk and return. Finding the balance that meets your own unique requirements lies at the heart of asset allocation.

TAKE A LOOK IN THE MIRROR

You can't even begin to draft a comprehensive asset allocation strategy until you have given some serious thought to your objectives. Are you building wealth to support yourself in retirement? Or are you accumulating capital to pay for your children's post-secondary education? Once you have articulated your goals against considerations like these and put them into a time frame, a little soul-searching with regard to your risk tolerance will be in order.

Risk comes in many forms, and we will explore the theme in greater detail later in this book. For now, we remain primarily concerned with the big picture, and as such are seeking something more like a blood pressure reading of portfolio volatility and your tolerance for it.

As mentioned earlier, a number of financial institutions have developed detailed questionnaires for the express purpose of gauging attitude toward risk. While we have no quarrel with the use of these questionnaires, we feel very strongly that there is no substitute for human interaction. Your responses to a questionnaire should be nothing more than the starting point to a deep conversation with your advisor on the subject at hand. This conversation about risk should be part of the fact-finding that we described in the last chapter.

Some factors that you and your advisor need to take into consideration before drawing up an asset allocation strategy for you include your:

- age (and that of your spouse, if applicable)
- career status (early, approaching retirement, already retired, etc.)
- sources of income
- financial resources, including your net worth
- current and anticipated financial obligations

Your objectives, tolerance for risk, and responses to the factors just listed will determine the direction that your asset allocation takes. Having someone push the dialogue along by asking thoughtful questions will help you and your advisor really get to the heart of the matter.

TACTICS AND STRATEGIES

Within the scope of asset allocation theory are two distinct methods of asset allocation: tactical asset allocation and strategic asset allocation.

Tactical asset allocation is an exercise in getting an appropriate balance among the three main asset classes: stocks, bonds and cash. The priority of the tactical asset allocation practitioner is to be in the right place at the right time to optimize the trade-off between risk and reward depending on prevailing market conditions.

Strategic asset allocation is all about striking a balance between risk and reward that meets the risk tolerance of the client. The investor utilizing strategic asset allocation uses the historic risk and performance characteristics of the three main asset classes as the primary determinant of how much of his or her portfolio should be directed to each respective category.

Tactical Asset Allocation

Tactical asset allocation strategies tend to focus more on maximizing the investor's rate of return than on managing risk, so by definition the investment time horizon here tends to be more short term than would otherwise be the case. Think of tactical asset allocation as taking more of a market timing approach to investing than its cousin, strategic asset allocation. As such, it historically has tended to be more suitable for trading-oriented investors or professionals. For many individual investors, tactical asset allocation is often best executed through a mutual fund, hedge fund or investment counsellor dedicated to the practice.

Tactical asset allocation strategies are notorious for their lack of breadth, yet we firmly believe they can be of great benefit to investors, particularly looking to the future. A growing number of investment industry leaders are expressing the belief that investment returns over the next decade will be much more modest than in the previous two. In this expectation, a significant debate has erupted over the relative merits of buy-and-hold investment strategies versus more proactive, opportunistic strategies. Those investors seeking to beat the major market averages may find particular appeal in tactical asset allocation strategies.

Strategic Asset Allocation

Strategic asset allocation differs from tactical asset allocation by tending to be more focused on investor risk tolerance and long-range objectives. It also takes on more of a long-term perspective, usually five years or greater.

---

100 Minus Age

There are dozens of cookie-cutter-type asset allocation strategies that appear to be wonderful in theory, yet often are sadly lacking in practice. One such example is the "100 minus your age" strategy. With this strategy, the investor subtracts his or her present age from 100 to find out how much of his or her portfolio should be allocated to equities. Or, inversely, that present age should be the percentage allocated to bonds and fixed income. The implied message here is that as investors age, their tolerance for risk subsides, and so also should their allocation to stocks.

This asset allocation strategy strikes us as one that raises more questions than answers. No consideration is given for changes in an investor's personal circumstances, such as sudden wealth. What happens if investors in question are a married couple with a significant age difference? The list goes on, but we won't belabour the point. In our view there is simply no substitute for a detailed conversation about your needs and wants with a qualified, experienced professional.

It's not unusual for an investor to employ both methods of asset allocation simultaneously, with tactical asset allocation as a component of a larger strategic asset allocation strategy.

THE EFFICIENT FRONTIER

First off, stop thinking about William Shatner! The efficient frontier has nothing whatsoever to do with *Star Trek*. What it does concern is a two-dimensional, historical analysis of how various mixes of asset classes have performed over extended periods of time.

Nobel Prize laureates Harry Markowitz and William Sharpe (yes, that guy again) took a scientific approach to examining how to build what they referred to as risk-efficient portfolios. They examined both the historic risk, as measured by standard deviation, and the historic return of a wide range of investments. They then were able to take this data and plot it on a graph to vividly illustrate how certain combinations of securities often can yield surprising results. Take, for example, their revelation that a portfolio composed 100% of U.S. Treasury bonds had a higher standard deviation (meaning it is subject to more price volatility, which many investors define as risk) than a portfolio split 40/60 between equities and fixed income. In addition, that 40/60 portfolio had a greater rate of return than the all-bond portfolio. Talk about revolutionary research!

Balancing Risk & Reward
The Efficient Frontier

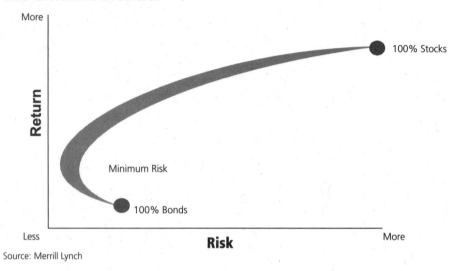

Source: Merrill Lynch

What the efficient frontier teaches us is that it is possible to arrange holdings in portfolios so as to strike an effective balance between risk and reward. It's interesting to note that the efficient frontier is a curved, not straight, line. Where do you belong in a curved-line scenario like this? All in stocks (and/or related equity products) and the risks could be too high; all in bonds (and/or fixed-income equivalents) and the investment returns could be too low. Nor is it a case of simply placing an X where you think you'd like your portfolio to be balanced. Your optimal point on the efficient frontier will depend on many considerations—your age, your resources, your financial and income needs now versus later, your tax bracket, your tolerance for risk, your sleep-at-night point—as well as the ultimate size your portfolio will need to reach to achieve what you want from your investments. Your position on the curve, and the road map to get, there are topics we will focus on in chapter 12. Suffice it to say at this point that correct portfolio balance is essential in both.

Yet, despite the best efforts of the investment industry's sharpest minds, asset allocation remains as much art as science. Capital markets are dynamic in nature. So too are investor wants and needs. It is for this reason that all of today's advanced technology hasn't been able to boil down asset allocation to an entirely mathematical formula. Hence, we encourage investors to put their asset allocation strategy down in writing, ideally as part of a comprehensive Investment Policy Statement.

For obvious reasons, we stop short of suggesting that asset allocation decisions be cast in stone. Your needs will change over time, as will your ability or desire to take on certain volumes of risk. It's clearly important that you and your advisor remain in regular communication. When clients inform us they intend to retire in two or three years, we can work with them at a thoughtful, pedestrian pace to adjust their portfolios to meet their changing circumstances. When they walk into our offices and declare that they are going to retire in two days' time there is little room for subtlety, and in the ensuing rush there is a significantly higher probability of an unfortunate oversight.

REBALANCING: LIPOSUCTION FOR YOUR PORTFOLIO

Over time, some segments of your portfolio will grow faster than others. The inevitable result is that its shape will begin changing in much the same way as a middle-aged guy with a tendency to overindulge in pizza and beer. Pizza guy will need months of cautious food intake, and grunting and sweating at the gym, to get back into shape. Mercifully, the health program for your portfolio needn't be as strenuous.

As we noted earlier, you'll need to set some parameters in your asset allocation strategy on how far you will be willing to let a segment grow. When a segment or security pushes past this predetermined threshold, you'll know it's time to trim back the position. This is in no way a repudiation of what we stated in chapter 2, where we paraphrased *Investor's Business Daily* founder William O'Neil's dictum that you should always take your losses quickly and your profits slowly. Stopping from time to time to trim back overweight positions in your portfolio is a good discipline that helps to ward off the risk of something else we described in chapter 2—portfolio concentration.

WHERE DO WE GO FROM HERE?

What should you do with the capital you've now taken from the fastest-growing segment(s) of your portfolio? The simple answer: reinvest into the sector of the portfolio that is under-represented. This is exactly what happens more often than not. On occasion, however, it may be prudent to reserve judgment on where to reinvest. This may be due to unpredictable market conditions, when wise investors will set aside some of their profits in the cash section of their portfolios for use later when, presumably, prices may be more advantageous to the buyer.

STRIKING THE RIGHT BALANCE

The search for the balance between risk and reward that meets your needs continues from the objective-setting stage through to an examination of the trade-off between risk and reward. You should view these two attributes in tandem. Understanding the characteristics of major asset classes, and even specific securities, will go a long way toward unravelling the riddle of *your* asset allocation.

The reward part of the risk-reward pairing, stated otherwise as investment return, is already almost universally understood. Rates of return are regularly published for major market averages, mutual funds, stocks and so on. With most fixed-income investments, the yield is known right from the start, assuming of course that you are planning to hold, not trade, these securities. What is much harder to quantify is the risk side of the equation.

STANDARD DEVIATION

Standard deviation has, over time, grown to become the investment industry's preferred method for measuring risk. It's a calculation of volatility of the investment returns of a given security. The higher the standard deviation number, the riskier the security. Take as an example two very different mutual funds. One, a bond fund, will carry a standard deviation rating that is substantially lower than the other, an emerging markets–based mutual fund. This is not to say that one is superior to the other. The standard deviation will be vastly different for each because one fund (the bond fund) has historically demonstrated much less pronounced fluctuations in value than has been the case with the emerging markets fund.

The popular view among the statisticians who generate standard deviation ratings is that a minimum three-year time horizon is necessary to effectively come up with a standard deviation rating for a security. Three years is considered a long enough period of time to establish a trend for a given security, reducing the risk of the analysis being tainted by abnormal short-term fluctuations. By using standard deviation, investors can then make a more direct comparison between similarly mandated securities.

One criticism frequently levelled against standard deviation is that it tends to treat above- and below-average performers in exactly the same manner. It's fine and dandy to declare that your mutual fund carries a below-average standard deviation, but poor investment returns are still poor returns. Chances are, what you are most concerned about is the possibility of losing money. That's why we prefer to use other means of measuring risk and reward in addition to standard deviation.

PEAKS AND VALLEYS

An alternative to standard deviation is to take a look at an asset class or a security's best and worst 12-month periods. Arguably, this is a much more "back of the envelope" means of understanding risk and reward characteristics. Nevertheless, it remains useful in that it offers a sense of an asset class or security's potential tendency for extremes by looking at actual performance figures.

Taking the probability of capital loss into consideration, it becomes readily apparent that time *in* the market is as important, if not more important, than the timing of entry points. John Templeton used to make the case very convincingly, as illustrated in the accompanying chart. This is particularly true of equity investments, provided, of course, that a portfolio is sufficiently diversified and stocked with high-quality names.

The "Best" Time To Invest
Average Annual Rates of Return 1972-1996*

Investment Made at:

Market high each year	16.9%
Market low each year	18.0%
DIFFERENCE	1.1%

Conclusion:

> **The best time to invest is whenever you have the money.**

*Results of $5,000 invested each year for 25 years in the Templeton Growth Fund
Source: Templeton

We'll be the first to admit that the prospect of avoiding losses is not what gets investor pulses racing. Rather, it's the prospect of having the money you've worked so hard to attain working even harder for you. The simple fact that you need your money to grow in order to fund your objectives (remember those?) then leads to the question of "How much is enough?" This is where a look back at historic returns can serve as a guide.

If you are looking for a high degree of growth over an extended period of time, following an asset allocation strategy focused primarily on capital preservation through the extensive use of bonds will lead to disappointment. Similarly, funding retirement income needs with portfolios composed almost entirely of growth-oriented equities is a recipe for disaster. The inescapable fact is that if you want superior growth, it will be necessary to take on incrementally greater degrees of risk in the composition of your portfolio. Similarly, if you are a risk-averse investor, and your portfolio is structured to reflect that preference, don't expect the kind of return on investment that would inspire a late-night infomercial. Alan Greenspan, the revered U.S. Federal Reserve Board chairman, perhaps summed it up best of all when he repeated an often-used colloquialism: "No one has yet invented the free lunch."

MUTUAL FUNDS AND ASSET ALLOCATION

It certainly would be nice if everything could be wrapped in a tidy package, kind of like the endings to most Hollywood movies. Unfortunately (or fortunately, depending on your point of view), life is seldom like a Hollywood movie. And this handy little bit of philosophy (which we offer to you at no extra charge) applies in equal measure to asset allocation.

Managed financial products, such as mutual funds, often have their own ready-made asset allocation. There is a wide assortment of mutual funds practising tactical asset allocation as part of their mandate. As well, virtually every fund company offers at least one balanced fund; that is, a fund that aims to strike a predetermined balance between fixed income and equities.

If you and your advisor are working on a detailed asset allocation strategy that includes, for example, a balanced fund in the mix, take a moment to crack open the fund to see how the assets are allocated. The best place to look for this information is in the governing prospectus, which will tell you what the constraints are and the maximum degree in any direction toward stocks, bonds or cash that the fund is permitted to move. Once you have this information, it becomes easier to see whether and how the fund will fit within your desired asset allocation.

INTERNATIONAL EXPOSURE AND ASSET ALLOCATION

For as long as many of today's generation of active investors can remember, the Canadian dollar has been the anaemic cousin to many of its international counterparts, especially the U.S. dollar. In 2003, however, the tables were turned when the mighty greenback began to fall from its very high perch as the world's pre-eminent currency. This, along with surging commodities markets, helped raise the value of the once-feeble Canadian dollar against a number of currencies—the U.S. dollar in particular.

Through the better part of 30 years, Canadian investors were taught that investing beyond Canada's capital markets was a sound means of adding additional portfolio diversification. As the Canadian dollar sank, foreign investments translated back into Canadian dollars received a currency-induced boost. Hence, adding global exposure often tended to increase a portfolio's performance while simultaneously reducing its risk profile.

With the rapid appreciation of the Canadian dollar by more than 30% against its U.S. counterpart between the spring of 2003 and the spring of 2005, the strategy of heavily emphasizing non-Canadian investments was turned on its head. Just as a portfolio would receive a currency-induced lift when international investments were converted back into depreciating Canadian dollars, those same international investments would drag down portfolio performance when converted into rising Canadian dollars.

Although Canada is one of the world's largest countries geographically, it is relatively small from an economic perspective, representing a mere 3% of world GDP and capital markets. And while a number of world-class investment opportunities call Canada home, it is obvious that there is a much wider, almost limitless, selection beyond our borders. Furthermore, the 2005 federal budget's elimination of foreign content restrictions on registered plans such as RRSPs and RRIFs makes it significantly easier for Canadians to invest more of their retirement savings abroad.

International investing makes perfect sense when the opportunity for growth exceeds the risk posed by currency exchange. We tend to steer away from global bonds as an asset class because there is simply not enough potential gain to overcome the risk posed by currency fluctuation unless you are an institutional investor with the capability and clout to bid for large quantities of bonds, negotiating a yield advantage. However, equity investment in other countries' companies or indexes is an altogether different story. If the growth potential offered by a non-domestic security is superior to what can be found closer to home, then you're on to something. If not, stay home—at least you won't have currency conversion risk issues to contend with.

GROWTH VS. VALUE

Selecting securities for the equity portion of portfolios brings investors face to face with the choice of taking either a value approach or a growth approach. Most mutual fund managers do just this, qualifying themselves as either growth- or value-style fund managers. Successful investors know that matching equal parts of growth and value funds in a portfolio is one way to add another layer of diversification to the equity portion.

The value style of stock selection has been made famous by legendary portfolio managers such as Sir John Templeton and Warren Buffett. Simply put, it means seeking out stocks that are trading for less than their intrinsic value. In other words, value investors are trying to buy a dollar for seventy-five cents. Benjamin Graham (once again, related to Michael only in spirit) saw underpriced securities as investments providing a margin of safety. Similarly, Warren Buffett has always liked a moat of safety around his investments. For risk-sensitive investors, stocks chosen through the value method of security selection are usually the most appropriate choices.

An investor who focuses on the growth method of stock selection is on the lookout for companies with the capability of growing their earnings at a pace fast enough to warrant a rise in the share price. This style of manager is typically less concerned with valuation than with putting growth funds into use in portfolios where investors have an above-average tolerance for risk.

In addition, there is a class of asset managers who are considered hybrids. These exotic birds refer to themselves as GARP (growth at a reasonable price) managers. Their definition of "reasonable" is somewhat subjective, and can vary quite significantly from one manager to the next. If you are considering the addition of a GARP style of mutual fund in your portfolio, take a look at the top holdings of the fund. That, together with an examination of the degree of volatility of the fund's unit price over a span of several years, will give you some insight into whether or not the fund fits your comfort level and needs.

AN OUNCE OF PREVENTION . . .

The highly disciplined application of strategic asset allocation helps all of us to avoid that natural human tendency of wanting to load up our portfolios with equities when stock indexes are in full flight, and to rush to cash in times of market turmoil. The inclination to fall victim to our own emotions of fear and greed can be found at the root of most, if not all, wounded portfolios.

Taking the time to work through an asset allocation strategy custom-tailored to your own unique needs before selecting investments will go a long way toward making more rational, less emotional investment decisions. You should also remember to include direction on both when and how to rebalance your portfolio, so that the delicate balance between risk and reward that you worked so hard to achieve at the outset of the investment process is not thrown into disarray by a rapidly appreciating or depreciating security.

CHAPTER 8

Show Me the Money

Investing for Income

Several years ago, Holiday Inn had a marketing slogan that promised "no surprises." This is exactly what you should be striving for if you are one of the millions of fully or partially retired Canadians who require an income from their portfolio.

The income stream generated by your investments should be reliable and highly predictable. You cannot rely on peeling off rising market values as a substitute for an income stream. Capital appreciation should come from growth investments, such as stocks or equity-based mutual funds. In order to have a reliable income stream generated by your investments, turn to investment vehicles whose primary purpose is generating a steady, reliable stream of income. To do otherwise is a little like having a wild bucking bronco from the Calgary Stampede brought in to give pony rides at a children's birthday party.

GIVE ME A BRAKE!

Investing for income is often viewed as the domain of widows and orphans. This view is grossly misleading. Even the most aggressive growth investor will at various points in time have a need to place some portion of their portfolio in fixed-income investments. A portfolio with no fixed-income representation is like a car with no brakes. In this chapter, we will introduce you to securities and strategies that can be used to generate an income, yet can also be used as risk management tools where appropriate.

LOANING AND OWNING

Loaning and owning are the two components that define investing. Loaning is contractual and finite. Owning is entrepreneurial and residual.

To put it another way, bonds, GICs and most other fixed-income instruments are, for the most part, a case of what you see is what you get. You are lending your money to the issuer. The bond (or GIC, etc.) is in effect an IOU from the issuer to pay back your money at a specific point in the future, and to pay you a prescribed rate of interest in consideration for having the use of your money. This is the essence of fixed-income investing.

Equities are another matter altogether. Buying shares in a corporation means that you have taken an ownership stake in the company. You have become an owner rather than a loaner. Here there is no maturity date, no guarantees on a return of your capital. Your earnings can be much greater or much less than the return on a comparable size fixed-income investment. It all depends on the success of the company in turning a profit. We'll focus on the owning aspect of investing in the next chapter. In this chapter, our focus will remain primarily on the loaning side of the equation, but we will occasionally cross over into the owning side as it pertains to income-generating equities such as income trusts and preferred shares.

RISKS AND REWARDS

Like equities, fixed-income securities can have "good" or "bad" prices during their income-generating lives to maturity. Also like equities, there will be times when they represent exceptional investment value, and others when they are overpriced and need to be sold, trimmed or best avoided. Michael vividly remembers the mid-1980s when bond yields were in the mid-teens and real (after-inflation) yields were of a magnitude seldom seen; in other words, bonds were at a stage where their returns simply could not be ignored. There are risks associated with bond investing, too. Like equities, there can be no escaping *en passant* investment risk, whether direct or indirect.

Credit Risk

Directly, there is the risk of the borrower being unable to meet interest and repayment commitments. It's a risk that can inflict considerable damage on portfolios. Investors who lent their precious savings to household names such as Air Canada,

Confederation Life, Royal Trustco, and Stelco and now Nortel will never forget what credit risk can come to mean.

Occasionally, creditworthiness can go wrong even at the highest level. An irony of history records Alberta as the last Canadian province to have defaulted on its debts—back in the "dirty thirties," the 1930s. A more recent example of how even the debt of a sovereign nation can be hurtful is Argentina, where damaged creditors eventually agreed to swap US$102 billion of that country's bad debt for US$25 billion of new bonds—at that point the largest restructuring in history. The cardinal rule of knowing what you are investing in applies as much to fixed income as it does to equities.

Asset-Backed Commercial Paper

Asset-backed commercial paper (ABCP) is a short-term debt instrument issued by a limited-purpose trust. These securities traditionally were the repository for consumer loans and receivables as well as mortgages of various descriptions. Over time, the ABCP market grew and assets held within these instruments came to include more exotic creatures such as credit default swaps, leveraged derivatives instruments and collateralized debt obligations.

Asset-backed commercial paper issued in Canada has been long rated by Dominion Bond Rating Service. Each asset within the ABCP trust is then separately rated, in many instances by more than one rating agency. For this reason, much of the ABCP in Canada was rated by Dominion Bond Rating Service as R-1 (high)—the highest rating DBRS could award. This led many to conclude that ABCP would serve as an excellent short-term "cash equivalent" type of security for risk-averse investors.

When there is a vibrant, healthy market for the underlying assets held within a particular ABCP security everyone is, for the most part, pretty happy. When the underlying asset's market value is called into question, though, problems ensue, and that's exactly what happened here in Canada.

The ABCP market lives and dies by the vagaries of the underlying asset market. If that market were to dry up, investors would be trapped by what is known as "liquidity risk." As the U.S. subprime mortgage market deteriorated from bad to worse, investors in Canadian ABCP became justifiably concerned that as a result of U.S. subprime exposure, certain Canadian entities could be saddled with credit quality issues.

In the summer of 2007, the sponsors of several ABCP trusts announced that because of the adverse conditions in the Canadian markets, it would not be possible for them to place new paper to replace maturing obligations. Many of the ABCP instruments in the market at the time had an extendible feature, meaning that the sponsor could, at their discretion, extend the maturity of a given ABCP. Where such an option existed, many sponsors chose to extend their maturities. This created a substantial liquidity problem for many ABCP holders, who are often among the more risk-averse individual investors in Canada. This was, after all, supposed to be a no-brainer, low-risk investment—a veritable widows and orphans investment.

In September 2007, an industry committee was formed to oversee a proposed restructuring process pertaining to certain ABCP products sold to Canadian investors. It was a lengthy, unnerving, often frustrating process for the thousands of Canadians who had invested what for many had been all-important retirement savings in one or more of these instruments. Ultimately, numerous Canadian financial institutions did what was felt to be right for their clients by providing the liquidity necessary for these investors to get their money back in a reasonably timely manner.

We won't use this space to apportion blame on a crisis that we hasten to add did not involve the five major Canadian chartered banks. That's best left to others far more acquainted with the intricacies of the matter, and quite frankly our role is to enlighten you on steps you ought to take to reduce the risk of being caught up in a similar crisis at some point in the future.

The sad reality is that investor education often lags behind new development in the financial world. On occasion, investors will assume that they are exposed to a different set of risks than their predecessors. More often than not, these risks are not apparent until market stresses begin to appear. Canadian investors caught up in the ABCP crisis had made their investments in good faith, believing the "good housekeeping" seal of approval from debt rating agencies suggested a high degree of safety. You must always remember that ABCP is commercial paper and is not comparable to debt instruments of a sovereign government. In fact, under particular conditions, ABCP has proven to be much riskier than traditional commercial paper securities.

More Lessons of History

The lesson we take from this episode in Canadian corporate history is that there is no substitute for the security provided by thorough diversification, meaning diversification of issuer, of asset type and of maturity. We know it's very much a case of Monday morning quarterbacking for us to write this, but it needs to be stated: take nothing for granted. Things are not always what they seem. Never compromise the safety and stability of the fixed-income portion of your portfolio in order to boost your yield. History is littered with examples of investors who thought they were getting a sweetheart deal—high yield with no risk—only to learn too late that it was an illusion. This risk of falling prey to the allure of high-yield, seemingly safe fixed-income investments is particularly acute in an era of exceptionally low interest rates. You simply have to accept the fact that you will have to take on more risk in order to lift your portfolio's yield in a time of ultra-low interest rates such as today. If you accept that premise, then at least do yourself a couple of favours: 1) Make sure you are going to be well rewarded for taking on additional risk, and 2) Be certain of the liquidity provisions of a given security. In other words, you need to know where the emergency exits are located. More often than not in a time of low interest rates, the additional yield you are seeking will not be found in the fixed-income market, but rather amongst equities, in the form of dividends. We'll save our discussion on dividends for the next chapter.

Because credit risk can be iceberg-like, that is, largely lurking beneath the surface and invisible to the untrained eye, fixed-income investors have come to rely on debt rating agencies such as Standard & Poor's Rating Services, Canadian Bond Rating Service and Dominion Bond Rating Service to provide valuable (though not infallible) assistance in grading credit risk. Their expertise should be a mandatory first step in checking the quality of the fixed-income investments being considered. We prefer bonds with an "A" or "I" rating and steadfastly ignore debt instruments with lower ratings or no ratings at all. No matter how enticing the yield, we prefer to stay away from inferior credit ratings. Our belief is that if the fixed-income element of your portfolio is destined to be the safe money, you don't want to obscure its purpose by taking on heightened risk. Bond traders have a name for investors who scrounge through the markets in search of above-average yields: yield pigs. There is also a quaint little aphorism that every bond trader has committed to memory by the end of their first day on the job that describes the ultimate fate of yield pigs: *Bulls make money. Bears make money. Pigs get slaughtered!* Fixed-income investing involves enough risks anyway; credit risk just isn't worth it—not at any price.

INTEREST RATE RISK
AND THE INVERSE RELATIONSHIP

Over the lifespan of fixed-income investments, the twin risks of rising interest rates and inflation can take their toll on the market price of an investment, despite eventual repayment at par (assuming a good credit rating).

Rising interest rates diminish the value of existing bonds in the market. As the price of a bond declines, the yield offered to a potential purchaser increases. The faster interest rates rise, the more dramatic the drop in a given bond's price, until the yield offered reflects the "going rate" of the day. The opposite occurs when interest rates drop. Bond prices appreciate, sending yields lower to reflect, once again, the prevailing yield of the day.

This phenomenon of bond prices falling when interest rates rise and rising when rates fall is what is known as fixed-income securities' unique *inverse relationship* with interest rates. All things being equal, the longer into the future the maturity date of a bond, the more susceptible it will be to price fluctuations from changing interest rates.

For this reason, it is a good idea to keep your bond maturities fairly short if you are expecting interest rates to rise over the near term. If, however, your expectation is for a steep drop in lending rates, the strategy then shifts to extending the average term to maturity in the fixed-income portion of your portfolio. This will enable you to lock in today's soon-to-be-high rates for as long as possible, and offer a boost to the market value of your portfolio as the bonds appreciate. If you learn nothing else from reading this chapter, let it be the concept of the inverse relationship between fixed-income securities and interest rates. Keeping this front and centre in your thinking will dramatically improve your results as a fixed-income investor.

The temptation for some investors is to trade bonds and other fixed-income securities for quick profits despite the interest rate risk, in a manner not dissimilar to what day traders do with equities. Short-term trading of any kind is not for the faint of heart, and in the overwhelming majority of instances is best left to qualified professionals.

THE RISING COST OF LIVING

Inflation eats away at the purchasing power of the fixed interest payments as they are received over the life of a bond. As a result, the return that really counts is the "real" return; that is, what remains after deducting the rate of inflation from the current yield. Real returns can fluctuate widely, as the following chart illustrates.

Government of Canada 10-Year Bond Yields
Actual & Real Returns, 1990 – Mid-2009

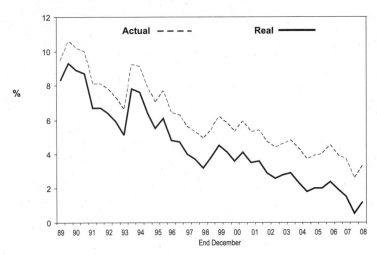

Source: Bloomberg Finance L.P.   Acknowledgement: Claudia Terrigno

Note: Actual yield (thin line) at end of quarter, real yield (thick line) after deducting CPI y/y %.

Over time the true, inflation-adjusted lending rate at which one can lend in meaningful terms emerges at about 4%. Above this historical level of real return, bonds and equivalent fixed-income instruments offer excellent, sometimes even outstanding, value. Below this level, warning flags should begin to fly. If real returns fall to zero or turn negative and remedial portfolio action hasn't been taken, the results can be very sobering. Remedial action would, in this instance, include shortening the average term to maturity in the fixed-income section of your portfolio and/or raising the cash/cash equivalency levels (money market funds, Treasury bills, bankers' acceptances, etc.). This defends the value of your portfolio against the risk brought on by rising interest rates.

FIXED-INCOME STRATEGIES

The fact that bonds are repayable at maturity reflects increasingly in their market prices the closer they get to maturity. Certainty of principal repayment (assuming creditworthiness) also means interest rate risk and volatility can be hedged against along the way. The strategies to do so are many and sometimes can be quite complex. We covered the most frequently used strategy earlier when we examined the inverse relationship between bond values and interest rates.

Bonds and Ladders

The simplest means of protecting your portfolio against the shifting fortunes of rising and falling interest rates is by staggering the maturities of your bonds. This is where you have bond maturities occurring at regular intervals into the future. A bond ladder has the advantage of giving built-in protection against both interest rate scenarios. If rates are set to rise, the shortest term-to-maturity bonds in the ladder can be reinvested at maturity into longer-dated and presumably higher-yield bonds in an act that bears some resemblance to a game of leapfrog. If rates are on the decline, the bonds out at the long end of the ladder will appreciate in value and help to preserve the overall value of the ladder.

When constructing a bond ladder, we ideally like to divide the total dollar value of the fixed-income component of the portfolio by 10. We then look for bonds (or related debt equivalents) of a more or less equal amount maturing successively in each of the 10 years from whatever date the ladder begins. As each bond matures, the proceeds can be reinvested in another future maturity, either going out another 10 years or shortening the new maturity if rising interest rates are foreseen, but repeatedly keeping a number of rungs to what becomes a perpetual ladder.

Arnold Schwarzenegger's Favourite: The Barbell Strategy

If an investor's portfolio does not contain enough capital to build a proper bond ladder, a sensible alternative is to invest half the fixed-income section of the portfolio in shorter-term securities and the other half in longer-term maturities. This is what is known as a barbell strategy. This strategy can be especially opportune when the yield curve is flattening and there is no great advantage to leaning one way or the other.

Monthly Income Portfolios

Bonds that pay their interest out to investors, and not all do, generally make their payments every six months. For an investor looking for a reliable, consistent income stream from their investments, getting paid only twice per year can be inconvenient. To counter this, build a ladder made of at least six bonds with successive annual maturities, but with each paying their semi-annual interest in different months (e.g., January and July, February and August, March and September and so on). This way, the bond section of a portfolio can be made to generate income every month of the year, as illustrated in the accompanying example of an account Michael advises on. You'll notice how the maturities are balanced between 2010 and 2016, with a gap in 2015 that should ideally be filled. You'll also see that this portfolio generates interest income every month with the exceptions of April and October. It's not an absolutely perfect ladder, but is still quite functional.

Laddered Bond Portfolio

Amount		Security	Coupon	Maturity	Income
$50,000		HSBC Financial Corp.	4.00%	May 03, 2010	$ 2,000
50,000	$100,000	Wells Fargo Financial Cda	3.60	Jun. 28, 2010	1,800
25,000		Gtr. Toronto Airp. Auth.	4.40%	Feb. 28, 2011	1,100
50,000		Trans Alta Corporation	6.90	Jun. 01, 2011	3,450
25,000		YPG Holdings	5.50	Aug. 01, 2011	1,375
15,000	115,000	Suncor Energy	6.70	Aug. 22, 2011	1,005
50,000		EnCana Corp.	4.30%	Mar. 12, 2012	2,150
65,000	115,000	Inter-America Dev. Bk.	4.25	Dec. 02, 2012	2,763
25,000		Royal Bank of Canada	4.15%	Nov. 04, 2013	1,038
50,000	75,000	Loblaw Companies	5.40	Nov. 20, 2013	2,700
25,000		Royal Bank of Canada	4.97%	Jan. 05, 2014	1,243
25,000		Terasen	5.56	Sep. 15, 2014	1,390
50,000	100,000	CIBC	4.75	Dec. 22, 2014	2,375
50,000		YPG Holdings	5.25%	Feb. 15, 2016	2,625
50,000	100,000	Bell Canada	4.64	Feb. 22, 2016	2,320
65,000	65,000	TransCanada Corp.	5.10%	Jan. 11, 2017	3,315
25,000	25,000	EnCana Corp.	5.80%	Jan. 18, 2018	1,450
50,000	50,000	Bank of Montreal	4.87%	Aug. 22, 2020 *	2,435
	$745,000				$36,534

* Callable Aug. 2015

Spring 2009

Ladders like these assure income while smoothing out interest rate risk. They also average out volatility and keep current the principal value of the fixed-income section of portfolios. Because bond prices customarily build in a premium to compensate for inflation, the continual adding of new maturities to the ladder automatically provides an element of inflation protection. By dividing the fixed-income section into equal amounts over a range of maturities, you can avoid the hazards of forecasting future interest rates—never an easy task at the best of times.

A BEVY OF BONDS TO CHOOSE FROM
Strip Bonds

For investors who do not yet need to derive an income from their portfolio, the semi-annual interest payments from bonds sometimes can be something of a nuisance. Often the payments in and of themselves are too small to roll over into another bond, or to add to a stock position. If the investment account in question is an RRSP, taking the cash out and spending it is not an option because of the onerous tax consequences. Many investors will allow the interest payments to accumulate as part of the cash reserve in their portfolio, but what do you do when that reservoir of cash is brimming over? Strip bonds are frequently the answer.

Strip bonds derive their name from the manner in which they are conceived. They are existing federal, provincial, municipal and sometimes even corporate bonds that have been separated into their component parts of interest payments and principal payments. These components are then made available to investors as individual securities. Strip bonds act a little like a compound GIC in that no interest is actually paid out until maturity. Strip bond prices, like the prices of all bonds, depend on current interest rate levels and can vary from day to day. Unlike more traditional fixed-income investments, these bonds always are priced below par. The interest earned on a strip bond is the difference between the discounted price and the bond's matured value of par (100 cents on the dollar).

Strip bonds can be sold prior to their maturity date, but like any other type of fixed-income investment, the price you receive will be a reflection of prevailing interest rates. This can work either for you or against you. Our advice to clients always has been to never buy a strip bond, or any bond at all for that matter, with a maturity that is longer than you are prepared to hold the bond for.

Canada Revenue Agency has determined that the difference between the purchase value and the maturity value of a strip bond constitutes accrued interest. As such, if you hold strip bonds in a non-registered investment account, the amount of interest that you are deemed to have earned in a given year must be reported on your income tax return. This creates a negative cash flow situation because you will be forced to pay tax on income that you have not yet received. It is for this reason that we recommend strip bonds be used primarily for RRSP accounts.

Convertible Debentures

Debentures are debt instruments offered by corporations. Unlike a bond, a debenture is not secured by any mortgage or any other lien on specific assets of the issuer. The line between bonds and debentures often gets blurred by investors who refer to all long-term debt obligations as bonds.

Convertible debentures offer the income-producing qualities of a bond and the capital appreciation potential of an equity. A convertible debenture offers the holder, for a predetermined period of time, the right to convert the debenture to a specific number of common shares at a specified price. This conversion right is valuable if the underlying stock escalates in value, but like the purchase of a convertible roadster, this feature comes at a cost. Issuers can usually price convertible debentures with a yield that is slightly below that of a comparable regular bond or debenture since the convertible has the capital gain potential that other fixed-income investments do not have.

Real Return Bonds

One way to protect against inflation is to invest in real return bonds. Also called inflation-protected bonds, real return bonds have the unique feature of the issuer annually raising the principal on repayment by the previous year's rate of inflation. Unfortunately, the Canadian market in these bonds is limited mostly to a few series of Government of Canada bonds. Even then, however, real return bonds can become over- or underpriced, and as such there are accompanying risks.

Corporate Bonds

Often, an investor who wishes to boost the overall yield on the fixed-income portion of his or her portfolio will look to the bonds of major corporations as the solution. This is a reasonable prospect, yet it is also one that can potentially turn up the risk profile of the overall portfolio by several degrees. We have witnessed situations where investors have bought the bonds of a company in distress, attracted to a yield that sits considerably higher than that of comparable term-to-maturity bonds. This is an act that is very similar to "catching a falling knife," which we described earlier in this book.

Great care must be taken in the selection of corporate bonds to make sure you have not bought an empty promise. Just as you would lend money to your brother-in-law only if you were confident he eventually could repay the loan, so it is with corporate bonds. Don't buy a company's bonds if you are not confident of its ability to make payments of principal and interest to you. This is where the debt-rating agencies can be a real lifesaver, but even they are not infallible. Our rule of thumb is that we will not buy the debt of any company if we would not gladly purchase its stock.

Never forget the relationship between risk and reward. The higher the yield, the greater the risk. Fortunately, there is a large variety of good-quality bonds available from many of the world's greatest corporations that really can add an enticing dimension to a fixed-income strategy. If there is research available on the stock of the company, it's a good idea to read it so you can gain further insight into the company and be able to spot debt-related problems before they become catastrophic.

Many corporate bond issues have a call feature that enables the company, under certain predetermined conditions, to call in bonds for redemption prior to maturity. This is a little like having the ability to renegotiate your mortgage well before maturity if interest rates drop. In the corporate world, these call features enable a company to reissue debt at more favourable terms to the issuer if market conditions permit.

For the holder (that would be you), this presents a problem in that the highly attractive yield that you may have become quite accustomed to receiving disappears when the bond in question is called. When shopping for corporate bonds, find out first if the bond you are interested in has a call feature. If it does, take a look at the bond's yield to call, not its yield to maturity. You may be forced by the exercising of the call feature to reinvest your money at a much less favourable yield; this is known as reinvestment risk. For investors are who are reliant on a stable income stream from their portfolios, the consequences can be lifestyle altering. If you are going to invest in corporate bonds with a call feature, your best defence is to have all the facts.

The bond market and, by extension, bond pricing tend to be anticipatory by nature. That means that bond prices are continually readjusted to reflect potential future events. If the bond has multiple call dates, focus on the yield to the first call date. Operating under the assumption that a bond with a call feature is going to be called away at the first opportunity, and focusing on the yield to that call date, leaves little room for unpleasant surprises.

Fixed-Income Exchange Traded Funds

For investors who may not have quite enough capital in their investment account to allow them to build a properly diversified bond strategy, the next best thing is the fixed-income exchange traded fund (ETF). Like their stock-based cousins, fixed-income ETFs permit you to have a high degree of both liquidity and diversification. There are ETFs structured on the basis of their term to maturity (short or long), as well as on the basis of their content. For example, the iShares family of exchange traded funds has an ETF that holds nothing but real return bonds.

If we had to choose between a bond-based mutual fund (more on these in a moment) or a bond-based exchange traded fund, our preference generally would fall in favour of the ETF. We become quite emphatic about this in a time of exceptionally low interest rates such as we find ourselves in today. The rationale behind this is simple: bond-based ETFs are more cost efficient than their mutual fund counterparts. The management expense ratio (MER) on the average bond-based mutual fund runs in the area of 1.55%. The MER of the average bond-based ETF is approximately 0.3%. At a time when the yield on a 10-year Government of Canada bond is well below 4%, in our opinion it makes plain sense to preserve as much of that yield as possible by keeping costs to a minimum. Though there are many portfolio managers we know who more than earn their management fees running portfolios of stocks, there is significantly less room to manoeuvre in the bond market and therefore less of an opportunity for a bond mutual fund manager to add sufficient value to compensate for the additional cost.

There are a couple of exceptions we believe are worth noting. The first concerns high-yield corporate bonds. This is an area of the fixed-income market that can be fraught with tremendous risk. A skilled fund manager can add their oversight and expertise to a portfolio of this type of bonds that is of enough significance to compensate for their management fee.

Playing for Time

A bond-based mutual fund also may be the better option for an investor who owns a portfolio of mutual funds that all have deferred sales charges attached. In a circumstance where reconstruction of an investment account is called for and a fixed-income component is a missing element, it will sometimes prove to be better for the investor to move assets within a given family of funds so that the fixed-income portion is represented by a bond-based mutual fund.

Investors can move from fund to fund within a mutual fund family without triggering deferred sales charges, which is a nice way of saying exit fees. These exit fees diminish over time. Once exit fees have fallen to zero or at least an acceptable level, an investor can then opt to move their assets from the bond mutual fund to another more cost-efficient means of fixed-income investing.

Playing the Yield Curve

For those who nevertheless want to run the interest rate gauntlet and capitalize on bond market swings, the ladder of maturities can be lengthened or shortened according to their forecasts. If you foresee rising rates, shorten the ladder of maturities; if you expect falling rates, lock in existing yield by extending term and adding more rungs to the ladder. What is then effectively being sought is the point in time where the advantage along the yield curve is greatest.

What Is the Yield Curve?

The yield curve is a curve that readily can be drawn by connecting the dots reflecting different maturities, all the way from 30 days to 30 years. It's also a curve regularly shown and updated in most financial newspapers. Sometimes ongoing interest rate and yield changes have a see-saw effect; if rates go up at the short end of the yield curve, they go down at the long end. Other times there are undulating patterns because some yields change less or more than others, and there is more relative advantage in one part of the yield curve than in another.

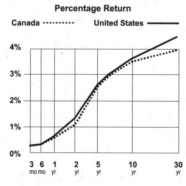

The Yield Curve Indicator
A Steepening Like This Always Augurs Positively

Short to Long Bond Yields

Percentage Return

Canada ··········   United States ———

August 14, 2009   **Gov't. of Canada and U.S. Treasury**

Of great importance to fixed-income investors is the overall slope, or steepness, of the yield curve, which helps them determine how adventurous or conservative they need to be.

When short rates and yields are higher than long yields, the yield curve is said to have an inverted slope. An inverted yield curve is generally regarded as a signal of pending economic slowdown. This is what happened in the early 1980s when central bankers dramatically raised interest rates to contain inflation and bonds became irresistible bargains.

Warren Buffett once famously wrote that there are times when "an absence of activity is not necessarily an indication of an absence of intelligence." We couldn't agree more. There is plenty of comfort in effectively keeping your fixed-income component waiting on the sidelines in the form of short-term instruments like 90-day government Treasury bills, a strategy that would have served all investors well in the early 1980s when interest rates were in an astonishingly rapid ascent. The same is true when the yield curve is flat, as happened in the early 2000s when the returns obtainable on all maturities, short and long, were essentially the same. At times like this, why reach out when you can comfortably sit and wait?

Realize, however, that at times like now when long yields are higher than short rates and the yield curve has a positive slope to it, the advantage becomes progressively greater, and waiting on the sidelines generally isn't the best idea.

Bond Funds

One of the oldest and probably corniest jokes on Bay Street concerns bond fund managers. We would be remiss in our professional duties if we did not take a moment to pass this comedic gem on to you.

> *What's the difference between a bond and a bond fund manager?*
> *The bond will eventually mature!*

Okay, that's enough fun and hilarity for now. Sit up straight, everyone, as we enter into the buttoned-down world of bond funds.

Bond funds are mutual funds that allow an investor to own a professionally managed portfolio of fixed-income securities. They are, in our view, ideally suited for the novice investor who has not yet amassed enough capital to build his or her own selection of fixed-income investments. We are defining "enough" in this instance as a fixed-income portfolio component of at least $50,000.

For those who do have enough, our preference, more often than not, is to bypass bond funds in favour of directly owning bonds and other fixed-income securities. We mean no disrespect to bond fund managers who work very hard on behalf of their unitholders and the majority of whom are exceptionally bright, energetic professionals doing their job. The problem as we see it is that, with few exceptions, most bond funds are not able to earn enough additional return over that of a simple bond portfolio to justify the underlying management expenses that are borne by the unitholder. As if that weren't enough, a significant number of the bond funds monitored by the respected tracking agency Morningstar have 10-year performance track records that fall below the widely recognized fixed-income benchmark, the Scotia Capital Universe Bond Index.

Of course, there are special situations where the cool head and unique expertise of a portfolio manager can turn out to be preferential to going it alone. The complexities of international currencies and knowledge of foreign debt ratings make a strong case for the use of a global bond fund manager. A similar argument can be made when it comes to high-yield corporate bonds. Often, corporations that offer exceptionally high yields on their debt securities are compelled to do so by circumstances such as poor debt ratings, high debt-to-equity ratios or precarious business conditions, such as the loss of a major customer. It is for all of these reasons, and more, that an investor would turn to a qualified portfolio manager for the day-to-day monitoring and quality control of high-yield bonds.

INCOME-GENERATING EQUITIES

The ultimate extension of term, that is the date when an investment eventually comes due, is into equities, which Michael facetiously refers to equities as perpetual bonds (never maturing) with floating rates of (dividend) return. It's because of these qualities that a steeply positive yield curve can effectively inhibit a bear market in equities by obliging investors to reach ever further out—and ultimately into equities—for desirable yield and total return. This need was undoubtedly a factor in the bull market in equities that began taking hold over the winter of 2002–2003 when central bank and related interest rates began falling to 40-year lows, long bond yields fell in tandem and income returns in portfolios came under inexorable pressure.

This exceptional fall in interest rates continued in 2008 and 2009 as central banks from around the world brought short-term interest rates to their lowest levels on record in the expectation that low rates would become drivers of new economic growth, and yields brought a welcome reminder that investing for income should also encompass dividend-paying stocks. Traditionally, these have been utility-type stocks known for their relatively high dividend payouts. In recent years, however, dividends have taken on a whole new importance as a rising source of income. It's a topic we'll pick up on in the next chapter, but we will note at this stage that investing for income can include much more than debt securities.

Income Trusts

This ode to bonds and other fixed-income investing would not be complete without including income trusts, a largely Canadian phenomenon that has bridged the developing income gap with great effect for yield-starved investors willing to forgo the security of capital offered by bonds in at least a fraction of their portfolio. The party came to a screeching halt on October 31, 2006, when federal finance minister Jim Flaherty brought forward legislation designed to end the preferential tax treatment on most forms of income trusts.

Previously, income trusts were exempt from having to pay income tax at the corporate level. The majority of the revenue of a trust is paid out to unitholders in the form of what is generally a steady stream of distributions. The unitholder receiving the distributions is then taxed unless the distribution is paid into the unitholder's RRSP or RRIF account. The Minister of Finance allowed a four-year grace period before the tax is due to be collected, which will go into effect in 2011.

This presented managements of income trusts with some tough decisions. Because any new units brought to market after the November 1, 2006, announcement would not be granted the grace period, trusts that needed to raise capital would be loath to issue new units. In response, a substantial number of trusts have converted from the trust structure to the corporate structure. This has altered the very nature of the entity, in many cases meaning a substantial drop in income received by investors, as dividends are generally lower than from what previously had been trust distributions.

Income trust management teams not looking to tap the capital markets were still faced with a dilemma: grow earnings sufficiently to have enough excess cash flow to compensate for the new tax starting in 2011, avoiding the need to reduce distributions, or simply cut distributions by an amount equal to the tax the trust would be required to pay. Either way, investors who had come to rely upon a stable, and in many instances, regularly rising flow of income from their trust investments were at minimum unlikely to get a "raise" any time soon and might even have to suffer a reduction in "pay."

One form of trusts, real estate investment trusts (REITs), were exempted from the tax rule change.

REITS are, as the name implies, income trusts built around income-producing real estate, such as shopping centres, retirement homes, and hotels. Some of the more widely known REITs in Canada include RioCan (shopping centres), CHIP REIT (hotels) and Retirement Residences Real Estate Investment Trust (just try to guess what that is into).

Even at this late stage, their unique and complex structure means that investing in income trusts, just like all other investments, requires due diligence. In essence, they are trusts that conduct their own investing through a combination of shares in an operating company (the underlying business) and high-interest loans to the same company. The interest on these loans is designed to eliminate profits in the operating company and flow that income to the trust, which, in turn, passes it and dividends received from the operating company through to its unitholders, who must then face the tax consequences of the income received.

In this way, the double taxation of profits (at the company level and on dividends paid to shareholders) is avoided. The flow-through income trust structure means income that would otherwise be taxed twice is now being taxed just once. As such, income received from income trust units held in a non-registered account is often taxed at a lower (personal) rate. In addition, interest income from bonds is fully taxable, sometimes even before it is received (refer back to the section on strip bonds). Often the income from an income trust includes a "return of capital" element in which the tax is deferred, as it will be deemed to be part of the capital gain when the units are disposed of at a later date.

This type of investment is not without risks, and, as investors in income trusts have found, also political risk. There may well be some "last puff" value in the sector. No doubt, those income trusts with sound underlying questions will either be acquired or merged before 2011, or, as has already begun to happen, they will convert back to their former taxable corporate structures. Here, once again, know what you are investing in.

The word "trust" denotes an investment of paramount quality, and of regular, reliable income distribution. Because of the attendant risks, income trusts should never replace bonds and other debt-related securities in the fixed-income section of portfolios. Instead, they should be looked on as a good accompaniment to fixed-income investments.

We've recommended and used income trusts to telling effect and continue to find a place for them—albeit diminished—in portfolios. Even in their changed capacities they can be a useful addition to a portfolio that is mandated to provide income.

Preferred Shares

Preferred shares are a little different from their common share cousins. Before a company can make a dividend to common shareholders, holders of preferred shares must receive their dividends. Furthermore, the dividends they must pay are usually cumulative, which means that any missed dividend payments must be made good before a common shareholder gets his or her turn. From a security standpoint, in the event of a company's bankruptcy, preferred shareholders rank after all creditors but ahead of common shareholders for a claim on the assets of the company.

Investors buy preferred shares for what most often is a stable stream of dividend income. Most preferred share issues pay a fixed dividend. If the dividends are paid by a tax-paying Canadian corporation, the dividend tax credit kicks in.

The dividend tax credit is a reduction in the amount of tax a shareholder must pay on the dividends received from Canadian tax-paying corporations. The purpose of the tax credit is to partially offset the effect of double taxation. The earnings that the company generated in order to pay dividends were first taxed at the corporate level. To have these same dollars taxed once they reach the shareholder without offering at least some degree of relief truly would be a double whammy. All of this is irrelevant if you were to hold preferred shares inside an RRSP or RRIF account because the income generated by investments held in these types of accounts is not taxed; only capital that is removed from the accounts is subject to tax. As such, the dividend tax credit would not apply under this situation.

The Many Different Breeds of Preferred Shares

These are some of the more common breeds of preferred share issues that you are likely to encounter in the market.

Perpetual Preferred Shares

Commonly known as straight preferreds, this type of share pays a fixed rate of dividend. Price changes are primarily the result of interest rate fluctuations. Perpetual preferreds do not have a maturity date, but do carry a redemption date. This redemption date is the time at which the issuer can call in the issue for redemption. Redemption is generally not mandatory on the part of the issuer.

Retractable Preferred Shares

Although most preferred share issues are redeemable, there is no guarantee that a call feature will be exercised by the issuer. A retractable preferred provides the investor with the ability (under certain predetermined conditions) to force the company to redeem the issue. If a retraction feature expires unutilized, the shares become perpetual preferreds.

Soft Retractable Preferred Shares

This is a feature found with retractable preferred share issues, in which the redemption value could be paid either in cash or in common stock of the company. The choice is up to the issuer.

Reset Preferred Shares

This increasingly popular "new" breed of preferred shares sets its terms at five-year intervals. They can be convertible and can be redeemed, but only on anniversary dates.

As is the case with fixed-income investments, credit quality is a highly important consideration when selecting preferred shares. For us, suitable preferred shares must have a rating of Pfd-1 or Pfd-2 from the Dominion Bond Rating Service or a similar rating from one of the other major rating agencies such as Standard & Poor's.

Many of the risks associated with fixed-income investments apply equally to preferred shares. Such risks include

- interest rate risk
- call risk
- credit risk
- liquidity risk

Interest Rate Risk

Just as bonds have an inverse relationship with interest rates, so too do most preferred share issues. This may not be much of a concern for long-term, buy-and-hold investors who are less concerned about fluctuations in market value and more concerned about stability of income. However, for the investor with a shorter time horizon (e.g., less than five years), fluctuations in value can be a significant concern.

Generally, preferred share issues with higher-than-average yields tend to be less sensitive to interest rate fluctuations. Yet one does have to question why an issuer is offering such a high yield in the first place. With preferred issues with very high yields, interest rate sensitivity may turn out to be the least of your concerns; instead, it could be solvency that is the overriding risk. Issues that are close to their call date also tend to display less-than-average interest rate sensitivity.

Call Risk

Many preferred share issues on the market today have call provisions attached to them. This is wonderful for the issuer because the call provision affords a great degree of flexibility, but it is usually not so terrific for individual investors.

The one distinct advantage that callable preferred share issues have over non-callable preferred share issues is that, all things being equal, the callable issue will carry a higher yield. The problem is that you may not have the issue in your portfolio long enough to truly enjoy the greater yield because it could be close to being called. Here again, just as in bond investing, the best defence against call risk is to know what you own; be certain to ask about call provisions if you are being offered a preferred share with an exceptionally attractive yield.

Credit Risk

Preferred share issues are commonly referred to as "junior" debt. This means that the obligation to pay dividends to holders of a given preferred share rank after payment obligations to other creditors and bond holders. It's why investors need to set minimum quality criteria when shopping for preferred shares.

Some preferred share issues have a provision that enables the issuer to defer dividend payments in the event of financial hardship. A non-cumulative issue is one where the issuer can skip dividend payments in the event of financial disaster, resume at a later date and not have to make up missed payments. We prefer cumulative preferred shares (pun fully intended). Under a cumulative issue, the issuer will have to make up any missed payments. For an investor who is dependent upon a steady income stream from a portfolio, it is wise to focus on cumulative rather than non-cumulative issues.

Liquidity Risk

This form of risk deals with the relative ease with which an investor can dispose of an investment at or near fair market value. For the buy-and-hold investor, this may not be much of a problem. For an investor who might need to remove money from the investment, though, liquidity risk can be quite significant. Will Rogers summed it up best when he said, "It's not return on my investment that I'm worried about—it's return *of* my investment."

One of the best methods we know of to check for the liquidity of a preferred share issue is to take a look at the spread between the bid and ask (offer) quotes. A preferred share offering with good liquidity will maintain a fairly narrow spread between the bid and ask quotes.

FINAL DOS AND DON'TS

The fixed-income or lending part of investing might best be summarized as securing required income while maintaining a vigilant lookout to take advantage of opportunities and defend against accompanying risks. It's a part of the process pivotal to overall investment success.

Diversify and guard against the associated risks and minimize the reinvestment risk through a laddered portfolio approach. Above all, don't succumb to the siren song of disproportionately high yields. The risk is seldom worth the reward.

Take basic steps like these and the fixed-income section of your portfolio could bring that extra degree of annual total return that, compounded annually over a multi-year term, makes the all-important difference in ultimate portfolio success.

Though very largely an ode to bonds, fixed-income investing is nonetheless the essential first part of a two-step process in which both steps must be approached in tandem. Now on to the second step, that ultimate extension of term into those "perpetual bonds with floating rates of return" referred to earlier; namely, to investing in equities with which to build the real wealth that will be needed to ensure our investments last longer than we do.

CHAPTER 9

Building Blocks of Wealth

Ownership Through Equities

In 2008, in an interview publicizing his latest book, *Wealth, War and Wisdom*, Barton Biggs, now a 75-year-old managing partner at New York hedge fund Traxis Partners and formerly the renowned global strategist at Morgan Stanley, said, " . . . markets are smarter than any expect.... The markets are going to make the right decisions in the long run . . . . I don't see how you can beat stocks."

The "stocks" he was referring to are equities. In turn, equities can take many forms and are synonymous with owning something, whatever it may be. Stocks, for their part, are proxies for the ownership of corporations which, if the investment turns out successfully, can translate into wealth that grows in remarkable fashion.

Hernando de Soto, author of *The Mystery of Capital*, indefatigably champions property rights for the poor as a way of breaking the cycle of global poverty. The growing worldwide success in allocating micro capital for the starting of the smallest of businesses increasingly corroborates his view. An eye-catching lead article in *The Economist* (February 14, 2009) wrote of how the new middle class that is springing up in emerging markets is producing a revolution of wealth creation and new aspirations that is changing the world.

Standout Canadian examples of what grass-roots entrepreneurship can come to mean are many. Roy Thomson, later Lord Thomson of Fleet, transformed a tiny radio station in Timmins, Ontario, into The Thomson Corporation, now Thomson Reuters Ltd., one of the world's foremost information service providers. Similarly, Ted

Rogers went on to build his father's small radio station into Rogers Communications, a world communications giant. Isadore Sharp, another Canadian pioneer, built his dream of providing service quality, which he defined as giving customers what they want, into the renowned Four Seasons international hotel chain. Mr. Sharp always believed in involving his employees in the decision making: "If they work for you, you work for them" is a *modus operandi* not dissimilar to entrusting someone with your savings and letting them run.

Jack Cockwell was hired by Edward and Peter Bronfman in 1968 to run Edper Enterprises, which now heads a vast multinational conglomerate whose crown jewel is majority ownership of another international giant, Brookfield Asset Management, formerly Brascan. Frank Stronach, who launched his company in a Toronto garage decades ago, built Magna International into a world-leading auto parts manufacturer, now with a pending 20% interest in the consortium, it leading to buy the prized Adam Opel GmbH from bankrupted General Motors.

Paul Demarais is another who began small, in his case by owning a local Sudbury bus company. Family-controlled Power Corporation of Canada is now a giant, internationally ranked management holding company. Similarly gigantic is the company of Mike Lazaridis and Jim Balsillie, Research in Motion, as well as its famous Blackberry, to which even U.S. President Obama is addicted. A list of Canadian entrepreneurial spirit and pride of ownership could go on and on and is truly impressive.

In the corporate and individual wealth stratospheres, let's also not forget Warren Buffett, who began his business career as a schoolboy delivering newspapers. Ventures that followed in refurbishing golf balls, selling shopping stamps, buffing used cars and reselling old pinball machines were stepping stones to the investment arena, where a string of successful private investment partnerships gave way to his acquiring control of an all-but-defunct textile manufacturer, Berkshire Hathaway Inc. in the mid-1960s. The rest is history, except to note that the spectacular growth in Berkshire shareholders' equity has been driven in large part by Buffett's early realization that insurance, if managed properly, leaves a "float" of premiums over claims that is available for investment—and in his case the accumulation and compounding of vast investment wealth.

At your authors' much more mundane levels, Michael was motivated to retire early to set up his own investment firm in his early 60s, Bryan to start his own small business in his early 20s. Best of all, in both instances, our passion for the cut and thrust of free enterprise isn't finished yet.

If there is a common thread in all of these examples it is that with the possible exception of marrying well, winning the lottery or inheriting the estate of a wealthy relative, the only means of building true lasting wealth (whatever you may deem that to be) is through the ownership of enduring enterprises. We may not have the ability to turn a tiny radio station into a communications giant, or an insurance float into mega wealth, but we can nonetheless enjoy the benefits of business ownership through shareholding stakes in the widest range of corporations—maybe even beyond our wildest expectations.

It's also a challenge that should take on added meaning as our life expectancies keep rising. Scotiabank used to run an eye-catching advertisement in which someone comments to a friend that he is ready for retirement, but his RRSP isn't. To avoid a real-life predicament like this, we must ensure that the resources generating the income that we are going to depend on last longer than we do. How? By successfully building equity wealth through investment ownership.

FIGHT OR FLIGHT

Many investors become discouraged when they suffer portfolio "injuries" with equities. The causes are many, with the most common detailed in chapters 3 and 4. Never forget, however, that you cannot build sought-after investment wealth without running risk. It's a four-letter word that must be properly understood no matter how deeply you may or may not wish to involve yourself in the investment process. Risk and reward are connected at the hip like Siamese twins. How you minimize the one and maximize the other is what will make all the difference.

Yet the inevitable adversities along the way are met almost without exception by the most basic, instinctive human responses of fight or flight. Investors choosing to fight back can fall prey all too often to a casino syndrome and take on still more risk in a bid to recoup lost capital. The invariable result of this response is a compounding of the initial loss.

RBIs—NOT HOME RUNS—WIN THE GAME

At the other end of the response spectrum is the investor who flees the market in panic. Losses will be averted, but seeking cover on the sidelines can prove to be very costly when taken over a span of years. Think back to chapter 1, when we recalled the time in the early 1980s when equities were terribly out of favour with the investing public and, with the benefit of hindsight, how costly such short-term thinking turned out to be as the bull market of a lifetime was in the process of being born.

Risk must be accepted, provided it can be diversified and hedged against. Building wealth through equity ownership without subjecting oneself to catastrophic losses is the real test. In baseball parlance, one should be consistently trying to get on base. Swinging for the fences with every at-bat only serves to increase your number of strikeouts.

THE EIGHTH WONDER

Home ownership is certainly one form of equity investment everyone can understand. Borrow in the form of a mortgage to buy a home that grows in value and the resulting differential is equity that belongs to you, the owner.

In recent years, homeowners in the U.S. have repeatedly refinanced their homes to take advantage of historically low borrowing costs and mortgage rates, and cashed in on this accumulated equity. Well and good, except when, instead of reinvesting the capital raised from these bonanzas, they spent it on ever more consumption. As was to be painfully discovered, a cavalier approach like this can escalate the reverse risk when interest rates rise, property values fall and home equity turns negative. That's when you end up owing the mortgage lender—an experience millions of American homeowners came to bitterly regret.

Still, few would argue against the wealth-building power of this most understandable and worthwhile form of ownership. Even after the devastating real estate crashes of the 1980s in Alberta and the 1990s in Britain, it wasn't long before shrewd investors began capitalizing on properties listed at fire sale prices to amass great wealth as these markets recovered and prices rose. The same could well be happening in the U.S. as foreclosed homes continue to be snapped up at distress prices. The quest in stock market investing should be similar, all the more so after major stock market pullbacks like 2008–2009; that is, to find bargain or reasonably priced or, better yet, fundamentally undervalued shares at what are effectively discount prices. This way, time can work the magic of compounding, once described by Albert Einstein as "the eighth wonder of the world," and there can be escalating boosts in the wealth-building process.

RISK VS. REWARD

In corporations, the shareholders' equity is what remains for the true owners, the common shareholders, after all other claims on the corporation's assets have been satisfied. Likewise, common shareholder earnings are what is left after all annual costs have been met, including contractual payments such as interest on outstanding debt. These residual "bottom-line" earnings are then available to be disbursed as dividends, or added to shareholders' equity for reinvestment in the business, or a combination of both. The opposite happens if a company is unsuccessful; then, bottom-line losses are subtracted from shareholders' equity, which is thus depleted. Over time, the success or failure of an equity investment will come to be recognized in rising or falling share prices in the stock marketplace.

Bottom-line shareholder earnings are dependent on variables such as sales, operating costs, write-offs, interest on debt, and taxes. It follows, therefore, that management capabilities must be a major consideration in equity evaluation. Similarly, just as management is responsible for handling the risks and rewards of running a business successfully, patience and cool logic to achieve an optimal risk-reward balance are essential ingredients at the individual investor level as well.

When everything is working smoothly, little else can compare with the wealth-building power of growing companies. Michael fondly recalls the five shares of Canadian Pacific Railway he bought for his daughter at her birth. Dividends were automatically reinvested through the company's dividend reinvestment plan, and by the time Julia Graham was ready to enter university, much of her tuition could be covered by that initial investment of a few hundred dollars.

In Canada, the newly introduced Tax-Free Savings Account (TFSA) provides a heaven-sent vehicle for multiplying similarly small initial—and annual—investments into very significant cumulative wealth. Individuals 18 years or older can contribute $5,000 annually, unused contribution room can be carried forward, and money can be taken out and put back without losing any such room. In succeeding years, unused contribution room is indexed to inflation. It's all tax-free. What a way for young investors to begin! We urge all Canadian investors to have a TFSA.

Types of Risk Factors

"That which does not kill us makes us stronger." This famous quote from Frederic Nietzsche easily could be used and attested to by hard-bitten equity investors. Even at the best of times, equity investing can be a humbling experience. Your authors can testify to costly forays in Air Canada, Bombardier, Nortel Networks, Massey Ferguson, Royal Trustco and others, each of which brought a sobering reminder that investing in the stock market can involve scrapes and bruises. To ensure that this often-unavoidable damage isn't terminal, it also becomes important to have a clear understanding of how much risk you are going to be exposed to—and can afford to run.

First off, understand that if you're going to invest in the stock market, either directly through the ownership of shares or indirectly through third-party money managers (mutual funds, exchange traded funds, wrap accounts, etc.), there is no such thing as a free lunch. Hence, because risk must always be present in some form, understanding the various types of risk becomes necessary to identify problems sooner, as well as to trigger remedial action before a situation progresses from difficult to dire.

Let's begin our quick tour of the wonderful world of risk with its two main varieties: systemic risk and unsystemic risk.

Systemic Risk

Systemic risk, sometimes also referred to as "event risk," influences a wide range of assets and is virtually impossible to insulate against. Think back, for example, to the 1995 Quebec referendum on sovereignty. Had the separatists carried the day, there would have been a major near-term dislocation of the Canadian capital markets. Similarly, in 2008 and 2009, had AIG, Citigroup, Merrill Lynch and other major financial institutions been left to fail, the systemic risks conceivably could have brought the entire American and world banking systems down with them.

Another example of systemic or event risk is the major and continuing longer-term decline of the once mighty U.S. dollar on the world's foreign exchange markets. It's a subject we'll return to when discussing related risks—in this case, foreign exchange.

Unsystemic Risk

Unsystemic risk refers to the kind of risk that is more narrowly focused. The most common example would be a negative earnings report that affects the value of a company's shares, but also possibly could have an adverse influence on the share prices of other companies in the same industry. It's this type of risk that is best guarded against through proper portfolio diversification, another discussion for later in this chapter.

Now that we've introduced you to the big two, let's get acquainted with some of the other forms of risk you're likely to encounter when investing in equities.

Foreign Exchange Risk

From a geographic perspective, Canada is one big country. Comparatively, however, our capital markets are a diminutive 2% to 3% of total world stock market capitalization. Accordingly, many Canadian investors wisely choose to add another layer of diversification to their portfolios by including securities from beyond Canada's borders. The foreign exchange risk they must then run is of the Canadian dollar rising in value against the U.S. dollar and other currencies. When the loonie rises strongly against the greenback, the U.S. equity sections of portfolios are all the more heavily penalized when converted back to Canadian dollars.

Removal of the foreign content limitation in RRSPs (and RRIFs) has left Canadian institutions free to invest worldwide. While investment in Canadian corporations is no longer as sheltered as it once was, this removal is seen as a distinct advantage for both Canadian investors and corporations that makes the foreign exchange risks worth running.

Interest Rate Risk

Rising interest rates are another risk that can be particularly detrimental to the shares of interest-sensitive securities such as bonds, banks, pipelines, utilities and income trusts, in other words, to securities that are known for their yields. Thus, a secure yield on a pipeline stock will be perceived as more valuable by investors in a falling as opposed to a rising interest rate environment. The stock markets usually can live with interest rates at any level, but become very unsettled when rates begin rising and volatility increases.

Market Risk

"Beta" reflects market risk and is synonymous with volatility. It's simply a tool to help investors understand how much risk they are likely assuming, given the security in question's volatility versus the overall market as tracked and measured over time. Beta also can be used to measure the degree of price volatility on a mutual fund versus a benchmark index such as the S&P 500. (This is distinct from "alpha," the value-add that good anticipatory research and stock selection can bring.)

A high-beta stock has historically greater swings in value than the comparable market index. Growth stocks typically have a higher beta than interest-sensitive stocks.

We hope we've driven home that regardless of the type and level, all stocks must run a gauntlet of risk for reward. You can't have the one without the other. In order to enjoy more of the sought-after reward, it is best to first cover off the risks to the greatest degree possible.

THE PRICE MUST BE RIGHT

Warren Buffett likes to answer "forever" when asked how long he holds stocks. The truth is that nothing is forever, and even he would agree there comes a time when circumstances change or better values emerge elsewhere. Hence, we repeat the rule about taking your losses quickly and your profits slowly. This said, there can be understandable reluctance to sell stocks on which dividends are being paid and when the prospects are that the price will keep appreciating over time. At the 2009 Berkshire Hathaway annual meeting, Buffett candidly admitted to his mistaken timing on a multi-hundred-million-dollar investment in ConocoPhillips at what turned out to be the top of the oil market, which he subsequently lightened at a considerable loss. Sometimes the wisest course of action is to trim back holdings. The same goes when holdings have become disproportionately large within a portfolio, or when they are judged sufficiently overpriced to warrant switching into investments considered to offer better value. Investing always involves a shifting sea of values in which everything is relative. Investors, Warren Buffett included, must be prepared to make appropriate adjustments in this knowledge.

VALUE IS IN THE EYE OF THE BEHOLDER

In art, what customers are prepared to pay lies in the eye of the beholder. In investing, the price you are prepared to pay, or the value you place on the shares of a company, can be similarly subjective. You invest in a company anticipating it will generate a stream of future earnings. That seems to be a reasonable proposition, but to get a proper fix on the worth of the investment, you (or your financial advisor and their research support) must estimate these earnings annually into the future and then discount them back to the present at an appropriate interest rate. Subject to these caveats, if the resultant present value is higher than today's share price, you'd have an investment offering value. If it is much higher, you could have unearthed a true investment bargain. On the other hand, if it is lower, you would be wise to invest elsewhere.

The same holds true in what should be an ongoing assessment of the relationship between your appraisal of the present value and the prevailing market value of individual stocks within portfolios. Judicious switching from one to the other for relative advantage could then become desirable.

VALUE INVESTING AND ITS HEART AND SOUL: THE PRICE-EARNINGS RATIO

Subject to creditworthiness (another risk), the regular payment of interest and the repayment of principal make investing in bonds a comparatively straightforward affair. It's also why bond yields can be useful benchmarks in equity valuation, beginning with the markets as a whole before getting down to the individual equity level.

Canadian Equities vs. Bonds
A Relative Assessment

TSX Composite (10,848) *	8,000		12,000
Earnings (operating)			
2008		900	
2009E		650	
2010E		825	
Price-Earnings Ratios **			
2008	8.9		13.3
2009E	12.3		18.5
2010E	9.7		14.5
Earnings Yields			
2008	11.2		7.5
2009E	8.1		5.4
2010E	10.3		6.9
Gov't of Canada 10-year *		3.5%	

* August 14, 2009   ** Long-term average 15-16X

> Conclusion: Equities remain cheap historically despite lower 2009-10 earnings; equities superior on earnings-yield basis.

Source: TD Newcrest, UBS Canada

The accompanying table shows the average price-to-earnings (P/E) ratios within a widely set range on the S&P/TSX Composite Index. Inverting the P/E ratio gives an average earnings-to-price or earnings yield on representative Canadian stocks for comparison with prevailing bond yield benchmarks, in this instance using the yield on 10-year Government of Canada bonds.

In an exercise like this the obvious equity risk lies in the accuracy of earnings estimates on a very broad stock index. Nonetheless, it's worthwhile in establishing the relative attraction of one principal asset class against another. Study the box and you'll see how equities emerge as relatively more attractive, even at the high end of a widely cast range. Now apply this same approach at the individual level where the higher the P/E, the lower the earnings yield, and generally the less favourable the comparison.

IT'S ALL RELATIVE

Optional refinements can round out a basic valuation exercise. For example, it is useful to compare the P/E ratio of a company being considered against the P/Es of others in the same industry to get a sense of how its valuation compares with those of its competitors. If the company in question is a resource company extracting difficult-to-measure assets from the ground, you'll probably be better off judging the value on the basis of future cash flows rather than earnings.

EBITDA, an acronym for earnings before interest, taxes, depreciation and amortization, is another measure that is widely used by research analysts and investment professionals. Many investment managers prefer cash earnings before subjective non-cash write-offs as a favoured criterion. Still further criteria are the underlying physical assets translated into book value per share, or what these assets might be worth in current market-adjusted terms. Exercises like these can also be broadened to include liquid (i.e., cash and near-cash) assets on hand, and working capital, defined as current assets less current liabilities.

AND FUNDAMENTAL

The point of this exercise is to demonstrate some of the many methodologies available to choose worthwhile investment prospects. Those listed here fall under the general category of fundamental analysis, which involves analyzing the characteristics of a company in order to determine its value. Technical analysis, however, takes a very different approach. This form of analysis focuses on stock price movements. People who rely on technical analysis over its fundamental cousin are commonly referred to as *chartists*, with stock price charts their main tool for determining value.

Both forms of analysis are worthy of merit, but if we had to choose one style over the other, we would lean in the direction of fundamental analysis in an undertaking whose success is measured over a lengthy period of time. Explaining the styles and intricacies of technical analysis really would require a book unto itself, something others have done with much greater skill than we ever could.

Benjamin Graham, the father of value investing, built a reputation for searching out stocks below their book values—or, even better, below their working capital per share. What out-and-out bargains these could turn out to be! For investors requiring income, the search for value could also extend to a company's ability to pay dividends to its shareholders. We particularly like companies where there is a history of dividend increases over a span of years. More later on dividends.

THE WORLD ACCORDING TO GARP

A close relative to value investing is the GARP style of security selection—growth at a reasonable price. Whereas a value investor will hunt for companies that, in the words of Warren Buffett, offer a "margin of safety," or the protective "moat" he so likes, a GARP investor is willing to take on incrementally greater risk in the search for profit—and is an investor on the prowl for companies that demonstrate the potential to grow their earnings at a pace faster than their peer group. In this respect, GARP investors are not much different from growth investors, except that they set strict limits on how much they are prepared to pay for potential earnings growth, usually using the P/E ratio as their yardstick. Like Mr. Buffett, the GARP investor is also looking for some margin of safety, just maybe not quite as much as their value compatriot.

GROWTH AND MOMENTUM INVESTING

We've put growth and momentum investing together because, while often synonymous, they are not truly identical.

As stated previously, a growth investor is an investor seeking companies capable of delivering an above-average rate of growth in sales and earnings; as an extreme example, a biotech company with an exciting new development to treat a heretofore incurable disease. In this quest, growth investors may not be completely unconcerned about valuation metrics, but they are far less conscious of them than their GARP counterparts.

Momentum investing, meanwhile, occurs when an investor is looking for direction from the analyst community to uncover candidates for investment. The momentum investor combs through reams of analyst reports looking for an emerging consensus to raise investment ratings, price objectives or target prices. If the classic formula for profitable investing is to buy low and sell high, the momentum investor alters the formula to "buy high and sell higher." Momentum investors are most often the least concerned about valuation.

KNOW WHAT YOU OWN

We've earlier mentioned the Buffett-Munger insistence on understanding the businesses they invest in. In their book, failure to understand how a business operates and, more important, how it generates profits for investors precludes rational investment decision-making and makes it tantamount to speculation. It is because neither felt they had a sufficient grasp of the various forms of new technology that they consistently avoided the high-tech sector, a conviction vindicated by the bursting of the tech bubble.

You needn't be a geologist to invest in a mining company, but you should know that Company X mines copper and what the outlook for copper is before making a commitment to it. You don't have to know all the intricacies, but you do need to be aware of the rudiments of the business Company X is in. This is why Mr. Buffett always wants the managements of companies Berkshire Hathaway acquires to stay on: they know more about their business than he and Mr. Munger will ever know.

SURF AND TURF

The mismatching of stocks with investor needs is a sure path to pain and disappointment. Someone with a deadly shellfish allergy wouldn't be foolish enough to order surf and turf in a restaurant, yet it is alarming how many times investors unwittingly commit a comparable act. Portfolios should contain *only* securities that match investors' tolerance for risk. Thus, a conservatively ranked investor should not be in speculative mining stocks, nor should an investor who requires long-term capital appreciation own the preferred shares of a bank.

It's for this reason as well that we urge investors, regardless of whether they prefer active or passive management of their capital, to have at least some working knowledge of how their investments function. You should never be shy about bringing in outside help when you, and possibly your advisor, don't have the requisite skills.

Highly specialized market segments such as biotechnology, or lesser-known geographic regions such as emerging markets, are classic examples of this need. As professionals who earn their living from proffering investment advice, we are the first to admit that investing is far too humbling an experience not to seek expert counsel. Advisors should always welcome questions from investors, especially in the setting-up stage.

INVESTOR, KNOW THYSELF

Which equities are right for you in going about the challenge of best assembling those necessary blocks of wealth? The answers can require soul searching, as well as giving careful, often painstaking, consideration to

- your time horizon
- the financial resources at your disposal
- your need for income now versus capital appreciation later
- your tax bracket
- the time and energy you are prepared to commit
- how much you can afford to risk

A 20% annual gain on an investment is an enticing achievement few would ignore. Turn it around, though, and ask yourself how you might cope with a 20% loss. Behavioural finance is a veritable industry devoted to answering such questions. "What's *your* Number?" is an all-embracing question we will return to in chapter 15, but for now we will simply say that once again it's all about you.

SPREAD THE WEALTH—BUT NOT TOO THIN

The risk-busting rule of diversification is critical in building the equity component of portfolios to include the right blend of different stocks in different industries. If you were to poll a sampling of Canadian investment managers, you would find that each has their own limit, beyond which a portfolio can become unwieldy.

A World-Ranking Canadian "Top 30"
Resource (bold) and Non-Resource Choices

BANK OF NOVA SCOTIA	BNS	$44.24	**POTASH CORP. SASK.**	**POT**	**$105.12**
BARRICK GOLD CORP.	**ABX**	**37.15**	POWER CORP. OF CANADA	POW	27.70
BCE INC.	BCE	26.29	RESEARCH IN MOTION	RIM	79.90
BOMBARDIER INC.	BBD.B	4.29	ROGERS COMMUNICATIONS	RCI.B	30.89
BROOKFIELD ASSET MGMT.	BAM.A	21.97	ROYAL BANK OF CANADA	RY	51.12
CAMECO CORP.	**CCO**	**31.27**	**SUNCOR ENERGY**	**SU**	**35.80**
CDN. NATIONAL RLWY.	CNR	53.92	SUN LIFE FINANCIAL	SLF	32.50
CDN. NATRL. RES.	**CNQ**	**63.74**	**TECK RESOURCES**	**TCK.B**	**28.90**
CDN. PACIFIC RLWY.	CP	52.73	TELUS CORP.	T	34.24
CANADIAN TIRE	CTC.A	59.15	THOMSON REUTERS	TRI	35.47
ENBRIDGE	**ENB**	**41.34**	TIM HORTONS	THI	32.48
ENCANA CORP.	**ECA**	**56.37**	TORONTO-DOMINION BANK	TD	63.55
HUSKY ENERGY	**HSE**	**30.64**	TRANSALTA CORP.	TA	21.78
MAGNA INTERNATIONAL	MG.A	52.54	**TRANSCANADA CORP.**	**TRP**	**31.47**
MANULIFE FINANCIAL	MFC	22.28	**VITERRA**	**VT**	**9.07**

* Prices as at August 14, 2009

Dr. Graham's Prescription

Drawing on his four-and-a-half decades of slogging it out in the trenches of Bay Street, Michael has developed a stock-picking pattern that has served him well. He begins with the basics: searching out industries where the conditions are judged to be favourable.

He then moves in closer to examine the earnings record of a company that may have caught his eye in a favoured sector, placing particular importance on the previous five years' worth of earnings to help identify any trends.

Next, he focuses on industry analysts' estimates of that company's current and future-year earnings per share. From these he can assess and compare the price-to-earnings ratios based on trailing and forward earnings (i.e., latest 12-month reported earnings and estimated future earnings), and work through the valuation procedure described previously. He particularly notes the payout record, the dividend currently indicated and the dividend yield.

Finally, Michael looks at the 52-week price record to get an idea of how the shares are favoured in today's marketplace. Out of a monitoring process like this he assembles a world-ranking Canadian "Top 30" list, as illustrated in the accompanying table. (If the famous Dow Jones Industrial Average can be made up of 30 leading—and representative—equities, why not the same in Canada?) It's a list laced with Canada's famed natural resources, but also includes a surprising number of non-resource entities—our standout banks (sadly not enough room to be able to include them all), our exceptional life insurers and other financial service (and wealth management) institutions, our diversified management holding companies, manufacturers, merchandisers, Canadian technology leaders who can compete with the world's best, et al.

Other indexes, like the Toronto Stock Exchange, may set up their groupings and their sub-indexes differently, but the point of the exercise is to set up a system whereby you and/or your advisor can keep on top of constantly changing prices and relative valuation assessments.

Remember that not every name on a shopping list like that opposite will make it into every portfolio. Also, remember that whereas an existing client may hold a stock that was once favoured for purchase, a newer client may not because the stock has risen to a level where it is no longer judged to be the relative bargain it once was. Just as it is always a good idea to go grocery shopping with a list to ward off unfortunate or impulsive purchases, so it is advisable to enter the investment markets with a shopping list clenched firmly in hand.

Even a perfunctory review of the accompanying "World-Ranking Canadian Top 30" table reveals the range of variables to be contended with and the related questions needing to be answered. Earnings growth is never assured, and earnings can fluctuate widely, in the resource and cyclical sectors in particular. It is the same with P/E ratios, depending on the expected degree of growth and associated risk. (Growth stocks traditionally have higher P/E ratios than cyclicals.) Dividends and dividend yields can vary, depending on reinvestment needs. Many internationally oriented companies report their earnings—and sometimes pay their dividends—in U.S. dollars, this practice requiring adjustment for currency conversion and risk.

Earlier, we recommended an optimum number of holdings in the equity section of portfolios. A continually fresh shopping list of 30 or so names will facilitate this optimum selection process. Here an able financial advisor and his or her supporting research can be of telling assistance.

6-Paks

From his selection lists Michael has developed his own distinctive Canadian 6-Paks, which have worked out very well, and while not every year, certainly for the periods of time since he first introduced them.

Six stocks are arguably too few for diversification purposes. Nevertheless, you'd be surprised at the degree of industry and sector exposure they can provide if chosen carefully.

An essential requirement is to purchase the six in more or less equal dollar amounts and thereafter to regularly rebalance so that the dollars in each of the six remain more or less equal. This means regularly trimming those that go up and become overweighted and, providing the fundamentals haven't changed, adding more to those falling behind and becoming underweighted. Keep this process going and you'll be pleased at how successfully the equity wealth builds.

2004–08 Canadian Equity 6-Paks
Maintaining Equal Balance With Broad Representation

Company	No. of Shares	Price End '08	Market Value	Indicat. Divid.	Dividend Income
BROOKFIELD ASSET MGMT. (BAM.A)	150	18.55	2,783	0.52*	95
CANADIAN PACIFIC RAILWAY (CP)	80	40.98	3,278	0.99	79
ENCANA CORP. (ECA)	75	56.96	4,272	1.60*	146
MANULIFE FINANCIAL (MFC)	125	20.80	2,600	1.04	159
TECK COMINCO (TCK.B)	150	6.02	903	–	–
THOMSON CORPORATION (TOC)	125	35.60	4,450	1.08*	164
			$18,286		**$643**

* in U.S. Dollars

Year	Level at Start	Level at Close	Total Return
2004–05	$21,080	$34,717	3.0%*
2006+	$30,464	$38,098	26.5%
2007+	$28,267	$27,806	0.1%
2008+	$30,941	$18,286	-37.8%

+ Rebalanced, new start level   * Annual average over two years

Such was the growth over the years 2004 through 2007 that Michael left his initial six unchanged, subject only to periodic rebalancing. That was before 2008, when his Canadian Equity 6-Pak began being heavily—and adversely—affected heavily by the huge stock market pullback, and was additionally torpedoed by Teck Cominco's catastrophic collapse in the wake of its ill-timed acquisition of the Canadian Fording Coal Trust. Though heavily damaged, the 6-Pak was still worth some 10% more at the end of 2008 than at the beginning of 2004, and the strong rise in the dividend income it generated over this period provided a further boost to the five-year total return. Nevertheless, Teck (now renamed Teck Resources) needed to be replaced and Michael selected TransCanada Corporation as its replacement. At the time of writing, the rebalanced 2009 model of the Canadian

6-Pak, including its newest member, has suffered some dividend income attrition, but is performing well.

Canadian Equity 6-Pak — 2009 Model
Revamped, Balanced, Diversified

Company	No. of Shares	Recent Price[1]	Market Value	Indicat. Divid.[2]	Dividend Income
BROOKFIELD ASSET MGMT. (BAM.A)	250	21.97	5,493	0.52[3]	143
CANADIAN PACIFIC RAILWAY (CP)	125	52.73	6,591	0.99	124
ENCANA CORP. (ECA)	90	56.37	5,073	1.60[3]	158
MANULIFE FINANCIAL (MFC)	225	22.28	5,013	0.52	117
THOMSON REUTERS (TRI)	175	35.47	6,207	1.13[2]	215
TRANSCANADA CORP. (TRP)	150	31.47	4,721	1.52	228
			$33,098		**$985**
STARTING LEVEL JANUARY 1, 2009			$29,543[4]		$1,141

[1] As at August 14, 2009   [2] Indicated annual rate
[3] Paid in U.S. Dollars   [4] Approximately $5,000 in each, excluding transaction costs

Quintessential Dividends

At the height of the tech stock boom of the late 1990s, Michael saved a cartoon from some forgotten business publication that spoke volumes for the ethos of the day. In it, three young employees gathered in the presence of a senior executive ask in astonishment, "And these dividends they used to hand out—where exactly did the money come from?"

Despite the twisted logic of those boom times, and throughout the savage bear markets of the opening decade of the new century, dividends remain what they've always been: cash disbursements from a company's earnings. Even more pronounced has been their ever-growing role for both tax and investment reasons, and the backstop support their payment can provide in volatile times and markets. There is also their role in helping income-dependent investors maintain income in a time of historically low interest rates.

Distinguished author Jeremy Siegel picks up on another growing role for dividends: as a boost of total returns and helper in building superior investment wealth. Another school contends that companies paying regular dividends generally outperform those that do not. The accompanying box summarizes all the good things that dividends can be depended on for—and then some!

A Dividend Is
The Case for Focusing on Reliable Dividend Payers

- a bear market "protector"
- something you can take to the bank
- a commitment to shareholders
- a vote of confidence in cash flow continuity
- a growing total return contributor
- a provider of stability
- a means to DRIP (dividend reinvest) your way to wealth
- an island of safety in the midst of a hurricane

> *"Today's markets present a rare opportunity for long-term investors to reinvest the proceeds of higher dividend yields at deep-discount prices."*
>
> **Jeremy Siegel**, Author of *Stocks for the Long Run*

Source: QV Investors, *Small Cap Update*, Nov. 23, 2008

Best of all is to seek out companies with leading industry positions, financial strength and exemplary earnings and dividend records. It's not so much the initial yield, but dividends and yields growing over time that make such stocks increasingly valuable investments. Compare current dividend levels with the per share payments to shareholders, say five or 10 years ago, and chances are you'll be gratified at how their yields have risen on the original cost.

For all these reasons, Michael broadened his 6-Pak approach to also include a Canadian Dividend 6-Pak. Once again, it's an approach built on more or less equal dollar investments in half a dozen top-flight, financially strong, world-class Canadian corporations capable of raising their dividend payouts to shareholders annually—an ironclad requirement for inclusion. His Canadian Dividend 6-Pak for 2009 is shown below. Not only is it delivering income and performing in superior fashion the backstop protection of a dividend-based package is amply evident.

Canadian Dividend 6-Pak — 2009 Model
Requirement of Annual Dividend Increases

Company	No. of Shares	Recent Price [1]	Market Value	Indicat. Divid. [2]	Dividend Income
BANK OF MONTREAL (BMO)	150	51.25	7,688	2.80	420
BCE INC. (BCE)	200	26.36	5,272	1.62	324
ENBRIDGE INC. (ENB)	125	41.47	5,184	1.48	185
POWER CORP. CANADA (POW)	225	27.70	6,233	1.16	261
TORONTO-DOMINION BANK (TD)	125	63.55	7,944	2.44	305
TRANSALTA CORP. (TA)	215	21.78	4,683	1.16	249
			$37,004		**$1,744**
STARTING LEVEL JANUARY 1, 2009			$29,614 [3]		$1,665

1 As at August 14, 2009

2 Indicated annual rate

3 Approximately $5,000 in each, excluding transaction costs

When you invest in well-managed companies that regularly raise dividend payments to their shareholders, you can also experience the equivalent of compounding. Reinvest these dividends in more shares of the same company and it becomes double compounding, in which Albert Einstein's "eighth wonder" growth effect takes over. Five of the holdings in the current Canadian Dividend 6-Pak offer dividend reinvestment plans to help you "DRIP" (dividend reinvest) your way to wealth all the faster. In *The Future for Investors: Why the Tried and the True Triumph over the Bold and the New*, Professor Siegel concludes that steady dividends and reasonable valuations always trump growth. We couldn't agree more.

In the Long Run

In his epic work *The Intelligent Investor*, Benjamin Graham wrote that "investing is most intelligent when it is most businesslike." They are the nine words his renowned disciple Warren Buffett singles out as the most important in all of investing. While investing is never easy, there is convincing proof that over time the longer-term returns on equities have surpassed those on all other financial assets. There you have the link between the two. Whether you do so actively or passively, work with your financial advisor or through a third party to invest in an intelligent, businesslike fashion and be all the more confident of the superior returns that are bound to follow.

The first of the accompanying Canadian-related charts illustrates how "time in" rather than "timing" the market is the best protector. There will always be losing years, sometimes periods of more than one year, and sometimes, though rarely, periods of five years, when the overall return is negative. But between 1935 and 2007 there was never a 10-year period when the overall return of a representative TSX compilation was negative.

The Canadian Experience
Time In The Market The Best Protector

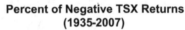

Percent of Negative TSX Returns
(1935-2007)

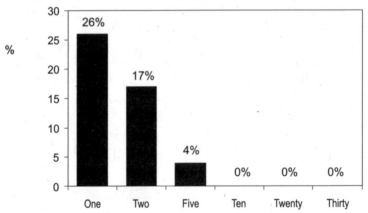

Source: Global Financial Data, Bloomberg, Dynamic Funds

The second chart illustrates the importance and the growing contribution of dividends to the total return on Canadian equities. Reinvest the dividends annually, allowing compounding to work its magic, and the wealth buildup would be all the greater.

Never forget that these charts are of averages. Think what the added advantage of investing—and reinvesting—in above-average equities and equity products could bring.

The Importance of Dividends
A Significant Part of Long-Term Total Returns

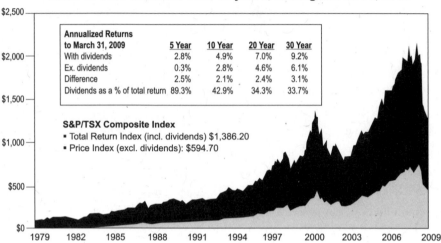

Value of $100 invested over 30 years, ending March 31, 2009

Annualized Returns to March 31, 2009	5 Year	10 Year	20 Year	30 Year
With dividends	2.8%	4.9%	7.0%	9.2%
Ex. dividends	0.3%	2.8%	4.6%	6.1%
Difference	2.5%	2.1%	2.4%	3.1%
Dividends as a % of total return	89.3%	42.9%	34.3%	33.7%

S&P/TSX Composite Index
- Total Return Index (incl. dividends) $1,386.20
- Price Index (excl. dividends): $594.70

Source: Bloomberg, Sionna Investment Management

REMEMBER INFLATION

Just in case you need more convincing that carefully selected equities or equity products must have a place in your portfolio, stop to consider the eroding effects of inflation. The double-digit inflation of the late 1970s and early 1980s may be a distant memory, but today's soaring government deficits and the flooding of economies with cheap money increase the risks of returning inflation—maybe even (perish the thought) hyper-inflation.

Those most vulnerable to inflation's long-term effects are on a fixed income, typically retirees. Look again at the accompanying charts. No other asset class offers a better hedge against the ravages of inflation than equities, and in these illustrations, Canadian equities. Though you may be investing primarily for income rather than growth, having even a small component of your portfolio devoted to equities will bring some protection against inflation and help toward sustaining the real worth of your investment assets.

BUILT TO LAST

The title to this chapter is intentionally ambiguous. Do we go about building blocks of wealth using equities, or are equities themselves building blocks of wealth? Whatever the answer, we submit that equities must play a role in everyone's longer-term well-being, and either way that the answer should be an emphatic yes.

Better still, there is a choice to be made in building that necessary wealth through equities, either directly or indirectly. There is also the protection of investment assets that the many new products in the life insurance industry are making possible, several also including an equity growth component (see chapter 12).

There is as well a final compelling reason for ownership through equities that we cannot ignore: we are living ever longer than the generations that preceded us. Hence, the bigger danger for many of today's investors is not that they will lose their money, but that they will outlive it. The way to head off this possibility and ensure our assets last longer than we do? Equities! Thankfully, modern-day Canada has more than its fair share of world-ranking equities and products for you, your financial advisor and your third-party manager to choose from.

Constructing a portfolio to meet long-range objectives absent of equities is akin to building a house of cardboard. Use the proper materials in a prudent and professional manner, and your portfolio has a better chance of not only meeting your financial needs of today and tomorrow, but also outliving you even as you beat the actuarial odds and live longer than the generations before you.

CHAPTER 10

Toys in the Attic

Three Ways to Own Equities Indirectly

If there is one thing the men and women of the Canadian financial services industry can take credit for it is the act of reinvention. With unfailing regularity the industry presents its latest version of the proverbial "better mousetrap"; ostensibly to make investing in equities safer, simpler and sometimes even more attractive from a price perspective. On occasion, all three of these attributes are achieved. Regrettably, there are still too many instances where the result of someone's eureka moment more closely resembles the work of Dr. Frankenstein than that of Thomas Edison.

What follows in this chapter is a review of three forms of indirect equity investing used extensively by individual investors today: mutual funds, exchange traded funds, and principal protected notes.

MUTUAL FUNDS

"I accept the need for building blocks of wealth called equities. But for all sorts of valid reasons—earning my livelihood, my hobbies, my commitment to raising a family and a lack of inclination—I would prefer others handle my investing for me." Statements like this are entirely logical. This is where mutual funds enter the picture. They offer the same long-term strategic focus, the same golden rules of balance and diversification and ultimately the same end goal as investments selected directly by investors. There are some important differences of approach, though, that you will need to understand.

Instead of shares and 6-Paks, there will be units in managed funds of your choice. You'll still own shares through which to build that necessary wealth, but indirectly rather than directly. Mutual funds are often used to good effect for representation in sectors where the investor and/or advisor have clear limitations. A frequent example is a need to understand foreign markets and accounting for international diversification. Often, it is more efficient to gain international diversification through a global or country mutual fund in which others have the "on-the-ground" experience and expertise you and your advisor may lack. The same applies in fast-growing, higher-risk sectors like technology and health care. Never hesitate to bring in outside experts where appropriate; failed investing is just too humbling to refuse outside assistance. Take note, however, that the market for mutual funds is a crowded field that should be entered with care. Hence, you must choose your mutual funds with as much deliberation as you would take in selecting individual stocks.

There are some important considerations to be made before dropping your precious savings into the lap of a mutual fund manager.

1. Always inquire about the track record of the mutual funds your advisor is recommending for you. How have they done over the past one, three and five years? How do their records stack up against other funds in the same sectors, as well as against established benchmarks like the S&P 500 and TSX Composite indexes? Try, where possible, to stay with funds and fund managers who have remained in the first or second quartile (see below for a definition of quartile rankings) relative to their peer group over extended periods of time. We recommend five years as a minimum time.

2. Fees charged by mutual fund companies to manage unitholder capital are a source of recurring criticism. We are always more than willing to pay a premium for performance; however, management expense ratios (MERs) that range between 2% and 3% of total fund assets can be all the more expensive if the fund doesn't perform as expected. An indifferent performance record and a relatively high MER could be the warning flags to steer you away from disappointment.

3. Pay attention to the manager of the fund you are considering, and the length of time he or she has been at the helm. If the fund in question has a terrific five-year track record, but the present-day manager has been there for only

five months, the past performance needs to be deeply discounted or maybe thrown out altogether.

Quartile Rankings

A mutual fund's quartile ranking is a measure of how its performance stacks up against similarly mandated funds over a specific time frame. A first-quartile ranking, for example, means that the fund's performance put it in the top 25% of all funds in its category. Having a second-quartile ranking is still good, but not as impressive as a first-quartile ranking. Some fund managers will nonetheless consciously try to deliver second-quartile performance on a regular basis. This could be because the fund the manager is responsible for has been designed with conservative investors in mind and an attempt at a first-quartile ranking may expose investors to higher levels of risk than would otherwise have been the case. While this is plausible, no manager can make the claim of trying to achieve third- or fourth-quartile performance. Funds with such performance are usually best avoided

---

Passive Vs. Active Management

The debate among investment professionals on the merits of active or passive management can rage with intensity reminiscent of the Hatfields and McCoys.

Passive asset management is achieved through the use of hybrid investment vehicles like index funds and exchange traded funds. Active asset management occurs when the services of a third-party manager enter the picture. This manager takes on the responsibility for selecting, buying and selling securities in accordance with a predefined mandate.

Under passive management, there aren't any fund managers making day-to-day security selection decisions. Instead, investment "decisions" involve the tracking or mimicking of a benchmark index such as the S&P 500, or a sub-index such as the TSX Composite financial services sub-index. With no manager to pay, and a low turnover of stocks, passive management fund vehicles often offer the attribute of rock-bottom pricing. It's a little like do-it-yourself home repair rather than having a contractor coming into your home to do the job for you.

Critics of passive management cite the inability to deliver returns superior to the major market averages on the upside, but the ability to deliver returns on the downside can be every bit as painful. Similarly, critics of active management point to the very small band of asset managers who consistently are able to beat the market and the higher attendant costs as reasons why they refuse to hire this type of manager.

EXCHANGE TRADED FUNDS

As the names imply, exchange traded funds (ETFs) are hybrid funds traded daily on the stock markets just like individual equities. They typically offer a passive approach to investing in either an entire stock market index, or one of the many sub-indexes. ETFs have grown immensely in popularity over the last several years with both individual and institutional investors. On some days, the most actively traded securities on the New York Stock Exchange and the American Stock Exchange are various ETFs. In 2008, the iShares TSX 60 Index Fund was the most actively traded security on the Toronto Stock Exchange.

The widespread appeal of ETFs can be boiled down to three issues:

1. **Cost efficiency:** Because an exchange traded fund passively holds a selection of stocks based on an index or sub-index, transaction costs and salaries are much lower than typically would be the case with an actively managed mutual fund, and the MER is significantly lower with an ETF than with a mutual fund. We have no issue paying a mutual fund manager, and paying that manager lavishly for that matter if he or she demonstrably can add value to an investor's portfolio. If the fund manager regularly delivers little better than index returns, however, there is little justification for paying for a manager's "expertise." The average equity mutual fund in Canada carries an MER of more than 2.5% per annum. An ETF? 0.5%. All things being equal, we're sure you'll agree that your money looks better in your pocket than someone else's.

2. **Transparency:** If "know what you own" is one of the cardinal rules of investing— and it is—then it only seems reasonable that an investor should want to know what's sitting inside a given fund. Because of the passive nature of ETFs, the composition of an ETF goes through infrequent changes. This makes it much easier to peer inside an ETF and see what it's made of. An actively managed fund such as a mutual fund can give you a glimpse at its holdings, but typically the list of holdings becomes stale the minute it goes to print. This is because of the simple fact that the fund's manager is making buying and selling decisions daily.

3. **Liquidity:** Exchange traded funds are bought and sold on a stock exchange, just like an individual stock. Mutual funds are ultimately purchased through a mutual fund complex. One can purchase an ETF in the morning and sell it that afternoon if they so desire. Not so with mutual funds. Orders to buy and sell are executed at the close of the trading day.

It is for these reasons and others that we often tend to refer to mutual funds as something of a blunt instrument. It should be noted that this is a sweeping generalization that applies mostly to broadly based funds. There are many excellent specialty funds that employ highly skilled asset managers to make crucial buying and selling decisions as well as provide ongoing monitoring and are worth every penny of their management fee. Your job is to make sure that your money, if it is going to be entrusted to the care of a fund manager, is with someone more akin to an agile and cunning fighter pilot—not a lumbering dodo.

Core and Explore

iShares, arguably the most prolific creator and marketer of ETFs, has spent considerable time and energy promoting what it refers to as the "core and explore" strategy, which can be built into the many different varieties of ETFs. The basic premise of core and explore is for an investor to build their core positions within their portfolio using ETFs. The primary benefit of this is to gain the advantage of wide diversification, eliminating the risk of a single stock causing massive damage to the portfolio. (This is known as single-stock risk,)

The *explore* part of core and explore involves using any number of more narrowly focused securities to add some "spice" to the total portfolio. Typically, an investor utilizing a core and explore strategy would use individual stocks for their exploration, but that doesn't necessarily have to be the case.

The core and explore investor takes a buy-and-hold approach to the core, while actively adjusting the assets outside of the core—the explore component—for maximum gain.

Turbo-Charged ETFs

The range of ETF investments in the Canadian marketplace has grown quickly in recent years. Amongst the new offerings, the most popular have been the leveraged and inverse leveraged ETFs.

Leveraged ETFs enable the investor to double, and sometimes even triple, the daily return of an underlying index or commodity. With an inverse leveraged ETF, an investor can earn double (or more) of the inverse return of the underlying index or commodity. Put simply, an inverse ETF that offers you 2:1 exposure will go up by 2% should the underlying index fall in value by 1%. This type of investing has proven to be very popular among traders and hedge fund managers, but is available to individual investors as well.

> **A NOTE OF CAUTION:** leveraged and inverse leveraged ETFs are not for the faint of heart nor are they suitable for a laid back, "buy and hold" type of investor.

Great care must be taken to understand the risks unique to this form of investing before committing any capital. Under certain conditions, these turbo-charged ETFs can perform substantially below an investor's expectations. Many investors mistakenly believe that if they hold leveraged ETFs long enough, they will realize gains that are double the returns of the index their fund is tracking.

It's easy to see why someone could be led to believe this, as "regular" exchange traded funds are meant to be held as a core, long-term investment. That is most emphatically NOT the case with leveraged and inverse leveraged ETFs, because this type of ETF is designed to track the daily return of the underlying index. At the close of each trading day, the ETF company must reset the fund for the next day. This is precisely the reason that this type of ETF should not be considered for a buy-and-hold strategy. The day-to-day volatility of the marketplace can and often is very easily magnified by this type of ETF.

A Clean Getaway

For an investor who is prepared to assume as much and even more risk than the market in order to achieve what are hoped to be turbo-charged gains, leveraged and inverse leveraged ETFs are a valuable tool. These types of ETF also are popular because they offer non-recourse leverage. When buying on margin or shorting on margin, the theoretical loss that can be sustained by an investor is unlimited, especially in the case of shorting (selling something you don't own by borrowing it, hoping to buy it back later at a lower price—a reverse of the usual sequence in buy low, sell high). When buying on margin, there is always the risk that you will be required to meet a margin call should the security bought on margin (using capital borrowed from your broker) drop to a level where it no longer provides adequate security for your loan. This will require that you either put up more capital or sell the margined security and pay off the debt.

One of the benefits of utilizing a leveraged ETF or inverse leveraged ETF is that your risk is limited to the amount of money you've invested into the fund. This means you've got the opportunity to make a clean getaway in case something goes awry. It's not that simple if you're using a short selling or margin buying strategy.

No margin call applies so long as you haven't bought the fund on margin, which we do not advise. Essentially what you have is a non-recourse loan. That means your liability is limited to your capital invested. It is for this reason that investors sometimes will be a little cavalier with this particular type of ETF, taking on more risk than they might ordinarily assume in a traditional shorting or leverage strategy. Never forget that leverage, no matter how it's executed, magnifies gains, but the quid pro quo is that it also magnifies losses.

Rent, Don't Own

Leveraged and inverse leveraged ETFs can be very useful to extend the reach of a growth-oriented investor. They are very different from other types of exchange traded funds. You may want to think of them as investment tools that you'll rent instead of own.

PRINCIPAL PROTECTED NOTES

Principal protected notes (PPNs) are essentially an evolutionary step from index-linked GICs. Like a GIC or a bond, these notes offer the investor a fixed term, but unlike a traditional fixed-income investment have no fixed yield. The performance of a note (if any) will be derived from the performance of a set grouping of underlying securities. This could include stock indexes, individual stocks, a portfolio of mutual funds or even a basket of commodities.

PPNs have grown immensely in popularity over the last decade as investors, still fearful from the bear market of 2000 to 2002, yet harbouring warm memories of bull markets past, seek to bridge the gap between the two.

An investor utilizing a PPN likely is someone who wants the growth potential characteristics of an equity investment but also the comfort of knowing that their principal will be returned to them at a specific point in the future. Sounds simple enough, doesn't it? It's actually anything but that. They're not all bad, but like most forms of investing they're not universally good, either. We'll take a look at the good and the not so good to help you to decide with some greater sense of clarity whether this type of security is right for you.

The Long and Winding Road: Path Dependency

One of the most persistent criticisms of PPNs is that a direct correlation between the rate of return of the note and the actual return of the underlying investment(s) may never exist, depending on how the note was structured in the first place as well as market conditions that exist during the life of the note. This is what is known as a return being "path dependent."

This is where misconceptions can lead to disappointment. With each passing year, the likelihood of reaching the peak return becomes statistically more difficult to achieve. This is because the indexes that stay within the portfolio the longest are likely ones that suffered large declines in value early in the term of the note. Before any index can generate a positive return and contribute to an investor's potential rate of return, the index in question must first pass "go"—the value that the index stood at when the note was initiated. Under the right set of circumstances, an investor may very well hit the limit in each and every year, but once again, from a statistical perspective the probability of this diminishes over time. Following a cataclysmic year like 2008, there will be many PPN investors who are about to become intimately familiar with the often overlooked "inconvenient truth" of path dependency.

Zero Coupon Structure

Of the two primary structures used in building PPNs, the simplest is the zero coupon structure. Under this method, the financial institution knows in advance how much capital they must provide a guarantee for. For the sake of argument, let's say the Fatbottom Hornblower note attracts $25 million in sales during the time that it is offered to investors (known as the offering period). A zero coupon bond is purchased (in this case by Fatbottom Bank of Canada) to provide for the principal guarantee. You may recall from the earlier chapter on fixed-income investing that a zero coupon bond is also known as a stripped bond and is in essence a future sum of money purchased at a discount.

Given today's low interest rates, a financial institution may have to put up 80% of the capital that they are ultimately seeking to protect. In our fictitious example, that means $20 million of the $25 million raised will be invested in an investment-grade zero coupon bond that is set to mature in seven years at a value of $25 million. The remaining $5 million (less fees) of the capital raised in the offering period will be used to purchase a call option package on the underlying securities.

It is important to note that as interest rates fall, the cost of the "insurance" rises, because more capital must be set aside to purchase the zero coupon bond. It is for this reason that one might find terms to maturity growing longer as rates drop. The inverse is true in a rising interest rate environment.

The zero coupon structure has its limits, and is therefore not as widely used as the second structure, which we'll explore next.

CPPI

Please do not confuse this style of principal protected note with the Soviet hockey team of the legendary 1972 Canada Cup series. We never could figure out how USSR translated into CCCP, but none of that really matters now, does it? You'll be happy to know that we did manage to figure out just what CPPI stands for—constant proportion portfolio insurance—but let's keep it simple and simply refer to it as CPPI.

The CPPI structure is the form of note structure that you are most likely to encounter in the marketplace today. Financial institutions prefer this method, as it is more flexible. When a PPN is built in this manner, the initial investment is made in the underlying security(s) equal to the principal invested minus fees. Principal protection is determined by the performance of the investment. If the underlying investment is rising in value, the note remains fully invested. If a provision needs to be made to provide for protection, a zero coupon bond is purchased. That protective zero coupon bond will be subsequently sold if it is no longer needed.

Hedging against market risk in this case is dynamic, as it is predicated upon movements in the markets. That means that the performance of the underlying investment must be continually monitored by the financial institution responsible for the management of the note. With the use of a fairly complicated formula, the manager of the note determines whether protection is required.

Look Out for the TKO

The danger for an investor in a CPPI note is the knockout event. This event occurs when, during the life of the note, the net asset value of the underlying investment equals the cost of protection. When that happens, full protection must be purchased, leaving no additional capital for investment. When a knockout event occurs, the return of the investor's original capital at maturity is the only remaining outcome, unless of course the investor chooses to sell the note at fair market value (meaning a loss) prior to maturity.

Some CPPI structured notes permit the manager to utilize leverage. As with any other kind of investment leverage, this has the ability to magnify both gains and losses, though it could be said that the risk in a principal protected scenario is limited to the opportunity cost if the note does nothing more than return the investor's capital. Remember that even a modest level of inflation erodes the purchasing power of capital that could conceivably be locked up within a note structure for years, waiting for the maturity date like a felon awaiting parole. Never forget the time value of money.

Too Many Cooks Can Spoil the Soup

PPNs have many moving parts, and regrettably in many instances several layers of costs not necessarily visible to the investor. In some of the more egregious examples we've seen, everyone seems to make money except for the individual who made the investment in the first place! This is where new rules pertaining to disclosure can be of invaluable assistance to investors. More on that to come.

The sheer variety of PPN offerings at any given point in time is virtually limitless. The financial engineers who create these instruments seem to be limited by only their imaginations, but the reality is not quite that sanguine.

The financial institutions that build PPNs are businesses just like any other. They want to be certain that before they go to the expense of creating a particular note, there will be buyers for that note. That's certainly fair enough, but a less charitable interpretation would be that financial institutions will bring to market note offerings that are less about what an investor needs and more a reflection of the marketer's vision of what investors want and will be prepared to buy. There's no doubt that there are numerous instances of where investor wants and needs are accurately aligned, though regrettably we've been witness to far too many instances where this has not been the case.

It is perfectly understandable that an investor, especially one nearing or already in retirement, should wish to strike a balance between a need for absolute security and growth that exceeds today's chronically low rates of interest. But before they make an investment in one of these notes, a PPN investor should know the conditions under which their capital will grow.

Don't kid yourself; despite the principal guarantee, PPNs are not risk-free investments. There is the not-so-inconsequential matter of the time value of money. You want to have at least a fighting chance to achieve a rate of return on the note that is greater than if the money were simply sitting in a daily interest bank account.

The Escape Clause

Though most notes offer the ability to sell them prior to maturity, the secondary market is very limited and can be shut down by the issuer at their discretion. Because the seller is dealing in a very narrowly defined marketplace, the market price for a note prior to its maturity may not be a very accurate reflection of the true value of the underlying securities.

New Disclosure Rules

Financial institutions that operate in Canada under federal law, as well as any agent selling the products of those institutions, must provide the following information to you both verbally and in writing at least two days before entering into an agreement to purchase a principal protected note on your behalf:

- the term of the note, how and when the principal that you invest is to be repaid, and how and when the interest (if any) is to be paid
- any charges and their impact on the interest payable
- a description of how interest is calculated, as well as any limitations concerning the interest payable
- any risks associated with the note
- the distinction between principal protected notes and fixed rate investments with respect to the levels of risk and return
- the circumstances in which a principal protected note could be an appropriate investment
- if the investment is not eligible for deposit insurance coverage by the Canada Deposit Insurance Corporation, the fact that it is not eligible
- whether the note may be redeemed before the end of the term and if so, the fact that you may receive less money than you had originally invested

- the terms and conditions of any secondary market offered by the institution
- whether you have the right of rescission; that is, the right to cancel the purchase of the note and, if so, how the purchase may be cancelled
- whether the institution is allowed to amend the note during its term and, if so, under what circumstances
- whether the manner in which the note is structured and/or administered may place the financial institution in a conflict of interest
- any other information that reasonably could be expected to affect your decision to purchase the note

If that seems like a lot, that's probably because it is. If when investing it comes down to a choice, however, between having too little information and having too much, an abundance of information is never a bad thing.

Though there are plenty of lousy PPNs languishing within the portfolios of millions of Canadian investors, so too are there many very good notes that quietly go about their job of complementing a diversified equity component of a properly diversified portfolio. On this point, we want to be perfectly clear: how you make a distinction between a PPN that is suitable for your needs and one that is not begins with a frank conversation with your advisor regarding your expectations regarding risk and rate of return. That will assist your advisor in sifting through the myriad of PPN offerings, narrowing the range of choices to those that are most likely to be suitable for your unique needs.

Considering the new disclosure rules and the information we've shared in this chapter, we can't guarantee that an investment in a principal protected note will work out exactly as hoped. We are confident, though, that you'll make an informed decision. And any time you are able to make a decision based on unassailable facts and sound reasoning your probability of success is magnified tremendously.

The three examples we've presented in this chapter are but a sampling of three of the more prevalent indirect methods of investing in stocks utilized by individual investors today. A fourth example, the guaranteed minimum withdrawal plan will be examined in detail in chapter twelve.

CHAPTER 11

Running With Scissors

Prescriptions for Managing Risk

Risk is common to all forms of investing, and yet a critical but often overlooked point is the relationship between risk and reward. The basic tenet of risk management is as fundamental as the laws of gravity: the rate of return should parallel the level of risk. In other words, the higher the risk, the higher should be the expected return.

This risk-return relationship is most evident in the bond market where, if a debt rating agency reduces the credit rating of an issuer, the yields on the bonds of that issuer rise in response to the heightened perception of risk. And here's the rub: the perception is often almost as significant as the actual risk itself.

In the summer of 2002, unexpectedly poor results by telecom leader Telus Corporation led to its debt securities being downgraded by Moody's to non-investment grade. Telus' bond prices plunged as investors shunned its now "junk-rated securities." The equity research analysts covering Telus were sufficiently unnerved to also drop their ratings and as a result Telus' shares also fell sharply. In the wake of this disappointment, the company was able to buy back its bonds at a significant discount. This debt reduction was financed by issuing new shares as investors warmly greeted the company's prudent balance sheet strengthening. The prices of Telus' bonds and stocks recovered fully, its shares soaring by some 800% over the next three years.

An earlier example with less happy results would be of investors who bought technology stocks in early 2000 in the hope that the new era of technology would lift their fortunes, and instead encountered a substantial decline in response to a heightened perception of risk that became substantial and lasting. Risk, whether perceived or real, is inescapable.

AN ALLY AND AN ADVERSARY

At worst, risk can dramatically, negatively and sometimes even permanently alter one's standard of living. This is why investors of all types need to spend time equating the accompanying risks with the associated opportunities. This is not to say you should run to the bedroom and stuff your life savings under the mattress, but to encourage you to recognize that, managed in a prudent manner, risk can be an ally and can be offset by the potential rewards.

THE MANY FACES OF RISK

Risk comes in many forms. Some are fairly benign, while others stand as a potentially deadly threat to your financial well-being. Nevertheless, it is possible to utilize investment strategies to safeguard against some of the more devastating types of risk. Our purpose with this chapter is to offer you some usable first aid rather than a medical degree on the vast topic of managing investment risk. You should emerge with a heightened level of awareness of the various forms of risk that can affect your portfolio, and with some time-tested strategies for managing risk in its various forms. If we impart just one message to you in this chapter it is that risk is an unavoidable yet manageable aspect of investing.

Here are some of the more common forms of risk that you are likely to encounter.

Market Risk

The type of risk that immediately springs to mind for most individual investors is that of the loss of capital, generally referred to as market risk. We've mentioned before how famous comedian Will Rogers used to worry not so much about the return *on* his investment, but the return *of* his investment. Many of the finer points on equity selection, where market risk is generally thought to be greatest, have been covered in chapter 9, so we won't repeat them here except to stress that it is possible to mitigate the degree of risk of capital loss by utilizing careful security-selection techniques.

One method of mitigating risk is to hold investments where there is a genuine concern of capital loss in a regular taxable investment account rather than in a registered non-taxable account such as an RRSP or a RRIF. Many investors make the mistake of holding their growth investments in their RRSPs in the belief that because equities generally should be assumed to be long-term investments, these investments should be made with long-term retirement savings. The flaw in this logic is that while capital gains realized inside a registered account are not subject to immediate taxation, there is no ability to utilize capital losses. In a non-registered account, capital losses can be carried back three years and carried forward indefinitely for the purpose of offsetting taxable capital gains.

Interest Rate Risk

Ever wonder why every word spoken by Ben Bernanke is so carefully scrutinized by professional investors, market watchers and the media? As chairman of the U.S. Federal Reserve Board, "the Fed," he has tremendous influence over the level of U.S. interest rates and, thanks to the widespread influence of the American economy, interest rate policies in much of the industrialized world.

You'd better believe that interest rates do really matter. Capital-intensive businesses that must raise large sums of capital on debt markets can have their fortunes significantly altered by increases and decreases in borrowing rates. Furthermore, the shares of companies such as financials and utilities that are considered to be interest rate sensitive can face greater-than-normal share price volatility depending on the direction and speed of interest rate changes.

Though bonds are often mistakenly considered to offer risk-free returns, their value will fluctuate continually depending on the levels of interest rates prevailing over their lifespans. For investors who tend to hold their bonds all the way to maturity, these price fluctuations in value may not be of much concern. However, for those who need to liquidate bond holdings prior to maturity, price fluctuations can come as a rude awakening. As previously mentioned, bond prices have what is known as an inverse relationship to interest rate movements. When interest rates are on the decline, bond prices customarily tend to rise; when interest rates are on the rise, bond prices more often than not tend to fall.

Default Risk

Another risk to be found within the seemingly risk-free world of bonds is that of interest and/or principal default. When a bond is issued, the borrower pledges to make periodic payments of interest to the lender, the bond holder. This gives the bond holder a claim on the assets that comes before the stockholder in the event of bankruptcy. In many cases this claim is insufficient to safeguard a bond holder's principal, and in situations where the borrower is highly indebted a bond holder may be able to recoup only part of his or her original investment. Default risk, or credit risk, can mean less-than-expected bond returns, the shortfall ranging from an interruption of interest payments while a financially troubled borrower like Stelco reorganizes its financial commitments, to an outright loss of capital because an insolvent borrower has substantially more liabilities than assets.

Bond rating agencies act much like credit agencies offering consumer credit ratings when someone applies for a loan. They compile volumes of statistics and work their way through a wide assortment of formulae to establish credit ratings on the debts of bond issuers. These ratings provide a signal of the degree of risk investors can expect from borrowers; the lower the debt rating, the higher the risk. This means, in turn, that riskier fixed-income investments should carry higher-than-average yields to compensate investors for taking on incrementally higher additional risk.

There are two major bond rating agencies in Canada: the Dominion Bond Rating Service (DBRS) and the Canadian Bond Rating Service (CBRS). The U.S. has three major agencies: Moody's, Fitch Ratings and Standard & Poor's. Below is a table that illustrates the classifications used by the two major Canadian bond rating services.

Credit Ratings and What They Mean

	DBRS	CBRS
Highest Quality	AAA	A++
Superior Quality	AA	A+
Good Quality	A	A
Medium Grade	BBB	B++
Lower Medium Grade	BB	B+
Moderately Speculative	B	B
Highly Speculative	CCC	C
In Default	CC	D
In Default/Low Liquidation Value	C	–

Source: Canadian Bond Rating Service, Dominion Bond Rating Service

Understanding a bond issuer's debt rating is of great importance in managing the degree of risk in what is ordinarily and mistakenly assumed to be the risk-free portion of portfolios. In fact, institutional investors such as pension plans usually set out in advance the minimum quality of debt instruments acceptable to their managers. Generally speaking, except for very short-term maturities, we prefer A-rated bonds or better in our clients' portfolios.

Opportunity Cost or Lost-Opportunity Risk

This form of risk deals not with what has happened, but with what has failed to happen. Lost-opportunity risk is perhaps best described as one of those "I could have kicked myself" moments when investors realize (always with the benefit of hindsight) that they sold a security too soon.

So what if Bernard Baruch, who gained notoriety for selling stocks well before they reached their peak, used to boast that he got rich by selling too soon? Who cares if profits from that recently sold investment continue to flow as freely as the beer at a stag party, but only for those who did not sell? Looking back with regret is costly and dangerous.

Of all the various forms of risk an investor can face, lost-opportunity risk is by far the most benign. This is particularly so as the lost ground can be made up by successfully reinvesting the proceeds of a premature sale in a new, bargain-priced investment, hopefully setting the stage for the next generation of profits.

Purchasing Power Risk—The Silent Killer

This form of risk is often the net result of not taking on enough risk in your investing habits, and is a particularly acute problem for investors accumulating assets to support themselves in their retirement years. Specifically, we're referring to the risk that someone who is blessed with tremendous longevity can see that blessing turn into a curse if their money is insufficient to support them in their later years. Over time, inflation will rob your money of some degree of its purchasing power. Stop to think, for example, of what it cost to mail a letter 10 or 20 years ago compared with today.

No doubt, rumours of the death of inflation have been greatly exaggerated. Mercifully, however, inflation in North America is not currently running at the breakneck pace of the 1970s and early 1980s, yet it remains with us still. It is precisely because of today's relatively tame rates of inflation that persistently rising prices are overlooked by investors planning their retirement. Low, single-digit inflation may not be particularly noticeable in a given year, yet the cumulative effect over what are an increasing number of retirement years for North American workers acts like a pounding surf continuously eating away at a coastline.

RISK MANAGEMENT

Every investor must be prepared to assume some modicum of risk in return for the kind of growth necessary to protect the long-term purchasing power of their invested dollars. Study after study has found that of all asset classes, equities offer the best inflation-protection qualities. Commensurate with equities' potentially greater reward is a proportionately greater degree of risk than is ordinarily found with other asset classes. Risk management is the art and science of striking the delicate balance between risk and reward—in equities perhaps most of all.

The following are some ways to manage risk in the equity portion of your portfolio.

Stop-Loss Orders

A stop-loss order is an open order left with your broker to sell a particular stock should it fall to a specified price. It is placed below the prevailing market price, and its purpose is to set a floor price at which a falling security is to be sold. Just where that floor price should be is a decision to be made by you and your advisor. For most blue-chip securities, we recommend setting a stop-loss order at least 10% below the current market price. That way, ordinary daily fluctuations will be unlikely to trigger the stop-loss order, but a downward trend or a catastrophic event will. Stop-loss orders can be very useful in situations where there is the perceived risk of a sudden and dramatic fall in the value of a security. Having a stop-loss order in place will also help to remove some of the emotion surrounding a selling decision, because the decision to sell is, theoretically at least, made well in advance.

Options

An option is a financial instrument giving the holder the right to buy or sell an asset at a particular price for a specified period of time. Though options could be used for everything from real estate transactions to the drilling rights for an oil-rich property, we'll confine our comments on options to their use within a portfolio of common stocks.

There are two types of options: calls and puts. A call option entitles the holder to purchase shares at a fixed price for a fixed period of time; a put option entitles the holder to sell shares of a specific stock at a fixed price over a similarly fixed period of time. They are used by investors to hedge against making an inaccurate prediction on the direction of a stock's price.

Options can also be purchased for stock market indexes, meaning the same rationale could apply to investor expectations for the direction of an entire index or the market as a whole.

Calls

A call option can be used when an investor expects that a stock or an index is about to undergo a significant increase in value. For just a fraction of the value of the underlying investment, the right to purchase can be locked in for what is hoped will be a substantial discount to the prevailing price at the time of the option's expiry. However, if the underlying stock or index drops in value, the investor would allow the option contract to expire because it would be "out of the money." The investor's loss would then be limited to the price paid for the option contract. It's for this reason that investors who use options consider them to be risk management tools.

Can You Take a Call?

Let's assume it's April and International Pumpernickel Inc. is trading at $5.75. An investor buys a call option, expiring in October, to purchase its shares for $6. The call costs 60 cents per option contract. If International Pumpernickel manages to climb to $9 before the option expires, the investor will have made a profit of $2.40. Here's how it would work:

The price of International Pumpernickel at the time of the option exercise	$9.00
minus	
The purchase price guaranteed by the option contracts	$6.00
equals	
The gain	$3.00
minus	
The purchase price of the option	$0.60
equals	
The net, pre-tax profit made by the investor	$2.40

An investor may choose to use a call option not only because of the mitigation of risk, but also because of the aspect of leverage and its ability to magnify gains. Remember, in our example, the investor made $2.40 on a 60¢ investment. If the shares of International Pumpernickel had gone the other way, let's say dropping to $3 instead of rising to $9, the loss would have been limited to the 60¢ spent to purchase the call option, which would simply have been allowed to expire worthless.

Short Selling, Call Options and the Great Marble Rye Crisis

Short sellers will frequently use call options to protect themselves against a rapid appreciation in the value of a stock they are hoping will decline in value. You'll remember that short selling involves selling shares you don't own. Let's take another look at International Pumpernickel to illustrate the point.

Use Calls to Cover Your Assets

You've sold International Pumpernickel at $6 per share. If the stock drops to $3 you will have made a $3 per share profit! Now let's assume for a moment that you've shorted IP at $6. Thereafter, events turn terribly ugly. There's a marble rye crisis in Flyspeckia! Fearful of not being able to have a decent sandwich, residents begin hoarding loaves of International Pumpernickel's world-famous pumpernickel bread. Loaves are flying off store shelves faster than pre-election patronage appointments. Shares of International Pumpernickel soar, hitting a 52-week high of $9. Ordinarily, this would spell disaster for a short seller, but let's say you were also savvy enough to purchase IP call options for 60¢ apiece. You exercise your options, covering the short at the prescribed $6 called for in the option contract. Your loss has now shrunk from $3 per share to just 60¢ per share.

Covered Calls

Perhaps you already hold shares of IP, in which case you may opt to write a call on the stock in what is known as a covered call. Covered call writing is done to protect the shareholder against a decline in the underlying price of a given stock and to increase the yield on a portfolio. There are plenty of instances when an option contract will expire worthless for the purchaser.

To the seller, the premium received by writing the covered call contract is an attractive additional form of profit. Of course, it too is far from risk-free. If circumstances are such that the purchaser is "in the money," meaning that it is worth their while to exercise their call option, your shares of International Pumpernickel will be called away; that is, sold at the price predetermined in the call option contract. This really stings when the stock in question is experiencing strong share price growth. Theoretically, the loss from writing a covered call is unlimited. As such, treat this strategy as a risky endeavour usually best left to professionals who specialize in this area of investing.

Puts

A put option is a contract that gives the holder the right, but not the obligation, to sell a given stock at a particular price for a specified period of time. An investor would want to purchase a put option when expecting the price of a particular stock to fall. Let's use another imaginary titan of industry to illustrate the point.

Put Your Foot Down

Shares of Catdiaper Industries are trading at $17.75. You, being the prescient investor that you are, have determined that its shares have an above-average probability of a serious drop in value. Hence, you purchase a put for $2.50 that entitles you to sell the stock for $14. If the stock drops as anticipated, you will be able to sell your put contract at a profit. However, if the shares of Catdiaper rise instead of fall, you, the holder of the put contract, will have to allow it to expire worthless and will lose the investment in the put. (All puts and calls have expiration dates.)

Buyer Beware

Puts and calls are useful risk-management tools widely used by investment professionals in their day-to-day activities. Be warned, however, that they are much more complex than they appear at first glance. Financial advisors who use options strategies require a special licence. Because of their costs, risks and complexity, in Canada, options strategies are offered by a relatively small number of advisors—and in our view it should stay this way.

AS INEVITABLE AS DEATH AND TAXES

We've said it before in these pages but it bears repeating: we believe the handling of risk to be a rudimentary skill every serious investor must strive to master. Be forewarned, however, that achieving mastery over risk is as elusive as the famed Loch Ness Monster. Nevertheless, attempting to shun risk altogether is not an answer either. For the majority of the investors with whom we have had the pleasure of working, some degree of asset growth is a vital requirement to ensure long-term financial prosperity.

We are most likely going to live longer, more active lives than the generations that preceded us. The need to maintain purchasing power from your nest egg decades after you've collected your gold watch means assuming some degree of risk in order to achieve a necessary degree of growth. Taking steps to mitigate that risk is the answer. Seeking absolute safety of principal is understandable, but is not in itself a risk management strategy. In fact, a no-risk strategy could turn out to be exposing you to one of the greatest risks of all: the risk that you will outlast your money.

CHAPTER 12

Gimme Shelter!

Using Insurance to
Protect Your Assets From Risk

A real sense of urgency has developed as the leading edge of the baby boomer generation enters what has traditionally been considered retirement age. The outright and justifiable fear that they could suffer a significant depletion in the value of their retirement savings on the proverbial eve of their retirement has shaped the way many Canadians think about their so-called nest egg. The desire for gain has been tempered by caution. This caution has been born out of two bear markets over the course of the past 10 years—a rare occurrence to be sure, though nevertheless one that has serious implications for those requiring a reliable, long-term stream of income from assets carefully built up over a lifetime of hard work and sacrifice.

SLEEPLESS IN SASKATCHEWAN

The number of Canadians who've lost countless hours of sleep worrying over the state of their finances grew immeasurably during the final four months of 2008 when the global credit crisis took hold, sending stock indexes around the world into a violent tailspin.

Though it has been an enduring pillar of the Canadian financial services industry for generations, the life insurance industry has been particularly astute in recognizing the agonizing dilemma faced by millions of Canadians: How do I achieve the kind of growth I need for my money to last longer than I do, without putting my savings at undue risk?

No one should ever claim that life insurance company products are going to make you rich quickly, or exponentially grow your nest egg in value. Actually, one should consider getting a second opinion whenever a claim like that is made. Many of these products will, however, help you sleep at night. Fears of running out of money and living on government assistance in your golden years could be put to rest.

Insurance company solutions provide for protection of your spouse after you pass on, orderly transfer of your assets to your children or grandchildren while maintaining control of those assets and, last but not least, tax-efficiency. All of these attributes can go a long way toward setting a troubled mind at ease. Far and away, the most appealing aspect of insurance products for sleep-deprived Canadians is their ability to guarantee the policyholder's income, capital or both, depending on the product.

WHAT'S BEHIND THE GUARANTEE?

It's all fine and well to have a guarantee, but is that guarantee actually worth anything? That's a pretty fair question to ask following the credit market drama of 2008 and the list of casualties that included some of the largest and formerly most respected brand names in finance. You have three backups if you invest in an insurance company plan:

1. Assuris
2. Regulated policy reserves
3. Reinsurance

Assuris

Assuris (formerly CompCorp), established in 1990, is a non-profit organization created solely to protect Canadians in the event that a life insurance company becomes insolvent. Within specified limits, this organization insures policyholders against the possibility that the life insurance company that they hold their policy with experiences financial hardship. There is no cost to consumers for this coverage; it is entirely paid for by life insurance companies. All life insurance companies in Canada are required by law to be members.

If a life insurance company fails, all the policies are transferred to a solvent life insurance company. At worst, you are guaranteed by Assuris to receive a minimum of 85% of your promised benefit up to specified maximums for each type of policy, which we will point out for each product we cover in this chapter. This is by no means an attempt to provide a comprehensive list of every product on the shelves of the insurance companies nor the Assuris coverage on each, so if you have a specific question about a policy or investment you own you would be well advised to speak to an insurance specialist or start by checking out the Assuris website at www.assuris.ca.

Regulated Policy Reserves

While Canada's banks enjoy the envy of first world nations because of the strict regulatory requirements that have kept them from the dire situations that the banks of other nations have found themselves in, Canada's life insurance companies are subject to even stricter regulation.

Regulations such as the MCCSR ratio—the minimum continuing capital surplus requirement (try saying that really fast five times!)—requires that insurance companies keep a minimum percentage of cash on reserve to further protect policyholders. If the reserve ratio of an insurance company falls below 150%, OFSI (the Office of the Superintendent of Financial Institutions) will take over supervision of the company. If you are already an investor in insurance company products, this may be greater than the discovery of sliced bread, or pantyhose. It means that for every dollar of insurance that the life insurance company sells, it has to have a minimum of 1.5 times what they owe you in *cash* to stay out of trouble in the eyes of the regulators. According to OSFI's 2007–2008 annual report, in 2007, the average MCCSR ratio in Canada was 218%. This solvency test should provide Canadians with a level of assurance above and beyond the call of duty, or above the expectations that should be had for corporate governance.

An interesting phenomenon that occurred at the end of 2008 in the middle of the market crash was that insurance companies took a majority of their profits and added them to policy reserves at the expense of their shareholders. This was done in an effort to comfort policyholders, but it had the opposite effect. As the insurance companies' stock prices fell, policyholders thought that meant their policies were at risk, and shareholders and financial analysts believed it meant the insurance companies were failing, or unhealthy to say the least.

Because of the strict regulation and inherently conservative nature of life insurance companies (a good thing!), their products and the companies themselves tend to fare well in down markets. Going forward, Canadians looking for security in their portfolios should find solace and comfort in the products of life insurance companies.

In addition to offering very useful risk-management solutions, life insurance companies provide investment products with a focus on income and capital protection, such as segregated funds (also known as variable annuities), segregated funds with guaranteed minimum withdrawal benefits, annuities, insured annuities and whole life or universal life insurance. More on them shortly.

Reinsurance

Reinsurance allows an insurance company to spread its losses among one or more companies, lessening the impact of claims. This provides protection from a few big claims affecting the solvency of any one insurance company. A great example of reinsurance in action occurred following the destruction of the World Trade Center in New York. Many insurance companies contributed a share of the losses because of the reinsurance agreements in place. If one insurance company had had to pay the tens of billions of dollars in losses alone, it might have faced bankruptcy. There are many different reasons why insurance companies might choose to use reinsurance, but spreading of losses is the primary reason.

SEGREGATED FUNDS

Segregated funds, or seg funds, are the insurance industry's fraternal twin of mutual funds. New to Canada in 1961, the product was initially used as a fixed-income product for pension funds and later offered to investors as a creditor-proof investment, although it is important to note that a seg fund is not *always* creditor-proof. Please refer to the section titled "Armour and Shield" later in this chapter for more detail.

In the late 1990s, mutual fund companies and life insurance companies began teaming up to provide a competitive segregated fund product with greater opportunity for market exposure and growth. As a result of growing up together, seg funds began to look a great deal more like mutual funds, offering similar investments and returns. For every asset class of mutual fund—be it equity, bond, index, foreign, domestic, etc.—there is a corresponding seg fund. So what's the difference? As with any life insurance company product: guarantees.

Have Your Cake and Eat It Too

Segregated funds are often used by people who want both exposure to the markets and guarantees on their capital. Small-business owners who want to ensure creditor protection often find them useful, as do elderly parents who would like to pass on their investments to their children while bypassing probate. Research by Investor Economics confirms the popularity of this product; in 2007, before there were any signs of an upcoming market correction, seg fund holdings in Canada were at an all-time high of $74.9 billion in assets, which shrank by 15.7% in 2008 to $63.2 billion. This decrease was much less dramatic than that of traditional mutual funds, which had $636.8 billion in assets in 2007 but $507 billion in 2008, for a decline of over 20%. Even so, net deposits were up in 2008 by 3.2% over the previous year.

The Segregated Fund Guarantee

A segregated fund contract is required to guarantee a minimum of 75% of capital, minus any withdrawals. So for every $1 that you invest, assuming you make no withdrawals from that investment, 75¢ is guaranteed by the life insurance company to be returned to you on the contract's maturity or to your beneficiary on your death, regardless of the performance of your fund. The maturity date of a contract must be a minimum of 10 years, so if you close out your account before your 10-year anniversary, you don't benefit from this guarantee.

It's Not Too Good to Be True

To be competitive in the marketplace, and due to a raw talent for making things confusing, the life insurance companies offer differing guarantees. Of course, with any guarantee there is a cost, and the cost of seg funds comes in the form of higher management expenses (MERs). The higher the guarantee, the greater the risk to the insurance company, and the higher the MER. It's the classic case of "you get what you pay for." To keep MERs lower, some companies provide the required 75% guarantee of capital in 10 years but offer an option of a 100% guarantee if you'll pay higher fees.

If the value of your seg fund account is less than the percentage that is guaranteed in your contract on maturity or your death, the life insurance company provides the difference. Later in the chapter, we'll discuss income tax considerations you should be aware of.

> **Protection for Your Heirs**
>
> Peter invests $25,000 in a 100% seg fund. He dies three years later and his account is only worth $22,500. The insurance company pays $25,000 to his beneficiaries, a 'top-up' of the fair market value of $2,500. Because Peter's original investment in the plan is equal to the payout, there will be no tax consequence.

Resets

Seg fund policyowners have the option to "reset" the guaranteed value after predetermined intervals ranging anywhere from three to five years.

The benefit of the reset option is that if the value of your account has increased from the $100,000 principal that you originally invested to, say, $125,000 at the time of reset, your guarantee of 75% to 100% now can be based on the $125,000 amount—protecting your growth as well as your capital.

Original Investment	75% Guarantee	100% Guarantee
$100,000	$75,000	$100,000
Value at Reset Date	75% Guarantee	100% Guarantee
$125,000	$93,750	$125,000

Amounts are examples only.

There's a catch to resets. If you choose a reset, it starts a new 10-year maturity date. So if you reset your guarantee in year 3, your policy will mature in year 13, not year 10.

The Taxman Cometh

You can purchase a seg fund inside your RRSP or RRIF, or you can buy them with non-registered money (an investment outside an RRSP). Inside your RRSP, seg funds are taxed the same as any other sheltered investment: growth is sheltered, and every dollar withdrawn is fully taxable as income. With a non-registered seg fund investment, you can benefit from preferential tax treatment of the underlying investment, such as dividend income and capital gains.

Even When You Lose, You Win

Capital *losses* are passed down to you, which does not occur with mutual funds, as income in a mutual fund is considered a "distribution" and losses cannot be distributed.

The Age Myth

Many people are told that they cannot or should not purchase segregated funds if they are over the age of 80, because of the limitations of the death benefit guarantee and maximum age of deposit. While many life insurance companies do limit the age at which a person can invest in segregated fund accounts, it is important to note that *not all of them do*.

The insurance companies that do offer segregated funds to people over the age of 80 may adjust the maximum death benefit guarantee to 75%. Some insurance companies continue to offer a 100% death benefit, with caveats. It is important to read your information folder.

The Assuris Guarantee

In the case of segregated funds, Assuris guarantees the death or maturity benefit portion of the policy. If the life insurance company becomes insolvent, 85% of the death or maturity benefit portion, or $60,000 (whichever is higher), is guaranteed on transfer to a solvent insurance company. The actual value of the fund is not affected by the failure of a life insurance company as the segregated fund is kept separate—segregated—from the life insurance company's general accounts. The fund will be transferred to another company and continue as it was.

GUARANTEED MINIMUM WITHDRAWAL BENEFIT PLANS

Guaranteed minimum withdrawal benefit plans (let's do us both a favour and simply call them GMWBs) are ideal if you've lost confidence in the equity markets but can't afford to miss out on the higher returns that could be reaped over a reasonably long time horizon. GMWBs are the insurance industry's response to the aging population's need and demand for income-producing investments and heightened fear of running out of money. Consider it a pension option for individuals that don't have access to a defined benefit pension plan.

The product was first created in 2006 and was designed to offer Canadians protection from market risk by providing secured, guaranteed monthly income with the advantages of stock market growth, access to capital at any time, and more upside potential than previously available with any fixed-income product. The end result is the opportunity to balance growth and security while creating a minimum floor on returns.

The changes in taxation of income trusts in November 2007 left in a quandary many retirees who had relied on income trusts to create income. So now what? The inescapable fact is that interest rates on fixed-income securities are still low by historic standards, often much lower than what is required to meet annual retirement income fund payments without encroaching upon the plan's capital. GMWB plans are designed to offer equity exposure without putting one's capital at risk of market value depletion.

A Little Background

In 2002, Hartford Life became the first company in the U.S. to come out with a GMWB plan. Within about a year and a half of that introduction, almost every insurance company had a GMWB contract as an option. John Hancock followed in 2003, and from that point forward in the U.S., the product began to evolve. There was a bit of a feature/design race where one company would come up with something and another company would try to come up with something a little richer. That continued to happen even up until 2008.

These plans got to a point where bonuses reached 10% per year during the accumulation phase, with lifetime incomes starting as early as age 45 at a fairly decent rate. Reset frequencies became as frequent as monthly and there was even one company that reset daily! The payout rates were usually around 5%, but some companies ventured into the 6% area at different age bands, and 7% in some cases. These kinds of guarantees are simply not realistic long term.

This kind of variable annuity in the U.S. attracted more than $180 billion in 2007 alone. Sales tapered off a little bit in 2008, but were still well over $150 billion. Clearly, there was substantial consumer demand for GMWB plans, and similar demand was projected in Canada as well.

In October 2006, Manulife Financial decided to bring this popular concept to Canada with its launch of GIF Select with Income Plus. "We had been researching it for about a year and a half before it was actually launched and we were pretty confident it was going to resonate well with consumers," says Michael Ondercin, AVP Segregated Fund Products, Manulife Financial. "We hired the research firm Investor Economics to take a look at the Canadian market to see how these products may evolve and they were predicting within five years upward of $50 billion in assets just because what happens in the U.S. translates into Canada."

Soon after Manulife launched their offering, in April 2007, Sun Life launched its SunWise Elite Plus GMWB product.

There are now seven insurance companies in Canada offering some type of GMWB plan. All of them have a lifetime feature built into them providing that, at a certain age, payments are guaranteed for life.

The Canadian insurance companies did not get caught in the same feature frenzy as their U.S. counterparts, sticking to a set design of 5% bonuses during the accumulation phase or 5% income, which insurance company executives across the board concur is a more conservative and sustainable approach. Today, U.S product design is gravitating more toward the Canadian example.

Risk Transfer

The amount of equity risk the insurance companies are taking on with this product is significant. Remember our discussion earlier about reserves? Let's take a closer look at the reserve requirements the companies are forced to adhere to for GMWB plans.

Reserves refer to the amount of cash each company has to have on hand to ensure they can pay their obligations. OSFI has set an amount of reserves the companies must maintain for any type of segregated or guaranteed income product. Manulife made front page headlines in 2009 regarding the amount of money it had to invest in more liquid pools of assets in anticipation of having to make good on some of these guarantees. It set aside money today that might not be necessary for 7, 10 or 25 years.

As markets decline, the insurance companies must set aside additional money on a quarterly basis. Total reserves just for segregated fund guarantees went from $500 million at the end of 2007 to more than $5 billion by the end of December 2008. When markets recover, these reserves can be released back into their income statements. In the meantime, the reserves are based on the incredibly conservative assumption that at any time in the market there will be an additional 30% drop in the markets and no growth over the next 10 years.

Reserves have been set aside for the unlikely event of a repeat of the market correction experienced in 2008. Since GMWB products are very long-term commitments for the insurance companies—investors are going to be counting on them for 20 to 30 years—this gives the markets time to recover, and insurance companies time to collect enough fees to pay for the insurance.

In Canada, you can expect some modest changes going forward, but none of the exotic, highly generous features being offered in the United States. Given the sad reality that equity investors have faced the rare spectacle of two severe bear markets in the span of a decade, it's not hard to see why investors would clamour for the kind of protection GMWB plans have to offer. The alternative is to get extremely conservative in your investment portfolio, which can be detrimental to the lifespan of the capital that is required to provide income in a low interest rate environment.

A Little Reality Check...

As with anything, there must be a balance between price and features. There is no silver bullet, no single solution out there that does absolutely everything you need. In today's seismically shifting global economy and capital markets, the challenge is more about product allocation and asset allocation to help retirees achieve their goals.

We are seeing a more holistic approach to retirement planning, using multiple solutions. GMWBs should not be seen as a "one size fits all" solution, but rather as a part of your asset allocation strategy. Insurance companies offer a breadth of products that is decidedly different than most other financial institutions.

And a Call for Clarity

We are concerned with two areas of misunderstanding that appear to be prevalent among people we meet regularly with in our professional lives.

First, you can *never* capitalize the 5%. If you need access to your investment capital, the only funds available for withdrawal in a lump sum are those in your market portfolio. So, even though the Guaranteed Withdrawal Balance (GWB) of your plan may have been credited the 5% bonus and future income is based on this, if the fair market value of your investments has not met or exceeded the notional "bonus" account, then you can only withdraw from the lowest of the two accounts.

It is only when you decided to go on "income for life" that you get to choose from the highest of the two accounts.

Second, this is not a tax shelter! You need to be aware of the taxation of the income generated by the GMWB plan. In a non-registered account the income is preferred but still taxable. It's preferred in that the income is considered a combination of return of your tax-paid capital and income. This is not a variation on the Tax-Free Savings Account, nor does it act like the tax-sheltered investment portfolio of a universal life (UL) plan (a brief discussion on UL plans can be found near the end of this chapter).

Although the GMWB plan has tremendous retirement advantages, it has limited estate planning applications because of the inability to purchase it after age 80, except for Desjardins' Helios plan which is currently available up to age 95. It is very popular among people who have been and remain long-term investors, but who are spooked about the markets. For those who want some protection against what at times feels like a never-ending downward spiral in stock markets, this product will give you the opportunity to pay an additional cost to gain access to guarantees—to set a floor for losses and still have access to growth. It's not only for people who have been hit over the head with losses, but definitely for those looking at retirement.

Secure Income

Retiring investor James Bond has never been affected by the markets. Investing in equities never has been an option for James, but he would like to invest in something that provides the same or better guarantee than a bond can provide, while gaining access to the potential for greater return through exposure to the equity markets that he never would have incorporated otherwise. Gone are the days of the 12% income trust unit returns, but also gone is the volatility associated with those investments. What exists today, with a combination of all the products in this chapter, is the "sleep at night" factor.

The Assuris Guarantee

As with all other segregated fund products, Assuris guarantees the death or maturity benefit portion of the policy. If the life insurance company becomes insolvent, 85% of the death or maturity benefit portion, or $60,000 (whichever is higher), is guaranteed on transfer to a solvent insurance company. The actual value of the fund is not affected by the failure of a life insurance company because the segregated fund is kept separate—segregated—from the life insurance company's general accounts. The fund would be transferred to another company and continue as it was.

ANNUITIES: NOT JUST FOR GRANNY ANYMORE!

An annuity is a type of insurance contract. Think of it as an insurance policy in reverse, or a mortgage turned inside out. When you buy a basic life insurance policy, you pay the life insurance company a certain amount of money each month, and at the end of your life, they will pay out to your beneficiaries a lump sum amount.

In the case of the simplest type of annuity—a single-premium life annuity without a guaranteed term—you pay the life insurance company a lump sum amount at the beginning and then the life insurance company pays you a certain amount of money each month for the rest of your life. The amount is fixed, and you can sleep at night knowing that that income will keep coming in no matter what the markets do, what interest rates do or even what the life insurance company does. You're locked in, which can be both a good and a bad thing.

Splitting Heirs

It's important to remember that you cannot "unring the bell." You cannot unwind the plan, and you cannot access your original capital. In short, you are locking in guaranteed income for life with the potential—in the case of insured annuities, discussed later—to transfer capital to beneficiaries tax-free and probate-free under the insurance death benefit. The biggest misunderstanding with annuities is that investors often do not fully realize that they are, in fact, *spending their capital*. Beyond a specified guarantee period, if one is chosen, there lies the potential that little to no benefit is paid.

Guarantee Period	Income	At Death
Zero	Highest income paid for life	No benefit for heirs
5, 10, 15, 20, 25 years	Income decreases with longer guarantee periods and is paid for life	During the guarantee period, heirs receive remaining income or commuted value
Beyond the guarantee period	Income continues for life	No benefit for heirs

Although annuities are an alternative to GICs and other similar guaranteed investment products, they are not just an interest-bearing investment. There is a reason they're different. Annuity income is not limited to interest rates. It is based on mortality, competitive pricing between insurance companies, and the amount invested. Annuity rates are based on long-term rates—much longer than an individual investor typically would invest in. This provides a rate advantage to annuities over the short-term GICs and short-dated bonds that individual investors are characteristically comfortable with.

When you buy an annuity, your capital is used to purchase a combination of various government, high-quality corporate and high-quality private bonds. The bonds are purchased in a manner such that coupon payments and bond maturities will coincide with the payments the insurance company is required to make to you. Payment amounts are determined based on the insurance company's expectation of what these assets will earn as well as what they actuarially consider to be your life expectancy.

Who Could Use a Life Annuity?

Typically, an annuity would be appropriate for a retired couple or single individual who does not have children or grandchildren to whom they would like to leave an estate. This means that for these individuals, retirement income is more important than an estate benefit. Why invest in an annuity? It's simple: to receive guaranteed income.

Basic Life Annuity Factors

The amount of money that you receive in return for your premium is dependent on a few different factors:

- **Your age:** Unlike life insurance, the older you are, the better! Life insurance premiums cost more as you age and, correspondingly, annuity payments increase as you age. In both cases, this is because of the amount of risk that the insurance company takes on. The closer you are to life expectancy, the sooner it is that the life insurance company will have to pay out a death benefit on a life insurance policy. This means that, in the case of annuities, the closer you are to life expectancy, the shorter the payment period is. You do not have to qualify medically for an annuity like you do for life insurance, so whether or not you smoke and therefore shorten your life expectancy is not taken into account. The exception to this is an accelerated or impaired annuity, which requires proof of poor health in exchange for higher income.

- **Your gender:** Typically, women live longer than their male counterparts, so in the case of life insurance your premium would be less expensive if you were female. In the case of annuities, the payment period is expected to be that much longer if you're female, so the income that you receive would be marginally smaller than that of a man of the same age.

- **Interest rates:** Current interest rates affect the payment that you will receive on your annuity policy. The higher the current interest rates, the higher your annuity income. What is good for your mortgage is not so good for your annuity, and what is good for your annuity is not so good for your mortgage. Because of the long-term nature of annuities, you can expect your payment not to be as strongly affected by interest rates as the five-year term on your mortgage would be, as the life insurance company will need to invest in long-term fixed-income products to protect your annuity. Long-term bonds will typically pay higher interest rates than a shorter-term bond.

There Are Almost as Many Annuities as Imelda Has Shoes

Term Certain Annuities

Term certain annuities are different from life annuities in one important and very specific way: a term certain annuity pays income for a fixed period—a "term certain." For these types of annuities, your age and gender are not factors in the income that you will receive. The only factors are the length of the term (which can be as many years as you want, limited only to your age 90) and the current interest rates.

Accelerated Annuities

Accelerated annuities (or "impaired annuities") differ from regular life annuities in that, in this case, your health becomes a factor and you will need to qualify medically. With an accelerated annuity, when an individual's life expectancy is significantly shortened—usually by a terminal illness—the life insurance company will guarantee a higher income as the payment period is expected to be so much shorter. Some life insurance companies do not offer this type of annuity, and those that do have their own strict requirements on when and if they issue an accelerated annuity. Rarely will the insurance company pay for any medical testing or reporting required to determine the health of the annuitant (the person who receives the benefits of the annuity or pension, or the life on which an insurance policy is based), and it is not guaranteed that the company will issue an accelerated annuity even if the annuitant has been declined for life insurance coverage.

Immediate Annuities

An immediate annuity starts providing income within one year of the life insurance company receiving the capital that the annuity is based on.

Deferred Annuities

A deferred annuity starts providing income at a future date, more than one year after the life insurance company receives the capital that the annuity is based on.

Bells and Whistles

There are a few options that you can get on your annuity to customize it to fit your needs. As is the case with most products, when you add a bell or a whistle, it will cost you. For annuities, a customization will cost you income. Depending on your situation, the benefit may outweigh the cost, or there may be a better way to customize.

To Inflate or Not to Inflate, That Is the Question

Once you have conquered the fear of outliving your savings by securing a life annuity, a few other fears may appear. One is that the cost of living will increase between now and the later years of your life. While many people find that their costs decrease as they age, some people feel that they need their income to buy the same lifestyle at age 80 as they had at age 60. In that case, you may consider adding indexation to your annuity. What this means is that the income that you receive from your annuity will increase by a fixed percentage amount (for example, 2%) each year. This will significantly reduce the amount of income that you receive at the outset.

The problem with using inflation protection with an annuity is that the insurance companies have to protect themselves from the highest inflation that they expect over a long period of time, whether or not inflation ever actually reaches that high. So you could be paying for something you are never going to benefit from. It is worthwhile to consider alternatively hedging against inflation by investing a portion of your portfolio in securities with greater growth potential at a much lower cost to you.

What Happens to My Investment . . . In the End?

And while you may be happy to receive income for life from your annuity, what happens if you get hit by a bus tomorrow? In the case of a regular life annuity, the income stops when you do. A very common way to mitigate this is to add a guaranteed term to your life annuity. You can add a term of any number of years, as in the case of a term certain annuity, up to your age 90. This will, again, significantly reduce the amount of income that you receive from your annuity. An alternative to this solution—and one that is frequently recommended when capital preservation is important to a client—is the insured annuity, discussed a little later on.

Non-registered Versus Registered Annuity

A non-registered annuity is one where the capital does not come from an RRSP or RRIF; a registered annuity is one where the capital *does* come from an RRSP or RRIF. Both the registered and non-registered annuity will provide the same income amount based on your age, gender, investment amount and current interest rates. The difference is taxation.

One hundred percent of the income that you receive from a registered annuity will be considered taxable by the Canada Revenue Agency (CRA) and is reportable on your income taxes each year. This is the same for all income coming from a registered account. You weren't taxed when you put the money in and you weren't taxed on any of the growth, but as soon as you start taking money out, you get hit over the head with the tax hammer. The Mounties always get their man and the CRA always gets its money.

A non-registered annuity, however, receives different tax treatment. As far as the CRA is concerned, a portion of the income you receive from a non-registered annuity is a return of the original capital that you put in. Since you already paid taxes on that money when you earned it, it's not fair to be taxed twice—and you aren't. There are two ways to structure a non-registered annuity and the way that it is taxed: non-prescribed and prescribed.

Non-prescribed Annuities

A non-prescribed annuity reports income as it is earned—higher in the early years and lower in the later years. You will pay more tax on the same amount of income in the first 10 years than you will in the last 10. But it's the same amount of income, and most retirees spend more money in the first 10 years of retirement than they do in the last 10 years of retirement. That's why some people prefer prescribed annuities.

Prescribed Annuities

Prescribed annuities level out the interest earned and distribute it over the life of the annuity. Each year, you are taxed on level amounts of annuity income, ensuring that you are not taxed higher in any year for the same amount of income and that there is more money in your pocket in those early years of retirement.

Non-Prescribed Annuity

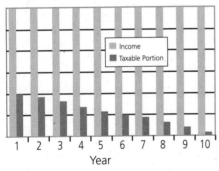

Prescribed Annuity

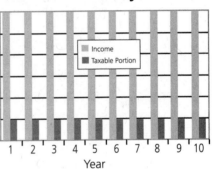

Source: Raymond James Financial Planning Article: The Prescribed Annuity Advantage

Planning Opportunities With Old Age Security and the Pension Income Credit

Old Age Security

Since Old Age Security (OAS) is an income-tested form of social assistance, not contributory like CPP, the way we can make sure you get more of it is to reduce your tax on income, without reducing income itself.

If you are 65 years old or older and in a higher tax bracket, the favourable tax treatment of a prescribed annuity could help you retain more of your OAS income.

If you are over 65 years old and in a lower tax bracket, you are probably already receiving 100%, or close to 100%, of your OAS. And if you are lucky enough to still be in your 30s or 40s and wondering if an annuity is the right thing for you, know that there is very little advantage. You might as well buy a GIC and have access to your capital.

Individual Net Income Amount	OAS Clawback*
Up to $66,335 annually	0%
Between $66,335 and $107,691 annually	15¢ of every $1 over $66,335
$107,692 or more annually	100%

* Based on Q3 2009 OAS rates

Few people are aware of how generous the OAS benefits are. The maximum OAS benefit (based on Q2 2009 OAS rates) is $908.75 per month. It's important to note that the OAS income clawback is based on the taxable income of an individual, *not* the combined taxable income of a couple.

Pension Income Credit

Life annuities—whether they are registered, non-registered, prescribed or non-prescribed—qualify for the pension income credit (PIC) on your tax return. This is a non-refundable tax credit (meaning they're not sending you a cheque) that reduces your overall taxable income. This can further assist you in your quest to increase the amount of OAS benefit you receive.

Federally, the credit is 16% of your taxable pension income (in the case of non-registered annuities, this is the taxable portion, not the entire income), to a maximum of $2,000 of income. This means that the maximum credit is $320. It's not a lot, but it doesn't hurt. Any provincial taxes will increase the effectiveness of this credit.

The Assuris Guarantee

In the event of the insolvency of a life insurance company, Assuris guarantees on transfer to a solvent insurance company a minimum of 85% of your monthly income or $2,000—whichever is higher.

THE TWO-FOR-ONE SPECIAL: INSURED ANNUITIES

Like fine wine (and your authors), insured annuities are among the few things that get better with age. The insured annuity concept combines two insurance products—the income of the non-registered "prescribed" annuity with the estate benefit of life insurance—into one little, neatly wrapped package. The price tag is the cost of life insurance. This cost is offset by higher income generated by a *zero* guarantee on the annuity.

Even after paying for the cost of life insurance, the favourable tax treatment enjoyed by prescribed annuities, especially for those people in the highest tax brackets, typically generates a much higher income than what can be achieved even with a laddered fixed-income securities portfolio.

If you are above age 55, in a 30% plus tax bracket, and have enough money to consider locking up capital that you won't have access to for the balance of your lifetime, the insured annuity will work for you. There are, however, two things that would stop you from investing in an insured annuity:

1. Health (you have to qualify for the life insurance)
2. Fear of hyperinflation

In the chart below, we contrast an investment of $250,000 into a non-registered GIC laddered portfolio earning an average of 4.5% over the lifetime of the investor with a $250,000 insured annuity. We've assumed that the investor is a male, age 65, in a 30% marginal tax rate. In both cases, $250,000 is available to this gentleman's beneficiaries when he dies. The insured annuity allows the funds to pass to his beneficiaries outside of his Will, probate-free.

$250,000 Investment 30% Marginal Tax Rate Male, age 65, standard non-smoker	Non-Registered GIC at 4.5%	Insured Annuity
Income	$11,250	$21,573
Taxable portion	$11,250	$6,816
Tax Payable	$3,375	$2,045
Cost of Insurance	$0	$7,669
After Tax Income	$7,875	$11,659

The GIC portfolio provides our healthy boomer with $7,751.21 in his wallet (after the CRA has taken a bit of cream off the top) each year. The insured annuity, even with the cost of life insurance, provides him with $11,584.50 in his wallet (also, after removing cream) each year. The preferred taxation of the prescribed annuity gives him an extra $3,834.29 to spend and the death benefit of the life insurance policy helps him leave a healthy lump sum of $250,000 to his children, grandchildren, favourite charity or whomever else might be important to him.

Nuts and Bolts: How Does This Thing Work?

Apply for the insurance part first, because you're not going to buy a life annuity without a guaranteed term attached until your capital is protected. Once you're approved by the life insurance company and accept delivery of the policy, then that very same day you can buy the annuity. Make sure that your annuity income payment date matches the timing of the insurance premium payment, to avoid any missed payments or shortfalls in income when the premium comes due.

If you don't qualify for the insurance because of past medical history or current health issues, you may be a good candidate for an accelerated annuity, as described previously.

The Assuris Guarantee

Each piece—the annuity and the insurance—is guaranteed individually by Assuris in the event that a life insurance company becomes insolvent. For annuities, a minimum of 85% of the monthly income, or $2000 (whichever is higher), is guaranteed. For life insurance, a minimum of 85% of the promised death benefit, or $200,000 (whichever is higher), is guaranteed.

UNIVERSAL LIFE: INVESTMENT OR INSURANCE?

Well, it's both actually. Universal life is a permanent insurance plan that came about in the early '80s because of demand from from consumers who were entering the higher income earning years—the accumulation phase of life—and they wanted to have more choices and a lot more flexibility than traditional permanent insurance plans. This is a subject that could take an entire book to cover. For the purpose of this chapter, we just want to make sure you know it's an option and spend time on why it's an option as an investment.

Tax Shelters 101

There are very few tax shelters the Canada Revenue Agency affords Canadian investors. Universal life is one of them. The amount of money you can deposit to the investment is directly correlated to how much life insurance death benefit you buy and measured by something called the Maximum Tax Actuarial Reserve (MTAR). All you need to know about MTAR at this stage is that it sets limits on how much money you can deposit to the plan; you cannot buy $1 of death benefit and put $100,000 into the tax-sheltered investment component of the plan.

Just as the government puts limitations on the amount of money you can put into RRSPs and TFSAs, they put limits on how much money you can put into life insurance plans. It's simply the government saying, "we're nice but we're not Santa, and although we'll let you invest in a tax-sheltered component of an insurance plan we are going to place some limits on the *amount* you can put in." The deposit you make to the plan must be in cash, you cannot transfer existing investments that you may own in your non-registered portfolio. Once the funds are deposited, then you can choose from a list of investments available inside the plan. The investments vary depending on the company you choose but are very comprehensive. The choices include everything from Money Market, GIC's and Bonds to mutual funds and links to the equity indexes.

What comes first, the chicken or the egg?

There are other tax shelters available to you, as we mentioned earlier, which you should consider maximizing first, before you enter into a Universal Life plan as an investment. Your house is the first one, and with primary residence status it's actually a great way to accumulate wealth (all the while providing an ever so convenient roof over your head) and it does great estate planning, too. You can sell it during your lifetime or leave it to your kids in your Will and there's never any tax to pay. This is unlike RRSPs and pension plans, where every dollar coming out is taxable as income because you didn't have to pay any tax on the money you put in.

There is a reason for bringing these other tax shelters into the picture. They make better sense than a universal life insurance plan and they come with fewer costs to you. So, implement them first. There's an order to accumulating wealth and it has something to do with the "life cycle."

1. Grow up, get married, buy a house…make babies if possible/desired, work, sleep less, and pay down debt (specifically the non-deductible kind).
2. Save money; maximize RRSPs, Pension Plan contributions and Tax-Free Savings Accounts.
3. Save *more* money; build up the emergency reserves, the non-registered taxable kind, whether personally or corporately.
4. Once the first three steps are completed, then and only then does it make sense to consider a permanent insurance plan as an investment.

UL Limitations

If this is something of interest to you and you find yourself at the right stage in life, you would be well-advised to do your due diligence. Nothing beats a little research and there is a lot of information to be found online. Also, ask your financial advisor about it. He or she can provide you with more information, if insurance licensed, or refer you to someone with the right depth of experience and expertise on the subject. We would suggest you request someone with the Chartered Life Underwriter (CLU) designation.

The Assuris Guarantee

Assuris guarantees each part of the universal life policy in the event that the insurance company becomes insolvent. The insurance portion is guaranteed for $200,000 or 85%, whichever is higher. The account value portion is guaranteed for $60,000 or 85%, again, for whichever is higher.

ARMOUR AND SHIELD: CREDITOR PROTECTION STRATEGIES

A growing number of Canadians are moving from the ranks of salaried employees to the realm of self-employment. Often, this exposes people to types of risks they may not have encountered during their days as an employee. This includes the economic uncertainty that self-employment, especially in the early stages of a new venture, can leave one more vulnerable to financial hardship than may have been the case when a steady paycheque was a fact of life. Often, litigation risk is a risk that is given little consideration by a salaried employee, yet is a risk that the self-employed must remain constantly vigilant over.

All of the insurance investments discussed in this chapter can help to mitigate these risks because they all give you access to a beneficiary designation. Creditor protection can be achieved by naming a beneficiary but the beneficiary must be a member of your close family—a spouse, child, grandchild or parent. The policy is protected from your creditors from the time that the designation is made.

Another option is to name an irrevocable beneficiary, in which case the beneficiary does *not* have to be a member of your close family (but it cannot be you or your estate). Of course, once you have elected an irrevocable beneficiary, you cannot later change the designation without the written consent of the person you named irrevocably. Although this is an attractive planning tool, losing control over an asset isn't always a desirable outcome; rather, it's a con that needs to be seriously considered and weighed against the benefit.

The risk of challenge is further reduced to some extent if the strategies are part of a plan implemented for some other purpose, such as estate planning, and especially when deposits to the plan are not made in anticipation of a creditor issue.

It's Beneficial to Have a Beneficiary

In addition to creditor protection, another advantage of a beneficiary designation is that you don't need to rely on your Will to give an asset away, which means no probate. Unlike income taxes on a RRIF balance at death, which can often propel an estate into the highest tax bracket, probate is a nominal fee but still one worth avoiding. The advantages of using a beneficiary designation for probate planning are:

- it doesn't cost you anything to implement
- you can change your mind at any time, so your beneficiaries still have to be nice to you
- you still own and control the asset for as long as you need it

In Alberta, the flat fee of $400 probate is a non-issue, but in provinces like British Columbia and Ontario where probate reaches 1.4% and 1.6% of the value of your estate, it's worth jumping through some hoops to avoid. The icing on the cake is that beneficiary designations cannot be challenged by anyone who might argue the fairness of the distribution of your assets through your Will. Your capital ends up entirely in the hands of the person you want it to go to.

Some people mistakenly believe that because segregated funds pass to beneficiaries outside of their Will and probate, the fund pays out to the beneficiary tax-free, as life insurance does. This is not the case. If the guarantee "top-up" mentioned previously is used, that portion is not taxable, as it is considered a life insurance benefit. If the guarantee top-up is not required because your account value exceeds your principal guarantee, these gains will be taxed in the same manner as any other investment account that you hold at death.

PRODUCT SUMMARY

	Pros	Cons	Ability to Name a Beneficiary
Segregated funds	-guaranteed return of 75% to 100% of your capital at maturity or death -access to capital if you need to make a lump sum withdrawal	-higher MERs to pay for the guarantees -expensive MERs eat up growth that might be required to fund retirement income	Yes
GMWB plans	-worst-case scenario is a 5% (net of fees) rate of return, with upside potential of the markets built in	-difficult to understand, with many product features and caveats to be aware of -known to be "fee intensive," making it difficult for the market portfolio to return >5% net	Yes
Annuities	-guaranteed income for life; no risk of outliving your capital -no market volatility or ongoing investment decisions -preferential "prescribed" tax treatment when purchased with non-registered funds, which can avoid OAS clawback	-no capital left for beneficiaries beyond the "guaranteed" period -cost of inflation protection is expensive, so most client don't choose it and are at risk for going broke slowly over time -no access to capital, ever!	Yes

Insured annuities	-guaranteed income for life; no risk of outliving your capital -no market volatility or ongoing investment decisions -preferential "prescribed" tax treatment when purchased with non-registered funds, which can avoid OAS clawback -your deposit is guaranteed to be paid to your beneficiaries tax-free and probate-free regardless of how long you live	-no access to capital, ever! -cost of protecting the capital for beneficiaries reduces spendable income	Yes
Universal life insurance	-can be used as a tax shelter for wealth accumulation and later to create income -removes income tax on an annual basis, resulting in lower tax brackets and more OAS -subject to qualifying medically, cost is less than the taxes you would otherwise pay to CRA on passive investment income -more money for you to spend or leave behind for beneficiaries	-must qualify medically, therefore reasonable health required -costs are deducted annually regardless of returns earned on the investment account -there is usually an 8- to 10-year surrender charge depending on the company you purchase the plan from	Yes

THE LIGHT AT THE END OF THE TUNNEL

Investment products of all shapes and sizes are available to investors and they attract the hard-earned savings of investors for different reasons. Insurance company products are simply another form of allocation. It's product allocation versus asset allocation. There is no magic to any one product and it's certainly not one size fits all. The product you choose will be driven largely by your needs—the need for safety, the need for income, the need for guarantees that your money will last, and the need for control over who gets what's left in the end.

PART THREE

STAYING HEALTHY

CHAPTER 13

The Unfair Advantage

Using Reliable Research to Make Better Decisions

One of Bryan's passions is auto racing. His favourite race-car driver of all time, Mark Donohue, was remarkable for his ability to win races in all manner of cars. Donohue credited much of his success to an "unfair advantage" through a highly focused strategy and detailed preparation of the car in advance. Michael is similarly reminded of a British officer whose meticulous preparation resulted in his commando group accomplishing their D-Day mission with scarcely a loss.

The moral of stories like these is simple: don't leave any stone unturned. Prepare thoroughly, and your goal will become that much more attainable. The most successful and best-known investors all have an aversion to unmanageable risk. None would want to be sidetracked by an unexpected turn of events. Warren Buffett still takes great care to have the relevant facts available to him before committing to an investment.

NO DARTBOARDS ALLOWED

While he certainly does not stand as a paragon of virtue, Gordon Gekko, the central character in the Oliver Stone film *Wall Street*, accurately summed up the attitude of true investors when he said, "I don't throw darts at a board. I bet on sure things."

The value-driven Benjamin Graham always sought his unfair advantage in correct facts and reasoning, because he would then be building his long-term strategy on a sound foundation. Our portfolios should demand no less. Like Mark Donohue and that D-Day commander, we too should give ourselves an unfair investment advantage through meticulous preparatory research.

Michael counts himself privileged to have been in on the pioneering of investment research in Canada. However, his nostalgia about the groundbreaking 1960s quickly gives way to awe at today's research tools. The information may not always be as trustworthy or as transparent as it should be (a painfully unfortunate discovery in the crisis of 2007–2009), but there is now instant fingertip access to information at every turn. In addition, at the corporate level separate investor relations departments, meetings and conferences are routinely held to review latest results, and "guidance" is regularly provided on expected future results. On the research coverage side, there is an ever-growing global army of investment professionals possessing the prestigious Chartered Financial Analyst (CFA) designation. The media feature non-stop expert assessment and comment of every type, and the Internet has opened up a floodtide of accessible investment-related information. Not only was there nothing like this before, but it keeps becoming more and more expert—and businesslike.

However, if there is a weakness, it is that the information available to today's investor can be overwhelming. On rare occasions, it also can be calculatingly false and misleading, as witnessed by this decade's sorry litany of fraud and deception. Window-dressing remains an undesirable part of the information and research process—taking unfair advantage in the worst sense.

Nevertheless, travesties like Enron and AIG only enhance what good research should be all about and is increasingly capable of providing. They have also taught us that interpretation, valuation and portfolio application are bridges better crossed with the correct facts. In due course, a great company will invariably ensure its own success. Unearth such a company early through fact-based research and the rest will take care of itself. Miss out on the basic facts and the risks of a poor investment will escalate. Protect yourself by doing your own digging, or have someone do your digging for you. The net result could well be a diamond in the rough.

This doesn't mean individual investors need to have the knowledge or tools of full-time research professionals. It does mean they shouldn't be deterred from acquiring basic investment knowledge in their own interests. This way, they will be better equipped to ask their investment advisors pertinent questions and to better follow what is being done on their behalf. The key is to have a modicum of knowledge of the very real advantages that reliable research can bring.

EMPIRICAL YOU

After over 40 years in the business, Michael has become more and more a believer in empirical observation to help him arrive at his investment conclusions. Just as his Ph.D. supervisor believed housewives are the best day-to-day economists, we can become our own best investors—not necessarily with the expertise and specialist knowledge we pay others to provide, but by keeping our eyes open, looking around us and asking logical questions from which helpful investment ideas might meaningfully flow.

Asking Why

Why is the economy supposed to be slowing down when shopping malls, flights, restaurants, and entertainment and sporting events are full? Conversely, how are we to believe that prosperity is just around the corner when the critically important automotive industry is cutting back drastically and fighting to survive? Or when economy-wide job losses and unemployment keep rising? Why should or shouldn't we be investing in companies that are being affected by activities and developments like these?

Such questions should leave your investment advisor thinking, too; both of you could be agreeably surprised where the answers lead. These questions also should be asked in the knowledge that even the greatest investment managers are not above getting their leads similarly.

We commented earlier on how Peter Lynch, the legendary manager of Fidelity's flagship Magellan Fund, always preferred to kick tires, knock on doors and observe what went into shopping baskets to what economists or strategists could tell him. One of his memorable put-downs was that spending five minutes listening to an economist was to waste three. Mr. Lynch even liked linking potential investments to what children could draw with a crayon. Talk about a grassroots approach that worked—spectacularly!

Michael (with his training in economics) begs to differ respectfully with Mr. Lynch, and has always preferred to go about his research preparation and security selection in top-down fashion, looking at the bigger economic picture before working his way down to good investments. This way he feels he can better gauge whether the investment tides are flowing in and lifting all boats, flowing out and taking stock markets and supporting investment values down with them, or are at a choppy in-between stage, which can spell added investment opportunity.

Opportunities always will abound if you go about your research properly. We'll never forget the massive bull market that no one believed could be building in the white-knuckle summer of 1982. This decade, despite not one but two unexpectedly severe recessions and bear markets, there nonetheless have been numerous exceptional investment opportunities to take advantage of; for example, at the macro level, on China's bursting onto the world economic and investment stage, the paradigm shifts in oil prices and world energy, and the impressive turnaround in a debt- and deficit-ridden Canada that was next on the World Bank's stewardship list in the mid-1990s.

Another current example of empirical research is the watershed transition currently playing out in the all-important U.S. economy and investment marketplace, along with the accompanying downward adjustment in the U.S. dollar, which nonetheless remains the world's premier reserve currency. Examples like these provide prescient investors all sorts of scope to get a jump on the crowd. Be patient, another successful investing discipline, and the resultant leg-up stands to be all the greater. There could also be the escalating advantage from one of investment's oldest adages: "The trend is your friend."

You may not have the research and valuation capabilities of today's economists and investment experts, nor do you need to. To compensate for the lack of the sophisticated tools of the professional investor, ask the "right" questions through your own powers of observation. You'd find yourself in distinguished company, along with the likes of Warren Buffett, whose legendary success has always been predicated on a simpler-the-better approach that everyone can understand.

KNOW WHAT YOU OWN

We commented previously on Mr. Buffett's refusal to invest in high-tech because he and his partner, Charlie Munger, couldn't understand it. But they have never had any problem with basic activities such as chocolates, paint, bricks, underwear, jewellery, furniture, newspapers and mobile homes. Or with sophisticated machine tools, or the growing world roles they see for China and energy. Throughout, though, their overriding requirement remains to be able to understand what they are investing in, which further enables them to have views on the U.S. economy, the U.S. dollar, the extreme dangers of derivatives and the bleak future for newspapers, to touch on some of their current thinking.

We have every right to ask similar questions of our investment advisors. Our portfolios can only benefit if we do.

IT'S THE SELECTIONS THAT COUNT

Regardless of the approach, investment ultimately boils down to choosing individual stocks and equity products with which to build (and/or protect) desired longer-term wealth. In other words, to a bottom-up, or micro, selection of securities. Thorough research is also all-important at this point-of-entry stage, whether by dint of our own efforts—direct or indirect, rudimentary or sophisticated—or with the help of others. Or, perhaps better still, through a combination of outside expertise and our *own* individual ideas.

In the final instance, nothing beats correctly assessing the fundamentals. The research summary questionnaire that follows illustrates the basic research approach Michael has always favoured. Filling in a summary questionnaire like this is not all that difficult; you could do it too. In the process you'd equip yourself with revealing answers to many key investment considerations.

RESEARCH SUMMARY QUESTIONNAIRE

Below are some of the typical questions we like to get answers to:

- How have sales or revenues grown?
- Has this growth accelerated or decelerated?
- Have bottom-line earnings grown faster or slower than revenues?
- What do profit margins reveal about management's effectiveness?
- How adequate is the cash flow, and how has it grown?
- How strong is the balance sheet and to what extent is it leveraged by debt?
- What have been the returns on the common shareholders' equity, and how do they compare with others in the same field?
- How have the stock markets rated results?

The longer the number of years data like this can be measured over, the better. Thus, a period of 10 years will likely have brought both up and down cycles, not to mention other assorted challenges for management. Rising trends over the

RESEARCH SUMMARY QUESTIONNAIRE
(absolute numbers in millions)

Consolidated Income Statement	Latest Year	Previous Year	5 Yrs Ago	10 Yrs Ago	Annual Growth (or changes) Latest	5 yrs	10 yrs
Revenue							
Operating Income/Profit							
Net Income/Earnings							
Dividends							
Cash Flow							

Consolidated Balance Sheet

Total Assets
Working Capital
(Current Assets–Current
  Liabilities)
Long-Term Debt

Shareholders Equity

Total Capital
Debt: Total Capital (ratio)

Share Data

Earnings Per Share
- Basic
- Diluted (if applicable)

Cash Flow Per Share

Dividends Per Share
Payout %

Equity (Book Value) Per Share
Return on Equity (ROE)

General

Share Price (year-end)
Shares Outstanding
Market Capitalization
  (price × shares)
Price-Earnings Ratio
  (annual average)

period being analyzed normally would be construed favourably. It's even better if annual growth rates and profit ratios are higher over the second half of the chosen period than the first half; and, best of all, if they are highest in the latest year. If the statistics don't measure up in ways like these, you'll need to dig more deeply before making your final decision. Successful investing is no mistake and it has little to do with luck.

Given today's plethora of available information, it shouldn't be difficult to obtain basic information for rudimentary analysis. The most recent annual report is invariably the best source. Warren Buffett devours annual reports from all over, and likes to tell how he often gets great investment ideas this way. Michael customarily writes in for the annual report of every company in which he has an investment. At the very least, the annual report, particularly the pages containing management's own discussion and analysis, will be worth a cursory leaf-through. All annual reports include a summary of past results, usually for five years and sometimes, preferably, for 10. If the summary doesn't go this far back, ask the corporate secretary or investor relations department to provide you with the numbers you need.

In due course you might become expert enough to "eyeball" annual reports and summaries for the sought-after answers. To be that much more sure, you might find it easier to set up a basic spreadsheet along the lines of the research summary questionnaire for regular updating on your home computer.

You might also want to compare and measure companies you are considering against others in the same industries, if only because superior investing is a relative affair we should all be obliged to measure up to. This way, we'd also be able to establish where the best relative investment values might lie.

No matter how rudimentary, there is no better discipline than basic fundamental analysis. Ultimately, such analysis will enable you to gauge how bottom-line earnings and returns on shareholders' equity are faring, and how adequately they are being reflected in the prevailing share price. EBITDA, alpha-beta analysis and other refinements can come later. Throughout, remember to keep things simple.

Michael has always preferred filling in basically simple tables (like the accompanying research summary questionnaire) and going about his research the old-fashioned way. This is not to preclude you developing *your* way to become *your* own best research analyst. Most likely you'll want some outside help in the process—and even better if this adds to the awareness of what good research can bring.

FEELING THE PULSE

Discipline yourself to stick to it, and even the simplest research approach soon will lead to the ability to feel the pulse of companies you are considering or are invested in, whether the pulse rate is speeding up or slowing down, and whether changes (good or bad) are being signalled.

In essence, this is what technical analysis (and research) is all about, be it charting the tempo in the markets as a whole, or plotting relevant dots, lines and patterns in different sectors and stocks making up the markets. Connect the dots and draw the lines between different points on stock and market charts, and the resultant patterns can often be highly revealing.

Thus, lines drawn through annual peaks or annual lows can highlight important up or down trends. Similarly, lines connecting past annual lows can indicate support levels for future buying, while lines drawn through past peaks can highlight ceilings that will need to be penetrated for any sustained upside breakout.

Moving-average lines based on closing prices over a set number of days are another widely watched and used technical indicator. When this average is calculated on periods as long as 150 or 200 days at a time, the moving-average price line also can be indicative of longer-based trends. It's always a comforting sign if prices remain above the moving-average line through periods of market turbulence; on the other hand, prices falling through their moving-average line can often signal further weakness to come.

Like its fundamentally based counterpart, which we must confess to favouring, technical research can be as sophisticated or as basic as you want. Whatever your approach, it's nonetheless much better than reading tea leaves.

KITCHEN TABLE ANALYSIS AND OTHER APPROACHES

Michael will always remember the courtly Bob Farrell of Merrill Lynch, one of the all-time great technical analysts, telling him of the handful of key charts he filled in by himself on the family kitchen table. There's a lesson for us all when Wall Street's top market technician, with his own budget and support staff, nonetheless liked keeping his finger on the market's pulse in this most homespun of ways.

In his days as a bank analyst, Michael used to routinely plot the prices of bank shares, one against the other. An admittedly apples-to-oranges comparison helped alert him to which shares were more active and less active, which were growing the most and the least, and where the better relative values might lie. It wasn't mathematically pure, but it helped him keep his finger on the pulse of a key sector in the Canadian financial markets.

Recently deceased Tony Furgueson, another respected Wall Street veteran and friend of Michael's mentioned earlier, liked to note the percentage increase in the annual dividend, usually made at the same point each year along with one of the quarterly declarations. If the percentage increase is the same as the previous year, he took it as a sign that all is continuing well; if higher than previously, that the company anticipated doing better; if lower, that there could be difficulties ahead.

Others believe the consolidated balance sheet is where the true heartbeat of a corporation lies. We commented earlier on how Warren Buffett measures Berkshire Hathaway's progress in terms of the annual increase in shareholders' equity. Benjamin Graham used to look for changes in working capital and that part of working capital held in cash or liquid form. As in these instances, develop your own criteria, and follow them in disciplined fashion.

THE *ETHICAL* UNFAIR ADVANTAGE

At our mundane level it is also worth going through your monthly or quarterly statements carefully, if only to develop a feel for the individual holdings in your portfolios and, from these, for how well or poorly your portfolios are doing. Even a regular daily or weekly scan of the closing prices of the stocks and fund products making up your portfolio will help you develop an experienced eye to add to the unfair advantage and the better decision-making that reliable research always brings.

Regularly feeling the pulse can tell a revealing story. If doctors and nurses do it as a matter of good practice, why not also we investors?

MAZE OR LABYRINTH?

Research can often end in what seems a blind alley or a cul-de-sac. This doesn't necessarily mean it's been wasted. Rather than being discouraged, you should establish whether these efforts have led you through a maze or a labyrinth—much better the latter than the former.

Mazes are defined as blind alleys and wrong turns set up to deceive and defeat; labyrinths, a single journey with lots of twists, turns and obstacles that sometimes seem to take one far off course but ultimately turn out to be trustworthy paths to the desired destination.

Research by definition must involve exploring the unknown, the risk versus reward aspect of investing. However, go about it thoroughly and there will be a greatly improved chance of successfully travelling a road that might seem labyrinthine at certain points, but will lead all the more surely to targeted investment goals.

Many decades ago, Winston Churchill implored Franklin Delano Roosevelt to give his war-weakened nation the tools to finish the job of defeating the Nazis. We investors also need tools—research tools that are now available to us as never before, as basic or as sophisticated as we want.

Whether you are an everyday investor, a financial planner or an investment advisor, don't be afraid to demand the facts, to ask intelligent questions and to dig as simply or as deeply as you might want or are able. It matters not whether you perform the number crunching yourself, or if you rely upon an analyst to do it for you. The key is to have at your disposal the facts to help you to make well-informed investment decisions. Don't be ashamed to follow the "kiss" (keep it simple, stupid) principle. After getting started, you might progressively want to learn more than your beginner's research, in which case the Canadian Securities Institute has much to help you to the next stage. Who knows, you might even become sufficiently hooked to end up with the coveted CFA designation!

Whatever your choice, there *is* an unfair advantage to be gained by making better decisions with reliable research—to spot opportunities as they emerge and to identify trends that warn of gathering risk.

CHAPTER 14

Pay to Play

Fees and Commissions

For more than two decades, many Canadian investors have been under a grand illusion that when it comes to the management of their portfolios, they could enjoy the financial equivalency of a free lunch. It's an illusion that first materialized in the late 1980s with the advent of the deferred sales charge on mutual fund purchases.

Up to that point, the overwhelming majority of mutual fund purchases had been paid for with upfront ("front-end") fees that were relatively high compared with today's standards. The deferred sales charge, or DSC ("back-end" fees), meant that the commission paid to purchase a mutual fund was buried among the fund's management fees and expenses. Investors would be liable for an exit fee were they to pull out their money within a specified period of time, after which the exit fees would disappear.

The illusion was that if you stayed invested long enough, you had executed an investment free of commissions. The reality, of course, was and is that nothing is free and that managers instead charged fees and expenses directly through what has come to be known as the management expense ratio (MER).

THE $5,000 COCKTAIL NAPKIN

As the markets continued their upward spiral through the 1990s, discount brokerages waged intense price wars to attract the growing population of do-it-yourself investors. Some of the most creative minds in advertising launched elaborate campaigns designed to attract these investors into the do-it-yourself arena. More often than not, these campaigns addressed the issue of cost, yet the issue of value was obscured. They left the casual observer with the impression that investing was little more than trading and implied that a low cost of trade execution was largely what separated winners from losers. Though we are sticklers for receiving value for any fees and commissions paid by us and/or the clients we represent, please remember our basic credo that successful investing is a dynamic process—it is never an unconnected series of trades.

Rapidly rising markets provide a veritable tailwind for investors, resulting in many abandoning long-established investment practices and counsel in favour of what they hope to be quick and massive gains. The old investment industry adage of "never confuse a bull market with brilliance" is something that both professional and amateur investors need to constantly remind themselves of. Expertise and experience, when applied in a consistent, disciplined manner, are valuable commodities and should not be dismissed out of hand as relics of a bygone era.

There is a well-travelled story regarding the celebrated Spanish artist Pablo Picasso that illustrates the point we so emphatically wish to make. Legend has it that Picasso was dining one evening in a fine dining establishment in New York. At one point in the evening, when his companion had stepped away from the table, Picasso was approached by a woman widely known in New York at the time as having highly cultivated taste in art, with a sizable private collection to match. The society matron gushed at meeting Picasso, asking him to sketch her portrait on a cocktail napkin for her. Picasso obliged, completing the task in under a minute. When he finished, the woman reached for the napkin but the great artist pulled it away.

He looked up at her and said, "That will be $5,000, please." Astonished, the woman stammered back at Picasso, "Five thousand dollars? But it took you less than a minute to sketch that portrait!"

"Ah, there is where you are mistaken, madam," replied the artist. "To create that," he said, pointing to the napkin portrait, "has taken me a lifetime."

There is no shortage today of competent, good and excellent financial advisors in Canada. The heightened market volatility of the past decade and tougher regulatory controls, together with an increasingly experienced and sophisticated investing public, has done much to shed the Canadian financial services industry of many of its marginal practitioners. You may not have the equivalency of a master artist handling your portfolio (or maybe you do, how are we to know?) but that's not the point. The point is that good advice is worth something. Good advice will save you as much, if not more, money than it makes for you by helping you to sidestep catastrophic declines. The larger issue is one of *value* and that is highly subjective. A good advisor will not shy away from articulating to you exactly what it is they do to earn their fees and commissions.

COST VS. VALUE

Oscar Wilde once famously wrote that a cynic is "a man who knows the price of everything and the value of nothing." Much of the criticism that has been levelled at the financial services industry has been centred on the issue of cost. The matter of value is prone to more subjective measurement, with all too often very little attention paid to it.

Throughout *Financial First Aid* we've asked you to undertake some serious soul-searching to understand what you want to achieve through investing. We've also asked you to give serious consideration to the amount of time you are realistically able to commit to your investments, and your level of expertise and real interest in acquiring more investment knowledge. Once you have reached a point where you are able to articulate what you want, you can progress to finding out who or what can help you achieve these goals. This is where the issue of value enters the picture.

A Little Self-Analysis Now Can Reduce the Risk of Disappointment Later

Here are five questions you need to ask yourself to help determine if you should or should not be a do-it-yourselfer:

- Do I want financial planning help?
- Where am I going to get my investment ideas from, and should I have someone making recommendations to me?
- Do I want to be involved with the day-to-day investment decision-making, or should I turn it all over to a portfolio manager?
- Who is going to monitor the portfolio and how often?
- How much time am I prepared to give the ongoing research necessary for the effective running of my portfolio?

How much you spend on the proper care and feeding of your portfolio is dependent in large part on the degree of professional help you want to have.

Value-Added Services From the Discounters

For the do-it-yourself investor, the focus is often on the cost element, yet here too, value is an important consideration. While discount brokers do not offer advice, their ability to perform accurate and timely trade on execution is important. During the tech stock rally of the late 1990s, one of Canada's most popular discount brokerages experienced tremendous difficulty in keeping up with the burgeoning demand for service from its clientele because it had not anticipated or prepared itself for such a surge in demand. The result was a rash of disgruntled customers, some of whom moved their business to smaller competitors who charged slightly higher trading commissions but were able to execute orders quickly.

The value proposition for a do-it-yourselfer should not be limited to trade capabilities. Many of Canada's leading discount brokerages are affiliated with major full-service brokerages and investment banks. Does your discount broker offer you access to its parent company's research library? What about financial planning tools? These are just two of the features of a full-service brokerage that will often also cross over to the discount channel as value-added services.

How "Full" Is Your Full-Service Broker?

The competition among full-service brokers for your business is extremely intense. Advisors at these firms work hard to differentiate themselves by taking on additional service staff (usually at their own expense) to offer financial planning assistance to clients and more of a personalized approach than their nearest competition.

At the head office level, full-service brokerages are constantly trying to differentiate themselves from their competitors through a variety of means, some of which include

- publishing up-to-date research reports on a wide range of stocks, trusts, REITs, mutual funds, etc.
- employing market strategists to assist their advisors in positioning client portfolios
- offering exclusive access to third-party investment managers
- having estate planning professionals on staff to assist clients
- tying investment accounts to credit cards and lines of credit in a bid to capture both the assets and liabilities columns of a client's personal balance sheet

Asset-Based Fees

The latest incarnation of the cost/value continuum is asset-based pricing, which is a nice way of saying fees. An asset-based investment account is one where a client chooses to pay his or her advisor a flat fee for service rather than commissions every time a purchase or sale is transacted.

The most significant advantage to an investor of moving from paying commissions to an asset-based fee is the heightened transparency that the fee brings to the client-advisor relationship. Even though you may have been working with your advisor for many years and have built a relationship on a solid foundation of trust, it is not at all unusual (in fact it's likely human nature) to wonder occasionally if some trades are being recommended for the sake of the portfolio or for the pay packet of the advisor, who may need to generate some commission revenue, particularly as month-end approaches. If your advisor is being paid a flat fee, much of the natural suspicion of conflicted interests is eliminated.

Just as investors are freed from paying trading commissions when their portfolios are subject to a fee, this method of paying for financial services enables investors to purchase on a no-load basis mutual funds that are not ordinarily no-load funds. In addition, access is granted to "F" class mutual funds, which are identical to their front- and back-end load fund cousins with the exception that the management expense ratio is reduced, in many cases by as much as 50 basis points (0.50%). This is because the fund company has stripped out the ongoing compensation normally paid to advisors because "F" class funds are only available for purchase in fee-based accounts.

Fixed-income purchases within a fee-based account also receive preferential treatment. When an investor purchases a bond from his or her broker, the commission is not stated in the same manner as a stock purchase or the load on a mutual fund. The broker's commission is the spread between the wholesale price of the bond and the "net to client" or NTC price of the bond. In a fee-based account, bond purchases are made at the wholesale price, which can boost the bond's yield by usually anywhere from half to three-quarters of a percentage point.

Out of the Shadows

Depending on how you invest, there can be significant cost savings in pursuing a fee-based relationship with your advisor rather than the more traditional pay-as-you-go, commission-based method. Beyond the cost savings, there is something less tangible yet of equal or perhaps even greater value: the true cost of managing your portfolio emerges from the shadows, allowing you to make a more accurate evaluation of whether you are receiving value for the fees paid to manage your portfolio.

The Benefits Are Not Universal

Not everyone should be in a fee-based program. For some investors, a pay-as-you-go, commission-based structure will prove to be the better value. These are investors who would ordinarily have very little turnover of the securities in their portfolio. Thus, an investor with a portfolio largely made up of bonds, preferred shares and high-yielding, blue-chip common stocks that will be held for a long time would tend to fit the profile of someone whose needs are likely to be better served by having a commission-based portfolio.

Just the Facts, Ma'am

How should you make the determination of whether a fee-based program is right for you? The best way we've found is to begin by taking a hard look at your past investment habits. We suggest that you needn't analyze any more than three years in the life of your portfolio. Add up what you have paid in commissions, mutual fund loads, RRSP or RRIF trustee fees, as well as any other fees that may have been tossed into the mix over that 36-month period. Don't forget to add in the MER on any mutual funds that you hold or held during the period under review.

All of the information, with the exception of the mutual fund MERs, will be found on your monthly or quarterly investment statements. These latter costs are readily obtained by calling either your advisor or the fund companies themselves, or by looking up the fund through an online service such as Globefund (www.globefund.com).

Once you have the total of what you have paid, divide that number into the 36-month average value of the account(s) in question and multiply by 12 to arrive at an average annual cost. The net result will be a percentage that can then be compared against the annual fee an advisor will quote for managing your portfolio. The fee will be quoted in terms of an annual percentage of your assets under administration with your advisor. This will make for a relatively easy "apples to apples" comparison.

Asset Based Fee Pricing vs. Traditional Commission Model

Analysis for John Smith
Period of Aug. 30/04 to Aug. 30/09

Portfolio Value as of Aug. 30, 2009 $328,500

Current Costs	Percentage	Annually	Fee based	Percentage	Annually	Monthly
MER on Mutual Funds	2.54%	$3,755	Blended Fee	1.33%	$4,369	$364
Commissions	1.22%	$3,685				
Registered Acct Fee		$133	Less Tax Deduction	0.64%	$2,097	$174
Non-deductible		$0				
Net Fee	**2.31%**	**$7,573.00**	**Net Fee**	**0.69%**	**$2,272**	**$190**

Estimated Total Annual Savings After-Tax   **$5,301**

Notes:

MER is the annual Management Expense Ratio charged on all Mutual Funds and is expressed as an average of your existing funds

Commissions are on equities only and are quoted as an average over the last 36 month period

Calculation of Tax Deduction assumes a marginal tax rate of 48%

The Net Fee is calculated as the total of all current fees expressed as a percentage of the current Portfolio Value

Virtually all the fee-based programs offered by Canadian firms today offer discounts on a sliding scale in a bid to encourage investors to consolidate all their investment holdings with the firm. It is for this reason that if you and your spouse have several investment accounts, you should conduct the 36-month review on all of the accounts and then ask for a fee quote based on the amassed total.

Another Pricing Option

Most of the major investment houses in Canada offer the choice of having a blended fee or a flat fee. A flat fee is, as the name implies, charged as a percentage of your total assets under administration. A blended fee, on the other hand, charges different fees for fixed-income and equity investments; the fee for fixed income will be smaller than the fee for equities. A more conservative investor would stand to benefit over a more aggressive growth style of investor, as the conservative investor is likely to hold a greater percentage of fixed-income investments in his or her portfolio than their growth-oriented counterpart.

If you are worried that to gain a higher fee the advisor may recommend a more aggressive, equity-driven strategy than you need, the blended fee is not right for you. It should be noted, though, that if you are entering into a relationship with an advisor and the core value of trust is not present, then maybe you need to rethink the decision to enter into that relationship in the first place.

Keep On Smilin'

Suppose you've done your analysis and found you can save money by moving from pay-as-you-go commissions to a fee-based method of compensating your advisor. The markets are rising, and so is your portfolio. The schoolboy grin on your face is rivalled only by those on the apparently very happy men on television in the Viagra ads. Will you keep on smiling, though, if the markets enter a protracted period of decline?

It's easy to spot the value when your portfolio is growing, but how wide will that smile be if you're paying to watch your portfolio decline in value? Remember, just as a rising market tide lifts all portfolios, a falling market will exert a reverse influence. This is the time when your advisor can really earn his or her fees, by limiting the slide of your portfolio's value. This is the essence of relative versus absolute performance, a subject we will explore in the next chapter.

While it is reasonable to expect your advisor to work even harder on your behalf when markets are falling rather than rising, it is unreasonable for those in a fee-based model to abandon the model simply because they can no longer discern the advantage accruing to them. In many respects, your advisor is an employee and you are the employer. If you want to have advisors working as hard or harder for you than anyone else, don't make the mistake of radically changing the compensation model at the time when you need them the most. If your advisor is not doing the job you expect, don't take half measures. Replace an inadequate advisor with someone who is willing and able to do the job.

Apples and Oranges

Much has been written over the last decade decrying the level of fees charged by mutual fund companies as reflected in their MERs. The comparison often is made to index funds and/or exchange traded funds; however, this is a little like comparing apples and oranges. We're not here to apologize for the Canadian mutual fund industry or to castigate it. We are always prepared to pay for consistent performance. If a particular mutual fund is delivering only market returns in good and bad markets then maybe the managers are not earning their keep. Before making that determination, though, we would want to be certain we were evaluating its performance in the proper context.

Index funds and exchange traded funds are what are known as passively managed investments. No daily buy or sell decisions are made by the fund manager. Instead, this type of investment mirrors the entire market index or, in the case of exchange traded funds, a specific sub-index. Because there is no ongoing management, the cost structure of this type of investment is much lower than that found even with "F" class mutual funds. It is not unusual for the fee savings on an actively managed mutual fund to be 65% to 75% of the MER of an "F" class fund.

The quid pro quo is that active management decisions, such as how much exposure to have to a market sector, or for that matter to the equity markets altogether, are left to the investor. An actively managed mutual fund will take some, if not all, of the burden of that responsibility off of your shoulders but, as you might expect, will only do so at a cost. This brings us back to the issue of value. If a fund manager can make ongoing decisions better than you could on your own with an index fund, they will have added value and are, in our view, worth the price paid.

If the performance is not there, assuming of course that the performance criteria are clearly understood, you've got some decisions to make.

Fee-Only Planners

There is a small but hardy breed of advisors who do not invest any of their clients' money. In fact, they seldom, if ever, recommend specific securities. These are fee-only financial planners who more often than not are accountants and/or certified financial planners. As part of a suite of services for the clients they serve, these advisors will work to construct a detailed asset allocation strategy as part of a detailed Investment Policy Statement. Their appeal is that because they do not represent any one mutual fund company, or stand to benefit from the purchase of one type of asset versus another, their advice is deemed to be unbiased.

Fee-based planners on occasion will bill by the hour but, in our experience, most will quote a flat fee for their services. The fee-based advisor approach can work well when the client is on a flat fee with a full-service brokerage, using the plan drawn up by the fee-only advisor as a blueprint to guide the advisor in security selection. However, the process can become quite costly if the client pays a fee to the fee-only advisor and then turns to a full-service advisor and pays commissions on transactions. Some do-it-yourself investors will utilize the services of a fee-only advisor to draw up the plan, and then use a discount broker to execute the strategy.

One major concern regarding fee-only advisors haunts us: that because fee-only planners are not engaged in daily, hands-on dealing with securities, there is a tendency to take a rather academic approach to portfolio construction. Many investors who have used the services of a fee-only planner do not have an ongoing relationship with the planner. Remember that investing is a process, not an event. Markets are dynamic by nature, as are client needs and expectations. Even the best-laid plans, not just the securities in the portfolio that result from the plan, require regular review and updating. It is for this reason that investors should engage the services of a fee-only planner only if they are willing to enter into a long-term relationship.

NO FREE LUNCH

You probably learned long ago, and we've mentioned it numerous times, that there is no such thing as a free lunch. There are costs associated with the management of a portfolio, regardless of whether you use the services of professional management or you are a hands-on, do-it-yourself type of investor. The quest to reduce the cost of investing is very necessary, because any resulting savings will flow straight to your bottom-line profit. Do not, however, lose sight of the essential element of value. Take the time to think about the level of support you want and need. That is always a good starting point.

CHAPTER 15

What's Your Number?

Benchmarking Performance

Setting benchmarks against which you can measure, over time, the progress of your portfolio is an area of investing that often sends investors down blind alleys, ultimately resulting in inaccurate or inappropriate investment decisions. In this chapter, we will examine the measurement of portfolio performance from two distinct vantage points.

The first approach takes a financial planning spin. The investor (or their advisor) works from the future to the present, and following a series of detailed calculations arrives at an average compounded rate of return necessary to meet long-range objectives. In some sense, this approach is comparable to golfers focused on lowering their handicap, unconcerned with the scores of others in their foursome.

The second approach to benchmarking performance takes on, by comparison, more of an immediate tone. It is, to once more use the golfing analogy, somewhat like tournament play: keeping score in a game against one or more opponents. In some sense, your aims for your portfolio may be comparable to playing in a ProAm tournament. You would love to be able to brag of beating the pro, but the reality is that you really are striving to remain within striking distance of the pro's score.

FAIL TO PLAN—PLAN TO FAIL

Inevitably, we all reach the stage in our life when we have to spend some serious time determining whether we are going to have enough to sustain ourselves in the manner we would like in what should be the sunset rather than the twilight of our ever-lengthening lives.

We may determine that there are many adjustments to be made to enjoy the sunset. We will be able to make some without too much fuss, like selling the family home for something smaller and cheaper once the children have moved out. (Some might suggest that this should be done immediately once the last child has left the nest to ensure there is no return trip!) Dropping a seldom-used club membership and getting by with only one family car are other tactics readily used by retirees to conserve capital.

But what if we've cut back and downsized and still lack the capital for the Sunbelt time-share we were going to commit to? And what of those travel plans we had hoped to fulfill someday? For those who have had the misfortune to fall into poor health, rising health-related costs only add to the concerns. No one wants to depend on their children for financial support in their later years. What a scary thought that our main retirement problem could be that of living too darn long!

Unfortunately, there is undoubtedly a lot to keep us from concentrating on sobering thoughts like these. It's far better that these thoughts happen sooner rather than later, leaving enough time to undertake an individualized savings and investment program aimed at ensuring that ultimate "margin of safety" the great Benjamin Graham regarded as imperative—or the moat that his disciple Warren Buffett repeatedly emphasizes as a measure of portfolio protection.

Let's face it, we shouldn't want to be beholden to government support programs in an era of rising longevity, taxes at very turn and soaring health costs. A recent study conducted for the American Association of Retired Persons (AARP) concluded that the U.S. social security system could run out of money in the early 2040s, a decade when it is estimated that more than 70 million people will be counting on it as their main source of retirement income. In Canada, the Canada Pension Plan mercifully appears to be in much better shape. We also have our Old Age Security program. Nevertheless, their solvency will be tested increasingly as a rising proportion of the Canadian population enters retirement.

WHAT'S THE SCORE?

You've likely heard of cooperative games where no one keeps score. Supposedly, they foster team spirit and protect fragile egos from soul-crushing defeat at executive retreats and in the kindergarten classroom. (Do you really need us to make the painfully obvious joke here?) These games are more than a little reminiscent of the *Seinfeld* episode where George and Jerry are at a woman's apartment for a party to celebrate the New York marathon and cheer on the runners. Just as George finishes proclaiming himself to be "king of the idiots," the party host leans from her window to greet the runners, screaming a full-throated "You're all winners." With exquisite timing, Jerry turns to George and says, "Suddenly, a contender for the throne emerges."

Call us knuckle-dragging, unenlightened, slack-jawed mouth-breathers, but we want to know the score. You need to know the score, particularly when it comes to your financial situation. Are you winning or losing? We don't like to lose, and will work twice as hard to avoid the sting of defeat as to savour a victory. We're pretty certain that when it comes to your portfolio you feel pretty much the same. How will you ever know if you are ahead or behind if no one is keeping score?

This, in fact, is what *Financial First Aid* is all about: diagnosing what is wrong, and prescribing what to do to move toward an investment goal like secure retirement and staying financially healthy. An essential three-part process will become progressively easier with at least some basic investment knowledge, the provision of which is another purpose of this book. In addition, your personalized investing will need to be quantified and measured as you proceed down that retirement road aided and abetted by a portfolio of financial assets designed to last longer than you do.

RETIREMENT CALCULATIONS

Later in this chapter we will focus on benchmarking portfolio performance as part of the accompanying accountability that also will be essential. Clearly, the time available will be vital in determining how your retirement portfolio should be balanced between fixed income and equities, as well as the degree of risk that it prudently can be exposed to. The more time there is, the more compounding will be able to work its magic, and the lower will be the overall goal attainment risks. Conversely, the less time to work with, the greater the risks and the higher the likelihood of enforced retirement adjustments.

Considerations like these will help you draw your own personalized road map to retirement. They will also set the stage for the ultimate question every investor should be called upon to answer, ideally with the help of their financial advisor. In full, the question involves how much you need your portfolio to grow in order to retire in the style you would like, and what the necessary average rate of investment return will translate into. In short, it's a succinct "What's *your* (retirement) Number?"

The answer to this question will give an idea of the type of retirement we have to look forward to financially. It will also help us to determine what preparatory investment actions we sensibly should be taking to get to where we would like to be—the sooner and more purposefully, the better.

We suggest that as a first step, you find an online retirement calculator in which to input key data. There are plenty available on the Web free of charge. Or, you can visit the website of just about any major bank, mutual fund company or investment house you care to choose. There's also your financial advisor. All offer or can provide you with online financial calculators that are easy to use. Input your responses to such questions as:

- When do I plan to retire?
- By how much do I expect my annual income to grow over my remaining working life?
- What do I estimate my annual living expenses likely to be over this period?
- How will my annual pension contributions add up? Do I intend to contribute the statutory annual maximum to my RRSP (incrementally if I belong to a company pension plan, fully if I don't)?

And, best assisted by your financial advisor, answer such questions as:

- What average annual rate of inflation should be assumed?
- What rate of return might I realistically expect on a properly balanced, risk-weighted portfolio both up to and in retirement?

Now push the button to find out what your accumulated retirement nest egg will need to be and hey, presto! There's your Number. You could well end up staring at your screen in stunned disbelief.

INCREDIBLE? MAYBE NOT

Simple rules of thumb will corroborate that this seemingly incredible number is indeed in the ballpark. In his excellent book, *The Number*, Lee Eisenberg estimated that to stop work at 65 and live to 90 you would need to multiply your current income by 40 if you are 30 years or younger; by 30 if you're between 40 and 49; and by 25 if you are 50 or older.

Despite your dazed reaction, remember this target number is in future dollars and that compounding can be very powerful. Then go do the math and start feeling better, and also more determined.

Thus, if your retirement portfolio earned a reinvestable 6% annually, it would double in 12 years; if 8%, then over 9 years; if 10%, in a little over 7 years. Add permissible RRSP contributions, and determine how much you can add annually to your non-registered portfolio in cash terms, and you could well find your Number becoming a much less stomach-churning proposition.

On the other hand, if your estimates of what you can realistically invest in the time frame available to you keep coming up short, you'll have to consider alternatives to close the retirement gap and remove the worry of your retirement chart showing your portfolio being exhausted way too early.

One such alternative might be to weight your portfolio(s) more heavily with equities than you would otherwise have liked, perhaps even 100% in equities for their prospective higher-risk returns. If this risk is judged excessive given your personal circumstances and resources, another alternative might be to cut back on your retirement lifestyle expectations; for example, to face the reality you will have to get by on a pro rata 80% or 60% or 50% (rather than 100%) of your pre-retirement income. Or, the taller your retirement order remains, you might have to accept that you will need to work that many years longer, or plan on part-time work in retirement, e.g., doctors doing locums, business people taking on consultancy assignments.

"WAITERS"

While there is no single correct answer or perfect benchmark, and while your Number will depend on how you choose and can afford to live, the worst of all worlds surely is to have no answer at all to what you might need in retirement. Or to join that new class of citizens dubbed "waiters" by Barry Fish and Leslie Kotzer in their self-published book, *The Family Fight: Planning to Avoid It*—made up of financially unsuccessful people waiting for their parents to die so they can get "their share" of an unknown and possibly disputed inheritance. Or to depend on government or your children's largesse.

The answer may not be comforting when you go through what should be a mandatory retirement exercise for all of us. Nevertheless, we can vouch for the fact that you will feel better for it afterwards. It's likely you also will be heartened by what can be done, and the positive adjustments that could be in store once your retirement investment plan develops some self-generating, upside momentum.

In going about an exercise like this to settle on the number—or range of numbers—that's best for you, the younger you are and the sooner you begin a serious personalized investment plan, the better. The older you are and the later you begin, the less likely you'll achieve that desired retirement nest egg, and the higher the retirement sacrifices you are going to have to make. Time waits for no one, most definitely not in an exercise like this. What's *your* Number?

LET ME BE FRANK . . .

Frank is 38 years old, single and earning $85,000 per year. He is self-employed, and as such has no company pension plan. His pension plan is his RRSP, which is presently valued at $300,000. Frank would like to retire at age 60, and live on 75% of his present income so that he can indulge in his passion for visiting the world's wine regions and sampling their wares. He is able to contribute an average of $15,000 per year to his RRSP.

We begin the process of getting Frank's Number by figuring out what 75% of his present income will be 23 years from now. We've assumed an average annual rate of inflation of 2%. Using this assumption, Frank will be hoping to receive an income of $100,527 in his 60th year, growing this sum by 2% each year to offset the effects of inflation.

We've now solved the first part of the puzzle. We know that Frank has to have enough capital by age 60 to support an income of $100,000 (we're all friends here, so let's round off the numbers), indexed by 2% per annum. How much capital will be needed to generate that income stream for what could be 30 years or more? Breathe deep—it's $2.17 million. And remember, today's generation is more active in retirement and generally is living longer than the generation that preceded it. We may be shortchanging Frank by assuming just 30 years.

Using Frank's current RRSP balance of $300,000, and assuming that he will continue to make contributions of $15,000 per year, growing at 2%, we must find out what average annual compounded rate of return Frank will need to earn on his assets to have him sipping Syrah in Sydney. The math shows that if Frank were to earn an average annual compounded rate of return of 6.5% on his money, he should have no trouble in amassing the $2.17 million he will need to fund his retirement lifestyle needs.

The Courage to Underperform

Now that Frank has his Number in percentage terms, 6.5%, he can set out to develop an asset allocation strategy that will offer him the greatest prospect of consistently achieving it. The beauty of this method is that if Frank can manage to tune out the distractions of the market, he will be far less prone to making irrational investment decisions. Frank will have what Brian Milner, writing in the *Globe and Mail* in May 2009, termed as "the courage to underperform." He will know specifically what he must earn to meet his objectives. Every decision he makes will be focused on protecting what he has earned so far, and on achieving his target—not on trying to outpace that oblivious competitor, the market.

But what if the calculations came back with a required growth rate that simply does not square with historic experience? What if the number was 12% or 15%? This is where a responsible professional can offer a cool, rational point of view. A reliable advisor will point out that generating annual returns in the low to mid-teens with great regularity is a pretty tall order, particularly when we find ourselves in an era of relatively low inflation and low interest rates. If this were the case, we would ask Frank to consider his options.

- Could he work until age 65 instead of 60?
- Is he willing or able to contribute more capital each year than he is at present?
- Could he live on less than the desired 75%?
- Would he consider supplementing his retirement income with occasional consulting work?

Changing the assumptions ever so slightly, particularly when lengthy periods of time are available, can affect the outcome considerably—and often comfortingly.

BENCHMARKS

Once you've got your Number and battened down the required average annual return to reach it, the focus switches to relative performance. This is where an investor makes a comparison between his or her portfolio (or specific components of the portfolio) and one or more of the dozens of benchmark indexes to choose from.

Take a look through your portfolio, gaining a sense of where you have the most representation. If your portfolio is primarily composed of Canadian large-capitalization stocks (either through direct ownership or through the indirect ownership of a mutual fund or other manager-run investment product), then the S&P/TSX Composite Index is probably a good benchmark. If bonds take up much of the available space in your portfolio, then a representative bond index is a more appropriate measuring stick.

Apples to Apples

Regardless of which benchmark indexes you use to measure against the performance of your portfolio, make sure they reflect the investments contained within your portfolio. What you are seeking to avoid is a comparison of apples and oranges. You want, to the greatest degree possible, to be making apples-to-apples comparisons.

Beat the Street

It's only natural for investors to want to beat the market, thereby attaining or exceeding their targeted Number that much more readily. There is no shortage of investment books, articles, seminars and studies on the subject. The fact of the matter is that only a precious few managers consistently outperform the "street" (market index) on a consistent basis. It's all really a false set of expectations. The quest to beat the market when indexes are on the rise requires taking on increasing quantities of risk to produce ever-greater investment returns. Eventually, the heightened risk catches up with the investor in a boom-to-bust scenario.

We encourage our clients to remain aware of how they are performing relative to a benchmark so that there is always an effective barometer. What we discourage our clients from doing is adopting a benchmark as their personal target. It's simply a counterproductive exercise.

Widely Used Benchmarks

This is by no means a complete listing of all of the relevant benchmark indexes that investors can use to evaluate the performance of their portfolios. There also are countless sub-indexes that follow industry groups. These permit an investor to have the ability to compare the performance of a stock or sector-specific mutual fund against their counterparts. An example would be to compare the performance of Suncor Energy against the performance of the S&P/TSX Oil & Gas Sub-Index over a specified time frame.

We won't waste your time by cramming this book full of filler by giving you a tidy little description of every big-name index out there. The point of the exercise is to give you an understanding of the big North American, global and international stock indexes in order to get you started. You own a Japanese mutual fund? Then do an Internet search on the Nikkei 225 or the Topix. A European fund? Go to the Dow Jones website and have a look at the Dow Jones EURO STOXX index. Your fund company and/or your advisor should be able to give you some insights into what are appropriate benchmarks for your portfolio.

S&P/TSX Composite: This is the most widely followed benchmark index for stocks in Canada. The index is run by Standard & Poor's, and represents up to three hundred of the largest publicly traded companies. The S&P/TSX Composite is a market-weighted index, which means value can be heavily affected by the performance of the stocks that it tracks. For example, in the halcyon spring of 2000, a high-flying Nortel rose to represent some 30% of the index. Today, oil stocks and their related sub-index account for close to one-quarter of the index. Therefore, the index needs to be treated with some caution. Index investing proponents frequently treat a given index as the ideal representation of the market. Often these people ignore the natural distortions that can occur within an index.

Dow Jones Industrial Average: Commonly referred to as simply "the Dow," this index is the most famous and widely known of all stock indexes. Composed of 30 large, well-established American corporations that are widely considered to be among the leaders in their respective industries, the Dow is what is known as a price-weighted index. This is viewed by some as a key disadvantage because it means that a stock that trades at $100 but has a market capitalization of $1 billion (the number of shares outstanding multiplied by the share price) will receive a bigger weighting in the index than a stock that trades at $50 yet has a market capitalization of $5 billion. It is because of the price weighting and the representation of just 30 stocks that the Dow is dismissed by some critics as not being a fair representation of the whole market.

Standard & Poor's 500: This is the index most often cited by professionals as the best benchmark for U.S. stocks. As the name implies, it tracks five hundred companies chosen for their market size, liquidity and sector. While there are some mid-sized companies in the index, most companies are considered to be large-capitalization ones. The S&P 500 is a market-weighted index.

NASDAQ Composite: This index tracks all of the stocks listed on the NASDAQ exchange. Because so many "new economy" companies are listed on the NASDAQ, this composite index is considered a heart rate monitor of sorts for the more than five thousand largely technology stocks listed on this exchange. Though this makes the NASDAQ Composite a useful tool for gaining an expansive view of the market, critics claim that the index is composed of far too many small, illiquid stocks. The performance of these small names can sometimes be quite volatile, making the index itself more volatile than would otherwise be the case.

MSCI World: For a snapshot of how the global capital markets are performing, many professional investors turn to the MSCI World Index. This market-weighted index is a benchmark for large, publicly traded companies in approximately 150 countries around the world. It is frequently used as a benchmark for comparing the performance of many global mutual funds.

MSCI EAFE: The primary difference between this index and the MSCI World Index is the EAFE (Europe, Australia and Far East) constraint, which means that the MSCI EAFE Index omits stocks that are listed in emerging markets and in North America. Twenty-one individual country indexes are represented in this index, which is typically used as a benchmark for international funds. International funds differ from global funds in that a global fund manager normally must invest just about anywhere in the developed world. This compares with an international fund manager, who usually must invest anywhere in the developed world with the exception of North America. The MSCI EAFE Index is a market-weighted index.

ABSOLUTE VS. RELATIVE RETURNS

In his groundbreaking 2004 book on investing entitled *Bull's Eye Investing*, author John Mauldin built his case for the need to seek out consistent absolute returns rather than striving to achieve relative returns.

Absolute or Relative

Absolute return: The rate of return on a specific investment or investment portfolio, taken as a stand-alone number. Absolute returns are usually compared against a target return that an investor has stated as their desired investment performance.

Relative return: The rate of return that an investor has achieved relative to a specific market index. For example, if the S&P/TSX Composite Index is down 10% in a given year, but an investor's portfolio is down 2% over that same time period, that portfolio will be considered to have delivered a superior relative return.

Mauldin believes that for the foreseeable future, the world's capital markets will fail to match the kind of wealth-building growth that typified the 1980s and 1990s. His main reason for thinking this way is the demographic trends that have the baby boomer generation rapidly approaching retirement over the next 10 to 15 years. Approaching and safely achieving retirement is when the demand and need for consistent investment gains is of greatest importance for any investor. It is precisely for this reason that Mauldin urges his readers to focus on absolute return strategies such as those found through alternative investment managers.

Mauldin's reasoning is entirely understandable. As retirement draws nearer, the need for consistency in terms of investment performance grows. Swinging for the fences with each appearance at home plate brings an above-average probability of strikeouts. For a young investor, with many years of working for a livelihood and portfolio contributions ahead, temporary setbacks as the result of a financial strikeout can be repaired over time. However, that same luxury is not available to the investor approaching retirement. Far better to advance the runners on base, in our view, than to risk an "out" if retirement is five years or less away.

YOU'VE GOT THE DESTINATION, NOW GET A MAP

Instead of flying blind, that worst of all worlds, you should have your own road map to retirement. Tools like the MapQuest program that helped guide Michael to Borsheim's (a trip you'll learn about in the next chapter) are readily available and simple to use. Once you have arrived at your Number, you and your financial advisor can map out your journey using an Investment Policy Statement or equivalent investment plan as a guide. That document is where everything we've described in *Financial First Aid* will begin coming together in a cohesive plan. In the next chapter we'll explore what needs to go into a carefully crafted Investment Policy Statement and how, once it is implemented, occasional road closures and detours will never push you off your intended course.

Best of all, by going about it this way you will have considerably reduced—if not eliminated—the risk of you and/or your spouse living to 90 and having to ask your kids for cash. Chances are, knowing your Number will also bring you the quiet confidence from which carefully considered investment decisions flow.

CHAPTER 16

Following the Yellow Brick Road

Investment Policy Statements

Just as he has every spring for many years, Michael makes the journey—a pilgrimage of sorts—to Omaha Nebraska for the annual meeting of the shareholders of Berkshire Hathaway Inc. For three days, devotees of all ages descend from across North America and around the world for the annual "Woodstock of Capitalism."

An annual affair like no other keeps breaking every attendance record—this year 35,000, up from 31,000 in 2008. What a far cry from the few hundred when Michael first attended a Berkshire Hathaway annual meting in 1994!

Transport is essential in getting around a pleasant but spread-out heartland city. The driving can present its own challenges—finding one's far-flung hotel (accommodation is always difficult), getting to the functions and the annual meeting, negotiating a maze of highways, not to forget the inevitable road construction diversions. Roughly knowing one's way around isn't enough, and Michael has gotten lost often enough to come to depend on MapQuest or GPS support. In other words, he has learned to have a well-laid-out plan, without which he wouldn't be able to reach his intended destinations as readily and three days of exceptional professional development wouldn't be nearly as valuable. It's the same in successful investing, just that the targets are different.

SET THE COORDINATES

Replace the departure points and arrival destinations with where you are currently in terms of your finances and where you will need to be at some set time in the future. Instead of day-to-day events and expenses, substitute years and financial contributions for the attainment of lifetime goals. A thoughtful approach to investing must be guided by a set of clearly articulated objectives. The drafting of an Investment Policy Statement (IPS) should always be the starting point of a journey on which we should all be embarked.

Just as those annual trips to Omaha require careful planning and en route adjustments to get full value, so does a well-planned investment portfolio designed to serve as a vehicle to reach the long-term destination of financially independent retirement. The preliminary step in laying out an Investment Policy Statement easily can be summarized in a statement worthy of Yankees great Yogi Berra: You'll never get to where you're going if you don't know where you're going.

THE TRINITY

That all-important Number described in the previous chapter may be representative of the investor's goal(s), but a careful plan needs to be drawn up for how to achieve it. The execution of this plan also will need to be measured and accounted for along the way. The successful investing trinity includes three essentials that should function in unison: ongoing performance targets, accountability and the Investment Policy Statement itself to tie it all together.

Every investment relationship must begin with the prospective client supplying basic information about himself or herself: full name, address, date of birth, social insurance number, employment information, marital status, family particulars and the type of investment account(s) needing to be opened. The investment industry's mandatory Know Your Client (KYC) form also requires the disclosure of salient information about net worth (annual income, assets and liabilities), the level of risk to be run (high, medium, low), the objectives (short-, medium- and long-term; capital gains and/or income), previous investment experience (in stocks, bonds, mutual funds, etc.) and the knowledge of investing (sophisticated, limited, average, none). While the KYC document is a useful starting point, it is not enough by itself. A truly successful client-advisor relationship needs a whole lot more.

Opening an investment account is an undertaking in which the clearer the paper trail the better. To get things properly understood and started for ongoing reference and, heaven forbid, in case there are future disputes, even the most basic of investment needs should be clarified—in writing.

Many advisors are happy to work off the KYC Form. Others will also make their own notes during the initial interview and any further meetings to set up the account. Some like filling in more expansive questionnaires (for example, an estate planning questionnaire) to record the facts and understanding they will need. There usually will be follow-up letters summarizing what is planned. Some firms like to go through the paperwork page by page on the signing of an engagement agreement with a new client. Regardless of how it is done, have something down on paper to go by. Setting down in writing your agreed-upon points at the outset can go a long way toward avoiding potentially costly and damaging disagreements later on.

In a perfect world, simple point-form notes kept in your client file to record the minutes of your meetings would suffice. In a perfect world, there would be no misunderstandings, and neither would there be any forgetfulness. In a perfect world, investment decisions would be devoid of emotion. Let's get our heads out of the clouds and remember that the world we live in is full of imperfection. In the real world, what is required and agreed upon should be recorded in a properly considered and drafted Investment Policy Statement.

CHARTING YOUR COURSE: ESSENTIAL ELEMENTS OF AN IPS

Like the MapQuest or GPS that Michael finds essential in Omaha, a carefully crafted IPS takes the process one giant leap beyond the basic outline of assets, liabilities and risk tolerance found within the Know Your Client Form. A sound IPS addresses four basic elements:

1. Quantifying and time-bounding the investment objectives
2. Defining the asset allocation policy
3. Setting out management procedures (dos and don'ts for the portfolio manager)
4. Delineating performance benchmarks and the frequency of performance reporting (monthly, quarterly or semi-annually)

Outlining the Objectives

With an IPS, an investor can expect a document that clearly outlines what is expected from their investment portfolio and provides guidelines on what steps the advisor/

portfolio manager, etc. can and cannot take in the management of the portfolio. An example of this is in the minimum acceptable credit quality for fixed-income securities in the portfolio. A risk-averse client may have his or her IPS declare that fixed-income investments must carry a credit rating of single "A" or better.

An IPS is designed to map out in careful detail the investment goals and the measures and procedures needed to attain them. According to the Canadian Securities Institute's textbook on *Portfolio Management Techniques*, the role of the IPS is to "clearly state the client's objectives and constraints, as well as to detail the tools and strategies available to the manager to meet the client's objectives, subject to the client's constraints."

Familiarity with Investment Policy Statements is also a vital component of the Chartered Financial Analyst qualification, with CFA candidates even asked to memorize that the IPS consists of two primary factors: objectives and constraints. The objectives are risk and return; the constraints are time frame, degree of accompanying liquidity, taxes, legal and regulatory requirements, and unique needs.

Documentation like this usually is required in precise detail at the pension fund and institutional levels, where it is often also a legal necessity. A conspicuous example, the IPS for the University of California General Endowment Pool runs to approximately 60 pages, in which investment goals and policies, fiduciary oversight procedures, performance objectives, and asset class and manager guidelines are spelled out in copious detail and are supported by exhaustive appendices.

While preparation like this needn't be nearly as onerous at the individual investor level, a good IPS will bring necessary discipline to both client and advisor—even more so if it is written in clearly understandable language (as opposed to "legalese"). It will help to keep emotions in check through periods of market turbulence, when clients and their advisors will find they are better able to coexist and work together.

Define the Asset Allocation Policy

Now that your objectives have been clarified and quantified, the next stage in creating a workable Investment Policy Statement is to spell out the asset allocation that will strike the balance between risk and return on an ongoing basis. Embedded as part of this stage are guidelines as to when and how the advisor should rebalance the portfolio. Be careful here to allow your advisor enough latitude so that he or she will not be compelled to prematurely cut short winning positions. Similarly, a good asset allocation policy will set out minimum weightings for certain asset classes.

Here is a typical example of an asset allocation policy Bryan has set down for some of his clients.

- cash and equivalents: 5%–15%
- high-yield bonds: 0%–5%
- investment-grade bonds: 20%–35%
- real estate investment trusts (REITs): 15%–20%
- small-cap Canadian equities: 5%–10%
- mid-cap Canadian equities: 10%–15%
- large-cap Canadian equities: 25%–35%
- large-cap American equities: 15%–25%

From the above holding limits, it is then possible to recommend a portfolio. One possible portfolio that could have been initially constructed from these limits is illustrated below.

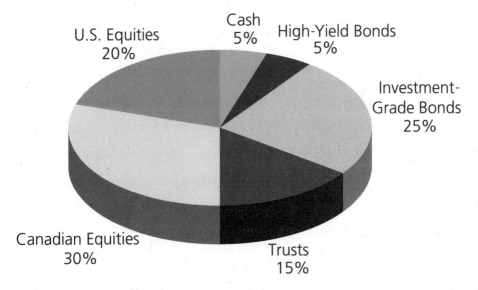

Under New Management

From an advisor's perspective, the heart of the IPS is the section that concerns the selection, monitoring and evaluation of the performance of the investments making their way into the portfolio. These same three elements can be used for situations where third-party investment managers have been utilized to manage a portfolio.

This is another prime example of where planning ahead and putting agreed-upon points in writing will make life a lot less acrimonious for everyone when markets become troublesome.

Just as constraints are placed in the asset allocation section on how much or how little representation each particular asset class should have in the portfolio, so too should there be clearly documented constraints on the inclusion or exclusion of certain types of investments, industry categories or geographic representations. As a matter of ethical concern, for example, an investor may not wish to have any tobacco-related stocks in his or her portfolio.

This section of the IPS also can be used to state what the minimum acceptable credit quality is for a fixed-income investment to make its way into the portfolio.

We Need to Talk

One of the most frequent causes of a breakdown in the relationship between advisor and client is poor communication. This can come in many forms, from regular conversations that fail to get to the heart of the matter, to long periods where the advisor and client are out of contact. The IPS should address the issue of communication clearly. It should spell out how often the client and the advisor are going to sit down to discuss the progress of the portfolio. The client should know in advance what will be covered in these meetings because it will be spelled out clearly in the IPS.

Investment Policy Statements (or their equivalent) should also be regarded as dynamic documents not to be locked away and forgotten. Instead, they should be kept handy for regular reference and for adjustment when investor needs and market conditions change, as they now seem to be doing more and more frequently. Whatever the form of documentation, carefully recording the relationship between investor and advisor can only facilitate the investment process to follow.

Benchmarking Performance: Milestones Along the Road

Hand in hand with the road map and the launching of the portfolio are the benchmarks that will be needed to measure how the "journey" is progressing. It is through the selection of benchmarks like the S&P 500 Index, the Dow Jones Industrial Average and the TSX Composite Index that you and your advisor will be able to determine whether your portfolio is on or off course to achieving planned targets.

In addition to needing to know how his or her portfolio is faring relative to the markets as a whole, every serious investor also will want to compare it with other similarly structured portfolios and/or mutual funds. It's not hard to measure the latest monthly statements against those of earlier periods. A comparison of the most recent portfolio total with earlier totals will provide the appreciation or depreciation over the period being measured (adjusted for any deposits or withdrawals).

Next, add the income that has been received and divide by the average value of the portfolio over the period to obtain the yield. Then add the two together—capital appreciation/depreciation and income yield—and you will have the total actual return on your portfolio, which you will then be able to compare with the returns on corresponding benchmarks.

An exercise like this is best done over a calendar year, or at least the preceding 12-month period. The market benchmarks usually are readily available in the financial press or from your advisor. If your portfolio is balanced between equities and fixed income, you'll want to average the benchmark returns to see how your return compares. If, for example, yours is a portfolio balanced evenly between equities and fixed income, and the total annual returns on related market indexes were 8% and 4%, respectively, then your benchmark return against which to compare would be 6%.

As we noted in the last chapter, the point of this exercise is to give you a reliable measuring stick against which you can track your progress. That progress almost certainly suffered a setback in a year like 2008, but how you fared still can be meaningfully compared with the misfortunes of the markets as a whole and universes of comparable mutual and other professionally managed funds. Portfolio performance never occurs in a straight line.

Distant Early Warning

All the more after an *annus horribilis* like 2008, you should be prepared to give your portfolio and your advisor a reasonable amount of time to do the expected job. We prefer to measure account performance over four continuously moving periods—five years, three years, one year and three months. We then compare these measurements with the markets as a whole, and also against comparable professionally managed funds.

What really counts in an exercise like this are the relative performance rankings over five years and three years; that is, periods long enough to include market ups and downs, as well as exceptional bear markets like 2000–2002 and 2007–2009. This gives an advisor or a portfolio manager ample opportunity to show their mettle. Equally, you don't need to wait three years before passing judgment on their work. Just as making dramatic transformations to the composition of your portfolio after a week or a month would be ludicrous, so too would be waiting an extended period of time before taking action to rectify a portfolio that is failing to meet reasonable expectations. We recommend you use a rolling 12-month period as your distant early warning system.

ACCOUNTABILITY

Back to the accountability leg of the proverbial "investment stool." It's an old term that takes on fresh meaning as new and improved measuring tools are developed, and debacles like asset-backed commercial paper, subprime-mortgage collapses and Madoff-type scams provide fresh challenges. Evidence of the need for improved accountability and transparency is increasingly evident in reporting systems that are enabling advisors to provide their clients with easy-to-understand performance-related information at the click of a button.

However, the numbers tell only part of the story. Analysis of performance over specified periods of time by someone possessing both experience and expertise inevitably will be necessary to keep your portfolio from straying too far off course.

The markets are dynamic by nature. Course corrections are inescapable. This is why it is imperative that the frequency and terms of performance reporting and communication, personified by accountability, play an integral role in the drafting of a worthwhile IPS.

In the final instance, investing must always involve the unpredictable and the unforeseen, never more than in recent years. What a difference if performance can be realistically measured and progressively accounted for through thick and thin! You can hold your advisor fully accountable, but you must be accountable, too. This way, one plus one could add up to considerably more than two.

Facilitating Owner-Partnership

At the meetings Michael never tires of attending, Messrs. Buffett and Munger treat attendees to a memorable annual lesson in owner-partnership, which is what they believe successful investing should be all about. Warren and Charlie simply love the idea of thinking and behaving like owners, and the idea of relationships between corporations and their stakeholders that are built on "seamless trust."

Near-term earnings and share price fluctuations don't matter to them, but results over a long period of time do. The Berkshire record speaks for itself. This record also suffered a setback in 2008, the worst year in the 44 years since Buffett and Munger took over, though much less than their S&P 500 Index benchmark. Between 1965 and the end of 2008, book value nonetheless grew to $70,530 from an initial $19 per Class "A" share, a rate of 20.3% compounded annually. In addition, the annual growth in per share book value exceeded the annual return on the S&P 500 Index (dividends included) in 39 of these 44 years. Some road map, some benchmark!

The accountability to their shareholders, i.e., their owner-partners, couldn't be more transparent or understandable. They are rightfully proud of their disciplined yet simple recipe for success. If these consummate value investors can use benchmarks so successfully, we should want to equip ourselves similarly. Accountability would then take on an added meaning for us as well.

AS TIME GOES BY

Just as Michael's trips in Omaha often take unexpected detours (even with MapQuest and GPS assistance), so too will your financial journey. A good guidance system in the form of a personalized and thorough Investment Policy Statement will help ensure that you reach your ultimate destination safely and on time.

The process itself of drafting an Investment Policy Statement is one that will strengthen the bond between you and your advisor, permitting the advisor to understand both your wants and needs on a deeper level than would otherwise be the case. Putting the outcome of these initial discussions into a written, time-bounded format will go a long way to ensuring that there is less room for misunderstanding or disagreement as time goes by.

CHAPTER 17

Outpatient Treatment

We set the background for *Financial First Aid* in the fear-filled autumn of 2008. More precisely, it was Monday, September 29, when a fateful vote by the U.S. House of Representatives inexorably ushered in a "new normal" world of big government, bailout, fiscal stimulus, state ownership, sweeping regulatory change, and soaring debts and deficits. General Electric CEO Jeffrey Immelt summarizes well what happened: "The Government has moved in next door and it ain't leaving." A setting like this can only bring intensified risks and new investor challenges—volatility, inflation and radically changing financial markets.

We have traced how investors endured and what they needed to do to survive two of the most tumultuous periods in stock market history—periods that have featured extremes in investor pessimism and exuberance. Over these years we've had the most spectacular bull market and two savage bear markets. Seldom have investors been put to the test against extremes like these.

As the markets continued their relentless upward trajectory in the 1990s and on into a Y2K-free new millennium, investors and their advisors showed increasing overconfidence. Few foresaw the financial bloodletting that was to follow, let alone took precautionary provision in their investment planning. This became the genesis for *Financial First Aid:* to diagnose the ailments that have afflicted so many portfolios, to prescribe necessary remedies and to engage in a fitness regimen for lasting financial health.

As opportunities lead to new-found prosperity, risk is magnified, and even more so when leveraging is involved. It's a dual-edged sword that all investors must contend with. And it's precisely because of today's enhanced opportunities and accompanying risks that more investors will, from time to time, need first aid to soothe the financial bumps and scrapes along the way. It's a situation that is somewhat analogous to the proliferation of sports-injury clinics as people become more active well into, and often beyond, middle age.

The legendary Lord Keynes's dour yet apt observation that "markets can stay irrational longer than you can stay solvent" is a sobering reminder of the need to temper optimism with prudence. Even at the best of times and now more than ever, risk is the investor's constant companion. The irrationality Keynes spoke of only makes it a more difficult beast to tame. Even when markets reach dizzying heights, risk is always lurking nearby. Being constantly conscious of risk—and how to handle it—ranks among the most valuable lessons we hope to leave with you.

QUALITY IS NEVER AN ACCIDENT

This doesn't necessarily mean one should take a fatalistic approach to risk. Instead, it gets us to another primary purpose of *Financial First Aid:* namely, to remind you that when it comes to investing, that old Rosemary Clooney hit—"Everything Old Is New Again"—is an apt description. Expect irrationality and be prepared to confront it head on. It may be trite to say this, but we want you to prepare for the worst and hope for the best, staying financially healthy in order to achieve the long-range goals you've set for yourself. We remain enthusiastic believers in the long-term viability of the capital markets provided we as investors treat market forces, which are in many respects like forces of nature, with care and respect.

Professional athletes, artists and musicians can make their challenges appear simple; however, the mastery of their craft doesn't happen without sacrifice. What they do with seeming effortlessness is the result of endless patience, dedication and determination, far from the roar of the crowd. Success in the arena that is the world's financial markets requires the same qualities as those of the virtuoso musician and the champion athlete. Just think of Warren Buffett and John Templeton to appreciate what we mean. Why not you? Never forget that exceptional performance comes as a result of persistence, willpower and discipline—never dumb luck.

Those who are not prepared to commit the requisite time and patience to their investing very easily can become overwhelmed. For many individual investors, going it alone is a far too daunting a task. Having a reliable, trusted advisor by your side to exercise dispassionate reason at those critical junctures when emotion overcomes logic can save you many times what you may have to pay in fees or commissions.

We're not so naive as to think that even with professional help there won't be a fair share of cuts and bruises along the way. Everyone, including your authors, has the battle scars to prove it. Instead, in *Financial First Aid* we've tried to point the way to a more consistently successful portfolio, to equip you with the knowledge and the confidence to deal with the inevitable setbacks as you remain focused on attaining well-planned investment goals.

EARLY DETECTION

Study after study has shown that the key to survival with many once-incurable diseases is early detection. Scores of men now are screened regularly for prostate cancer and an even greater number of women are checked regularly for early signs of breast cancer. The net result is a greatly improved rate of detection and survival. A similar situation exists regarding the long-term state of your financial health. Early detection through the careful measurement of your portfolio's performance against pre-selected benchmarks will go a long way to helping you identify and respond to trouble before it can cause permanent damage to your financial well-being.

To be a long-term investor is, by definition, to be an optimist. Our final piece of advice for you is to take lessons from history, but always look to the future if you wish to be a successful investor. Recent years have brought more than their fair share of exceptional challenges and opportunities. Optimists that we are, we believe the opportunities have outnumbered the challenges, though at times that seemed highly improbable. We see no reason why it should be any different in a more volatile and risk-laden future.

We hope we've left you with a renewed sense of confidence that the future is not pre-ordained. With *Financial First Aid* we've sought to offer you practical advice on how to overcome inevitable setbacks and push ahead to meet your goals. You always have choices. The sheer range of financial tools at your disposal today has never been greater. Your challenge, in fact every investor's challenge, is to ensure that you use the most appropriate "tool" for the job at hand. With virtually limitless choice that task can seem daunting, but you need not take on the challenge alone.

We are not suggesting that the obstacles faced by investors over the span of this first decade of the new millennium will be easily swept aside. For most of us, bull markets of innovation and productivity have led to an elongated upward sloping line of prosperity almost as far back as we can remember. As we write these words, there has been a reckoning of sorts. A corresponding bull market also has risen in hubris; leverage, a scourge we've warned about repeatedly in the preceding chapters, has laid low far too many once venerable financial institutions as well as private investors from all walks of life. Deregulation in many parts of the world (now to be succeeded by sweeping re-regulation) has exposed frailties in financial structures once deemed "too big to fail." Not anymore. Investors, particularly individual investors with their life savings on the line, can no longer afford to take anything for granted.

Bill Gross, the highly respected Managing Director of investment colossus Pacific Investment Management Company (PIMCO), summed up the current "state of the nation" succinctly in his April 2009 *Investment Outlook* report to clients: "we must now view ourselves as chastened adults, forced into acknowledging a new reality that is dependent upon bear market deleveraging and debt liquidation to deliver us to our new and ultimate restructured destination. Investing is no longer child's play."

YOU CAN DO IT

We live in an era of unparalleled access to information. We also live in an era of rapid, unforgiving change that can tear apart entire industries and national economies with little warning. This is the very essence of risk and reward and is the dynamic principle that drives all investing. Well-informed investors who rely upon facts and reasoning to guide their decision-making process will discover that for every risk there is an accompanying opportunity. For the ill informed, driven more by instinct than logic, this can be and likely is a very frustrating and frightening time.

In an interview with CNBC earlier this year, Warren Buffett couldn't have summarized today's investment challenge more aptly: "People are scared, and fear is very contagious. They're also confused. And if you're fearful and confused, you don't start to get over being fearful until you aren't confused." It is our sincere hope that *Financial First Aid* has helped place you in, or preserved your place in, the "aren't confused" category. We note as well that an animated version of Mr. Buffett will soon be aiming to also teach children about finance: "What better time to help educate our kids about financial responsibility."

The tools to attain your financial goals are all around you. Use those tools in a disciplined and practical manner, and we can assure you that as the years pass you will be simply astounded at what you can achieve.

Index

About the Authors

Michael Graham, Ph.D., is currently President of Michael Graham Investment Services Inc., an investment counselling firm which he formed in late 2007 to continue a career in the Canadian investment industry that dates back to 1962. Senior industry positions have included Director of Research at Wood Gundy, Chairman of Investment Strategy at Dominion Securities, Director of Investor Support at Merrill Lynch Canada and Director of Private Client Investing at Midland Walwyn. He is a longstanding Contributing Editor of *The MoneyLetter* and a columnist for Advocis' *FORUM* magazine, and has appeared frequently on radio and television, most recently the *Money Talk* show on BNN. He is also a frequent speaker to groups within the financial services industry.

Bryan Snelson is Vice President, Financial Advisor, and Branch Manager with Raymond James Ltd. He reaches over 500,000 listeners per week on Toronto radio station JAZZFM91 with his twice-daily market reports and weekly radio commentary, "Portfolio First Aid." Bryan appears frequently on CBC Newsworld and *The National*, and is a contributor to *The MoneyLetter*. He has spoken to many national and regional organizations on investing, including The Canadian Bar Association, The Ontario Nurses' Association, and the Canadian Association of Retired Persons.

Cindy David, CFP, CLU, is Vice President, Estate Planning Advisor, with Raymond James Financial Planning Ltd., with 15 years of financial planning experience. She is an accomplished speaker and frequent member of industry panel discussions. She has had articles featured in industry publications, local newspapers, and client newsletters.